The Dictionary of Economics and Commerce
English/French/Arabic

THE DICTIONARY OF ECONOMICS AND COMMERCE
ENGLISH/FRENCH/ARABIC

عناصر
لمعجم اقتصادي وتجاري عربي

Z. Nasr

First published in 1980 by
THE MACMILLAN PRESS LTD
London and Basingstoke

*Associated companies in Delhi Dublin Hong Kong
Johannesburg Lagos Melbourne New York Singapore
and Tokyo*

Filmset in Monophoto by
Type Planning Services Ltd. Hull, England.

British Library Cataloguing in Publication Data

Nasr, Z
   Dictionary of economics and commerce, English,
   French, Arabic.
   1. Economics – Dictionaries – Polyglot
   I. Title
   330'.03   HB61
   ISBN 978-1-349-03557-1   ISBN 978-1-349-03555-7 (eBook)
   DOI 10.1007/978-1-349-03555-7

«ما كان قياساً على كلام العرب فهو من كلام العرب»

ابن منظور – لسان العرب

"Formations by analogy with the Arabs' language
are part of the Arabs' language"

Ibn Manzoor: *Lissan Al 'Arab*

FOREWORD

The user of this glossary cannot fail to realize quickly how much Arab economic terminology owes to both English and French. The linkage in this process of borrowing from these two main international languages in the different parts of the Arab world reflects the colonial traditions of the past several decades. Usually trained in Anglo-Saxon or French universities, Arab scholars in the modern sciences, especially those that relate to social evolution, have displayed a considerable degree of imagination in Arabic word formation which has helped to enrich and modernize one of the few classical languages that is still a living medium of communication. However, we in the Kuwait Fund for Arab Economic Development, out of experience in working together with Arabs drawn from different cultural and historical backgrounds, have found that the process of word formation in economics was still in a fluid state. The need to coordinate and consolidate this process seemed therefore a pressing objective not only for better communication but also in order to enable Arab social scientists to concentrate on the more substantive, rather than semantic, aspects of cultural evolution.

Arabic, to be sure, has not always been at the receiving end of semantic interchange and it is a well-known fact that, during a good part of the Middle Ages and well into the Renaissance, Western European languages, including medieval Latin in particular, translated and borrowed from Arabic.[1] Such semantic interchange between different cultures is a natural process that goes on all the time and it is only to be expected that the more advanced culture would lend more than it borrows, though it should also be expected that other cultures would try to resist and preserve their own material. With time attitudes become more tolerant and foreign guest words more welcome, especially when they lose their identity and melt in the crucible of the host language's life.

There is no doubt that the present order of the day in the Arab world is before anything else economic, social and technological development, but one can harldy expect that this can ever proceed in isolation from other interacting aspects of the nation's modernisation efforts. Given the stakes involved there is in fact no escape from the necessity to launch strenuous efforts on the various fronts simultaneously, in the linguistic field no less than on construction sites.

I believe Dr. Nasr's impressive attempt in this glossary should be welcomed in the light of such an inevitable and protracted task. Better communication and understanding among the Arab countries in the field of economic cooperation will no doubt benefit from his work. It was often a pleasure indeed at the Kuwait Fund to accompany Dr. Nasr sometimes in a typically Arab intellectual quest: more knowledge of the heritage and of the possibilities of our own language.

ABDLATIF AL-HAMAD
Director-General
Kuwait Fund for Arab Economic Development

---

[1] Loan words from Arabic such as *cipher, algebra, alchemy, alcohol, alkali, admiral, nadir, zenith, elixir, lute, sirop, camphor, sugar, amber* . . . etc, are familiar examples, though the Arabic origin of words like *sine, arsenal, check, carat, talcum, spinach, Regulus, risk, hazard, ogive, naphta, cable* and others, is often forgotten. See Walt Taylor, *Arabic words in English*, SPE, Oxford 1933.

PREFACE

Most Arab economists would, I believe, agree that the Arabic language has achieved a reasonable degree of success in meeting the needs arising from modern economic life and thought. Arabic has been able to do so despite the various hurdles that confront the arabization of economic terminology no less than that of other branches of knowledge. The most important among these hurdles seem to be briefly as follows:

a) First, unlike some other languages such as French, German, Italian, Spanish and even Russian, a semitic language like Arabic is remote from the language that can without exaggeration, be regarded as the main vehicle for scientific thought at the present time namely English. No common words, common roots or common methods of word formation from Latin or Greek, come to the help of the translator into Arabic.

b) Second, modern colloquial Arabic with its various dialects seems to have lost its innate, and possibly quasi-genetic, links with Classical Arabic as the parent language. This has deprived us not only of the remarkable wealth characterising the original *koine* but also perhaps of that creative native spirit which imparts to every language the capacity to originate, to develop, and to overcome the inevitable casualties resulting from social change, by means of the language's own resources and assimilative powers. Various historical periods (including hopefully the present) bear witness however to the fact that Arabic itself does not lack such a capacity.[1]

c) One must, of course, add the obvious impact of scientific backwardness, which inevitably reflects on the level of linguistic usage and which directly contributes to the difficulty of modernizing the language and facilitates the introduction of foreign words in their original form and sound.

Despite all these difficulties, however, we do hope that this work will help the Arabic-speaking reader to avoid literal or semi-literal borrowings from foreign economic terminology, both through the attempt to compile what has already been translated and gained acceptance, and through the work's conviction that whenever necessary an effort should be made to derive and create new words from Arabic radicals and sounds. As a matter of fact, we believe that the level already reached by Arabic in the field of economics – despite whatever weakness, dependence and the necessity for translation – in no way justifies some of the works that we still encounter, works riddled with foreign words in Latin characters, with no inhibitions as to their constant repetition, almost as if incantations were needed to soothe the author no less than the reader.

We also hope that the foreign student of Arabic will find in this work an instrument for finding the equivalent in Arabic for English and French economic concepts. This explains why we have sometimes given a number of Arabic synonyms which would otherwise appear self-evident to an Arab reader.

Finally, we believe that readers may find some interest in the non-Arabic part of the work. French is also embarked upon an endeavour to preserve its integrity and many English economic terms still lack an established French equivalent.

This multiplicity of rather ambitious objectives partly explains the reservation qualifying the Arabic title of this work.[2] Such reservation also stems from our awareness that we have missed – either by inadvertence or by sheer ignorance – many concepts that should have been recorded, as well as many words from Classical Arabic which could have been used with advantage. A third additional reason for modesty is that we do not pretend having merely compiled established usage. In no few cases we have taken the liberty to make suggestions that may or may not succeed in introducing new terms into current Arabic economic literature.

---

[1] Who among Arabic-speaking people could consciously remember now that words like: *dinar – dirham – kirsh – sundook – iklim – Iblis – ibrik – ibriz – soundoss – kimia – arboon – sokkar – laimoun – falsafa – handassa – istiwana – camoon – bustan – bortakal – istabl* etc. are arabised words (or at least believed to be so). Compare this with words such as: *radio – television – ideologia – proletaria – benzine – petrol – gas – bank – garage – cinema – villa – diplomacia – barlaman – democratia – birocratia – logharitm – millione – motor* . . .which were copied more recently. This is not to deny however that the past has also known cases of literal borrowing (e.g. *mania, malincholia, sirsam*).

[2] *Elements for an Economic Glossary in Arabic.*

This latter endeavour has in fact raised a fundamental issue that transcends whatever significance this work may have on the purely technical plane, namely, the attitude that we ought to adopt towards Classical Arabic – that language "that time's hands have shattered"[3] and the advisability of trying to exploit its resources and to revive some of its expressions, either directly or through analogy, derivation or association.

One can well believe that, as happened and still happens to some other languages less copious and less extensive than Arabic, such as Turkish or Hebrew, an attempt at revival is not a symptom of mere nostalgia but a long overdue obligation that requires, rather than a justification, the continuation of efforts and more knowledge of both the relevant subjects and the language itself. Such a challenging credo was not unknown to medieval Islamo-Arabic culture during the period of reception, assimilation and development of the intellectual achievements of other earlier civilisations.

Needless to say, the real issue at hand is not and could not possibly be an attempt to go back to a language that ceased to be – if it ever was – a vehicle for oral communication centuries ago. What is at stake is simply the attempt to revive, whenever appropriate, the terms and patterns of Classical Arabic as a means of enriching current language of avoiding literal copying, and possibly narrowing somewhat the large gap that divides spoken from written and traditional Arabic, a gap which condemns the whole Arab region to a kind of bilingualism that, unlike other types of bilingualism, hardly opens new horizons of thought and culture.

No less persuasive in some of its arguments, however, is another viewpoint which contends that it is in the nature of any language to alter, that semantic change is inevitable, and that all is well, therefore, with current Arabic, a living language which adequately fulfils its various present obligations. In any case, resolving the problems of translation could not possibly lie in asking the user of a glossary to reach now and then for another bulkier and often less accessible one, in order to locate extinct origins and find the meaning of what time has in fact definitively made alien to modern Arabic.

Again, the outcome of this discussion depends, I believe, on an issue which is more general than those raised by mere translation into Arabic, namely that of the relative worth or merit of different languages or of the same language in different social contexts or at different stages of linguistic evolution. It is well known that some authorities believe that no preference can be given to a language over another unless it is better suited to the community using it. For instance, Pidgin English[4] as spoken in some former colonies is not in some way "inferior" to the English current in Anglo-Saxon countries. Each brand is appropriate to its users and adequately meets their requirements. Likewise, one could refer to a sophisticated language like French which mainly developed out of a corrupt Latin introduced during the conquest of the Gauls, a hint in this context to the sometimes timidly expressed hope that current colloquial Arabic should also some day achieve graduation and become the instrument of writing and thinking. One may finally, and rather skeptically, add that whatever path is chosen for translation into Arabic will hardly affect the possibility of catching up with modern civilisation and its achievements which is the real and most urgent order of the day. To be able to manufacture cars – like driving them – will not very much depend upon the name given to the steering-wheel, the engine, or the gearbox.[5]

The logic of such an argumentation would lead us to consider the corrupt vernacular current during the late Ottoman period no less acceptable than Classical Arabic. It would equally convince us that current Arabic has been enriched by Turkish contributions (such as *makhzangi – bostagi – kamangi – fustan – oda*, etc.) and continues to do so by borrowings from various Western languages, in fact not unlike what happened to older Arabic through Persian, Greek and Syriac influence.

The position that this work has adopted in this debate can best be described as simply eclectic. We have accepted without reservations foreign terms like "*cheque*", "*bank*", "*cartel*", "*trust*", "*camebiala*". . . all more or less easy for an Arab tongue (except perhaps the heavy "*teknololgia*")[6]. In most cases we have of course relied on current Arabic usage even when no established term among the economists was

[3]   Boutros Al Bustany: *Kotre Al-Moohit* (1869).
[4]   "*Pidgin*" seems to be derived from "*business*"
[5]   These are words which also show a dual existence in Arabic: in some foreign form and in an attempt at translation.
[6]   This word has had a better fortune than the Arabic for "productive arts" or "productive art" though it is derived from the Greek "*tekhne*" (art). The Arabic for "art" (*fan*) still remains however in the translation of "technical assistance" or "technical experts."

found. On the other hand, we have however also tried – within the available limits of time and effort – to benefit from Classical Arabic whenever appropriate. For instance, words for "moratorium", "foreman", "capitation tax", "tombstone", "second-best", "optimisation", "deflation", "conglomerates", "disaggregation", . . . etc. have been suggested, either by finding directly the proper Arabic equivalent or near-equivalent which was available but forgotten, or by derivation and analogy. Perhaps a typical example of what we have sometimes tried to do, or rather to avoid, in this respect is given by the word "bottlenecks": in current Arabic usage, this concept is often rendered by the horrendous "*ikhtinakat*" (from strangulation, suffocation) or even sometimes through loan–translation by the simple literal equivalent for "necks of the bottle". We believe the word we suggest ("*ma'azim*" or even "*ma'azil*", from the narrowing of a path) can more elegantly express the essence of the idea, though the original has fallen into disuse long ago.

We hope that these and similar suggestions will be successful and that time and better circumstances will allow others to pursue and deepen the effort in the same direction. There is no doubt in our mind that problems in this field as in other fields will finally be resolved through the choice that Arab countries will make in terms of the cultural paths currently facing them and in terms of the fields on which research efforts will be focused in the future. In the last analysis each nation only begets the language it deserves, the language it succeeds in shaping for itself and which best corresponds to the scope of its ambitions.

And now I would like to take leave from a work that could easily last a lifetime by expressing my gratitude to all my colleagues at the Kuwait Fund for Arab Economic Development whose continued interest and encouragement made the attempt possible. I particularly wish to express my thanks to Mr. Abdelatif Al-Hamad who – in the light of his experience in the various Arab countries – felt the need to develop and standardize Arab economic terminology, convinced us of the utility of such a glossary, and generously accorded the time required for its preparation. I also wish to thank Dr. Galal Amin, my colleague in the Kuwait Fund's Research Department and formerly in Ain Shams University, for having taken the trouble to read a first draft and for the valuable suggestions he has made from his past experience in a similar field.

I need hardly conclude by stating that any shortcomings, weakness or errors found in this work are to be imputed solely to my own limitations.

Zacharia Nasr

NOTES

1. In tracing the limits between economic terminology and that of other subjects related to economics (such as commerce, statistics, accounting or law) we have adopted a pragmatic approach. Concepts more or less current in economic literature have been included even when belonging to other subjects, though not to the extent that would have transformed a specialised glossary into some sort of *pot-pourri*.
2. The dualism of English in the genitive case has not always been taken into account. A reference to both forms is therefore advisable.
3. A number of equivalents in Arabic or in French may denote the availability of synonyms or the existence of different concepts.
4. Loan words still preserving their original form appear in italics.

١ – استطاعت اللغة العربية أن تحقق نجاحاً طيباً في
العمل على مواجهة الإحتياجات الناشئة عن تطور كل
من الحياة والمعرفة الإقتصادية الحديثة . وقد تمكنت
من ذلك على الرغم من العقبات التي تعترض سبيل
تعريب لغة الإقتصاد كما تعترض سبل تعريب الفروع
العلمية الأخرى . ولعل أهم هذه العقبات يتلخص
فيما يلي :

أ – بعد اللغة العربية عن اللغة الإنجليزية التي
تعتبر بحق لغة العلوم في الوقت الحاضر .
وذلك على خلاف لغات أخرى مثل
الفرنسية والالمانية والايطالية والاسبانية بل
والروسية أيضاً وهي جميعها أقرب إلى
الإنجليزية ومن ثم أقدر على النقل والاشتقاق
سواء منها أو من الجذور المشتركة في اللاتينية
والاغريقية .

ب – فقدان اللغة العربية الدارجة بمختلف
لهجاتها لصلتها العضوية (وربما شبه
الوراثية) باللغة العربية الأم . الأمر الذي
حرم إلى حد كبير الناطقين بالعربية ليس فقط
من غزارة الأصل وانما أيضاً على وجه
الخصوص من روح ذلك الأصل نفسها ،
تلك الروح التي تكفل لكل لغة القدرة على
الخلق والتطور وتعويض ما يميته تغير البيئة
من كلمات ، انطلاقاً من جذورها الذاتية
واستيعاباً للغريب من الألفاظ ، وذلك كما
حدث بالفعل للعربية في عصور مختلفة[1].

ج – يضاف إلى ذلك وطأة التخلف العلمي الذي
ينعكس بالضرورة على مستوى اللغة
المستخدمة ، كما يسهم اسهاماً مباشراً في
تعثر العمل على تطويرها ويسر من تقبل
استخدام الالفاظ الأجنبية على حالها .

٢ – وعل الرغم من ذلك كله فاننا نأمل أن نجد

القارىء العربي في هذا المؤلف ما يعينه على ألا يلجأ إلى
النقل الحرفي أو شبه الحرفي للمصطلحات الغربية في
الاقتصاد ، وذلك سواء بما احتوى عليه من الفاظ تم
تعريبها واستقرت أو بما يشير إليه أحياناً من وجوب
الاجتهاد في القياس أو الخلق ، معنى وزنة . والواقع أن
ما بلغته لغة الاقتصاد العربية حالياً – على قصورها
واضطرارها إلى الترجمة والتباعة – لم يعد يبرر بتاتاً ما لا
نزال نصادفه من مؤلفات تذر فيها المصطلحات
الأجنبية ذراً متكرراً لا يني إن انبى شيئاً الا بتعثر أو
لغف أو بالحاجة إلى عوذ يستعاذ بها .

٣ – كذلك نرجو أن يجد طالب اللغة العربية من
الأجانب ما يساعده على الالمام بالمقابل العربي
لمصطلحات الاقتصاد في الانجليزية وفي الفرنسية ،
الأمر الذي يفسر حرصنا على تفصيل العبارات العربية
أحياناً وايراد عدد من المترادفات التي قد تبدو بديهية
للناطق بالعربية .

٤ – وأخيراً أملنا أن يجد القارىء أيضاً بعض الفائدة
في الشق غير العربي من المؤلف . فقد أخذت الفرنسية
تعمل هي الأخرى على حفظ كيانها سليماً ولا يزال
كثير من المصطلحات في حاجة إلى ترجمة يتواضع
عليها ، الأمر الذي اضطرنا في بضعة أحوال هنا أيضاً
إلى اقتراح ما لم نجد له مستقراً بالفرنسية .

٥ – ولعل هذه الثلاثة أو الربعة من الاطماع المحلقة
معاً تفسر جانباً من التحفظ الذي يظهر في عنوان هذا
المؤلف . وهو تحفظ يجد تفسيره كذلك فيما فاتنا –
سهواً أو جهلاً – من مصطلحات ينبغي تسجيلها ومن
أصول عربية يمكن الاستفادة منها في الحصول على ما
هو أعلى لغة وأدق معنى . يضاف إلى ذلك أن ما نقدمه
لا يزعم دائماً أنه تسجيل لما تواضع عليه المختصون
وانما في أحوال ليست قليلة مجرد مقترحات منها ما قد
يؤخذ به ومنها ما قد لا يكتب له نصيب .

٦ – والواقع أن هذه المقترحات قد أثارت قضية
أساسية تتعدى ما قد يكون لهذا العمل من مغزى في
بحت . وأقصد بذلك قضية الموقف الذي ينبغي اتخاذه
من اللغة العربية القديمة – تلك اللغة «التي هشمتها
أيادي الزمان»[1] – ومدى ملاءمة العمل على
استغلالها واحياء الفاظها ، اما مباشرة واما بالقياس أو
الاشتقاق أو تداعي الأفكار .

٧ – فقد يذهب المرء – اسوة بما حدث ويحدث
للغات أخرى دون العربية ثراء وانتشاراً (مثل اللغة
التركية أو اللغة العبرية) – إلى أن محاولة الاحياء هذه

---

[1] من يتذكر واعياً الآن أن كلمات مثل : دينار – درهم –
قرش – صندوق – اقليم – ابليس – ابريق – سندس
– بستان – برتقال – اسطبل – ... الخ من الالفاظ المعربة ،
(أو على الأقل مما فيه شبهة تعريب)؟ ثم لنقارن ذلك بألفاظ
مثل : راديو – تلفزيون – ايديولوجيا – بروليتاريا – بنزين –
بترول – غاز – بنك – جراج – لمبة – سينما – فيلا –
دبلوماسية – برلمان – ديمقراطية – بيروقراطية – لوغا ريتم –
مليون – ميل – موتور ، ... الخ مما دخل حديثاً محتفظاً بكيانه
الأجني كاملاً . وهذا لا ينفي بطبيعة الحال أن الماضي عرف
أيضاً أحوالا من النقل الحرفي (مثل مانيا ، مالينخوليا ،
سرسام).

[1] قطر المحيط لبطرس البستاني (١٨٦٩)

ليست مظهراً من مظاهر الكنتية بل واجب لا يحتاج إلى تبرير وانما إلى مواصلة الاجتهاد وزيادة التعمق في شئون مادة المعرب وشئون اللغة معاً . وهو اتجاه عرفته الحضارة الإسلامية العربية أيضاً في عصر استيعاب منجزات الحضارات السابقة عليها .

٨ – وغني عن البيان أن الأمر ليس – ولا يمكن أن يكون – محاولة العودة إلى لغة لم تعد بالفعل لغة الكلام منذ قرون ، وانما هو العمل على تنشيط المناسب من الفاظها وتراكيبها بالقدر الذي يثرى اللغة الحالية ويغنينا عن النقل من الخارج بلا مبرر ويضيق بعض الشيء من تلك الفجوة الواسعة بين لسان الكلام ولغة الكتابة والتراث . وهي فجوة تحكم علينا كما هو معروف بازدواجية لا تفتح لنا ، على خلاف ضروب الازدواجية اللغوية الأخرى ، آفاقا جديدة من الفكر والحضارة .

٩ – ومع ذلك فقد ذهب رأي آخر لا يقل عن السابق اقناعاً في بعض حججه إلى أن كل لغة من طبيعتها أن تتطور وتتغير ومن ثم فاللغة العربية الحالية بخير وقادرة على مواجهة شتى التزاماتها . وليس حل مشكلة التعريب في أن يطلب من قارىء معجم أن يستعين بمعاجم أخرى ليبحث فيها عن أصول بائدة وعن تفسير لما جعله الزمان غريباً علينا بالفعل .

١٠ – واعتقادنا أن الفيصل في هذا التباين في الرأي مرده إلى قضية أعم مما يثيره التعريب وحده من مسائل . وهي قضية المفاضلة بين لغات مختلفة أو بين لغة واحدة في بيئات متغايرة أو في مراحل مختلفة من تطورها . فمن المعروف أن من علماء اللغة من يؤكد ألا فضل للغة على أخرى الا بمدى الملاءمة للمجتمع الذي يستخدمها . فالرطانة شبه الانجليزية التي تستعمل في بعض المستعمرات السابقة[1] مثلاً لا تقل مرتبة وفقاً لهذا المذهب عن انجليزية المجتمعات الانجلوسكسونية مادامت كل منها تناسب احتياجات أصحابها وتفي باغراض حياتهم . كذلك قد يشار في هذا الصدد إلى أن لغة متطورة كالفرنسية مثلاً قد نشأت وتبلورت انطلاقاً من أصول أهمها لاتينية ركيكة ادخلها الفاتح إلى بلاد الغول ، ومن ثم فالأمل معقود أيضاً على أن تتطور العربية الدارجة لتصبح يوماً هي الأخرى لغة الكتابة والفكر . وقد يضاف أخيراً أن اللحاق بركب الحضارة ومنجزات العصر لن يتأثر في أية حال بما يختار سبيلاً في التعريب . فالقدرة على صنع السيارات مثلاً ، شأنها شأن قيادتها ، لن يتوقف

<hr>

كثيرا على المفاضلة بين «دركسيون» و«عجلة قيادة» ، أو بين «محرك» و«موتور» . أو بين «دربوكس» و«علبة تروس السرعة» .

وبناء على ذلك قد نقبل القول بأن ما نسميه «عربية الحضر تلو» أيام الحكم العثماني كانت لا تقل عن العربية الفصحى مرتبة . وأن العربية الدارجة حالياً قد أثرت وتثرى بمساهمات التركية (مخزنجي ، بسطجي ، كمنجي ، فستان . أودة ... الخ) وبمساهمات مختلف اللغات الغربية ، مثلما أثرت من قبلها العربية القديمة بالفاظ فارسية ويونانية وسورية .

١١ – ولعل الموقف الذي أخذ به هذا المعجم أميل إلى محاولة الافادة من هذه الاتجاهات المختلفة . فقد قبلنا دون تحفظ دخول بعض كلمات أجنبية درج استخدامها ، مثل «شيك» (وهي كلمة رجعت إلينا بعد تصديرها في صورة «صك») ، «بنك» ، «كارتل» ، «ترست» ، «كمبيالة» ... وجميعها كلمات سهلة النطق بالعربية (باستثناء تلك الكلمة الثقيلة «تكنولجيا»[1]) . كذلك اعتمدنا في أغلب الأحوال على اللغة المستخدمة حالياً حتى فيما لم نجد له مقابلاً جارياً بين المختصين . ومع ذلك فقد حاولنا أيضاً الافادة من العربية القديمة ، في حدود ما استطعنا تكريسه لها من وقت وجهد ، كلما وجدنا ذلك مناسباً .

ومن الأمثلة على هذا اقتراح الفاظ مثل : «مكابلة» moratorium «وهين» foreman ، «فردة» ، capitation tax «مآزم» bottlenecks (بدلاً من «اختناقات») بل وأحياناً «أعناق الزجاجة»! ، «الشاهدة» tombstone ، «الثنيان» second best ، «الامثال» optimisation «أواطر» deflators ، «قضض» ، conglomerates ، «افضاض» ، disaggregation ، «بيب» pipeline... الخ مما نأمل دخوله في لغة الاقتصاد ومحاكاته على يد مختصين تسمح لهم ظروفهم بتعميق هذا الاتجاه على مر الزمن وليس من شك في أن الأمر سيتوقف أساساً في هذا الميدان مثل غيره من الميادين على ما سوف تختاره البلاد العربية من سبل حضارية وما سوف تركز عليه من مجالات لبذل الجهود في المستقبل . فلكل أمة في التحليل الأخير اللغة التي تستحقها وتصنعها لنفسها وترضى بها .

(١) كان لهذه الكلمة (التي يحسن كتابتها «تكنولجية») حظ أحسن من «فنون الإنتاج» أو «الفن الانتاجي» رغم اشتقاقها من أصل يوناني يعني «فن» tckhne ومع ذلك فالجميع يتكلم الآن عن «المعونة الفنية» لا «المعونة التكنولجية» .

(١) Pidgin English (والنعت تحريف لكلمة business)

xi

ملاحظات

١٢ – والآن أود أن أودع هذا العمل الذي يمكن أن
يمتد عمراً بتسجيل شكري لجميع الزملاء في
الصندوق الكويتي للتنمية الاقتصادية العربية الذين
كان لهم الفضل في انجازه بتشجيعهم واهتمامهم
المتواصل . ونشكر بصفة خاصة السيد عبد اللطيف
الحمد الذي اقنعنا أصلاً بجدوى القيام بهذه المحاولة
إثر زياراته للعالم العربي ولمسه الحاجة إلى مصطلحات
موحدة في ميدان الاقتصاد ، كما نشكره على الفرصة
التي أتاحها لنا لانهاء العمل . كذلك نشكر الدكتور
جلال أمين زميلنا بقسم البحوث بالصندوق حالياً
وبجامعة عين شمس من قبل ، على تفضله بقراءة
مسودة أولى كاملة وعلى ما أشاربه من تعديلات قيمة
استندت إلى خبرته السابقة في نفس هذا الحقل .
وغنى عن البيان أن أوجه النقص والمآخذ التي لا تزال
تشوب ما حاولنا تقديمه من عناصر لا تفسر الا بقصور
المؤلف وحده وتقصيره .

الكويت – يناير ١٩٧٦

١ – في رسم الحدود بين لغة الاقتصاد ولغة الفروع
الأخرى القريبة منه (مثل التجارة والاحصاء
والمحاسبة والقانون) حاولنا أن نسلك مسلكاً
عملياً يقبل تسجيل بعض ما هو دارج من
معان بين المشتغلين بالاقتصاد حتى لوكان ذلك
من فروع أخرى . ولكنه لا ينساب إلى ذلك
التساهل الذي قد يجعل من معجم متخصص
مسقطاً لشتى الالفاظ .

٢ – ان مثنوية تركيب الاضافة في اللغة الانجليزية
تجعل من المفيد الرجوع إلى كل من شقي
الإضافة تجنباً لافتقاد عبارة معينة .

٣ – تعدد المقابل العربي أو الفرنسي قد يشتمل على
مترادفات وقد يشتمل على معان مختلفة
للمصطلح الانجليزي الواحد .

٤ – العبارات المكتوبة بالبنط المايل مما استعارته
الانجليزية من لغات أخرى ولا يزال على
أصله .

AAA bonds	obligations de première qualité obligations cotées AAA	سندات ممتازة المرتبة – سندات الدرجة الأولى
Abandonment (*of goods, of an option*)	délaissement-abandon (*de biens, d'une option*)	ترك – تنازل (عن سلع ، عن حق خيار)
Abandonment value	valeur de délaissement	قيمة الترك
Abatement	abattement – dégrèvement rabais – diminution	خفض – خصم – نقصان
Ability to pay	capacité de paiement	قدرة على الدفع
Abrasion of a coin	frai d'une pièce de monnaie	تآكل المسكوكات
Absentee landlords	propriétaires absentéistes	الملاك الغيب
Absenteeism	absentéisme	تخلف عن العمل – غوبة – تغيب
Absolute advantages	avantages absolus	ميزات مطلقة
Absolute deviation	écart absolu	انحراف مطلق
Absolute poverty	pauvreté absolue	فقر مطلق – بؤس
Absolute rent	rente absolue	ريع مطلق
Absorb losses, to	absorber des pertes	استوعب الخسائر
Absorption capacity Absorptive capacity Absorption potential	capacité d'absorption potentiel d'absorption	طاقة الاستيعاب – قدرة الاستيعاب
Abstinence	abstinence	امتناع – اقتار – تكاف
Abstinence theory	théorie de l'abstinence	نظرية الامتناع – نظرية الاقتار
Abstract of account	relevé de compte	كشف حساب – موجز حساب
Abundance	abondance	وفرة – رخاء – يسار – رفه
Abundancism	abondancisme	مذهب الرفهية
Accelerated depreciation	amortissement accéléré	استهلاك معجل
Accelerated development	développement accéléré	نمو معجل – انماء معجل
Accelerated industrialisation	industrialisation accélérée	تصنيع معجل
Accelerated service (*transport*)	service express (*transport*)	خدمة سريعة (نقل)
Acceleration principle	principe de l'accélérateur principe de l'accélération	مبدأ المعجل – نظرية المعجل نظرية التعجيل

1

Acceleration clause	clause de déchéance du terme	نص تعجيل الأداء- نص اسقاط الأجل
Accelerator	accélérateur	المعجل – المعجال
Accelerator-multiplier interaction	interaction accélérateur-multiplicateur	تفاعل المعجل والمضاعف
Acceptance credit	crédit par acceptation	قبالة – اقراض بالقبول – اعتماد بالقبول
Acceptance house	maison d'acceptation	بيت قبالة
Acceptance of a bill	acceptation d'une traite, d'un effet commercial	قبول ورقة تجارية – قبول كمبيالة
Access to capital markets	accès aux marchés financiers	امكان دخول الأسواق المالية – ولوج الأسواق المالية
Access to modern technology	accès à la technologie moderne	الافادة من فنون الانتاج الحديثة اتاحة التكنية الحديثة
Access road	route d'accès – route transversale	طريق مستعرض – طريق موصل
Accident insurance	assurance-accidents	تأمين ضد الحوادث
Acclimatisation	acclimatation	تأقلم
Accommodation bill	billet de complaisance	كمبيالة مجاملة – سند مجاملة
Accommodation note	traite de complaisance	
Account	compte – position – liquidation	حساب – تصفية
Account day	jour de liquidation	تاريخ التصفية
Accounts payable	dettes à payer effets à payer dettes passives	حسابات دفع – التزامات دفع
Accounts receivable	créances à percevoir dettes actives	حسابات قبض – حسابات مستحقة
Account-holder	titulaire d'un compte	صاحب حساب
Accountancy	comptabilité profession comptable	محاسبة – مهنة المحاسبة
Accounting	comptabilité	محاسبة
Accounting agency	organe comptable organisme comptable	جهاز محاسبي – مكتب محاسبة
Accounting framework	cadre comptable	اطار محاسبي
Accounting period	exercice comptable – période comptable	فترة محاسبية
Accounting practices	pratiques comptables	أساليب محاسبية
Accounting prices	prix comptables – prix de référence	أسعار محاسبية – أثمان اعتبارية
Accounting profits	bénéfices comptable	ربح محاسبي-أرباح محاسبية
Accounting rate of return	taux de rendement comptable	معدل العائد المحاسبي
Accounting system	système comptable	نظام محاسبي
Accounting unit	unité de compte	وحدة حساب – وحدة محاسبية
Accounting value	valeur comptable	قيمة محاسبية – قيمة دفترية
Accredited bank	banque accréditée	بنك معتمد – مصرف معتمد
Accrual (*of interest, etc.*)	accumulation (*d'intérêts, etc.*)	تحقق – تراكم – تجمع (فوائد ، الخ)
Accrual basis, on	d'après sommes courues sur la base des constatations d'après patrimoine	على أساس المتحقق
Accrual system	système des sommes courues	نظام المتحقق (محاسبة)

Accrued interest	intérêts courus – intérêts accrus intérêts accumulés	فوائد محققة – فوائد متحققة
Accruing interest	intérêts à échoir	فوائد مستقبلة
Accumulated labour	travail accumulé	عمل مجمع – عمل مركوم – عمل متراكم
Accumulation of capital	accumulation du capital	تراكم الرسمال
Accumulation of stocks	accumulation de stocks	تكديس المخزون – تراكم الكداس – تجمع الركام
Accumulator	accumulateur – accapareur	مجمع – جامع
Acid test	ratio de liquidité	نسبة السيولة – معيار السيولة
Acquaintance mission	mission de contact	بعثة اتصال – بعثة تعرف
Acquired rights	droits acquis	حقوق مكتسبة
Acquittance of a debt	acquittement d'une dette	سداد دين – وفاء دين – قضاء دين
Acreage	surface cultivée – superficie	مساحة مزروعة – مساحة زراعية – مساحة
Acting manager	directeur intérimaire directeur par interim	قائم بأعمال المدير
Action programme	programme d'action	برنامج عمل
Activation	activation	تنشيط – استخدام – اعمال
Active account	compte actif	حساب نشط – حساب فعيل
Active approach (aid policy)	approche active (politique d'aide)	منهج ايجابي (السياسة الاعانية)
Active balance	balance excédentaire	رصيد موجب – ميزان موجب
Active population	population active	قوة العمل – السكان العاملون
Activity	activité	نشاط
Activity analysis	analyse d'activité – analyse actionnelle	تحليل النشاطات
Actual costs	coûts réels – coûts effectifs	تكاليف فعلية
Actual value	valeur effective	قيمة فعلية
Actuarial reserves	réserves actuarielles	احتياطات اكتوارية – احتياطيات احتسابية
Actuary	actuaire	اكتواري – محتسب
ad valorem duties	droits ad valorem – droits proportionnels	رسوم قيمية – رسوم نسبية
Added value tax	taxe à la valeur ajoutée	ضريبة على القيمة المضافة
Additional freight	surfret	تكاليف شحن اضافية
Additional income	revenu supplémentaire	دخل اضافي
Additiomal premium (insurance)	surprime (assurance)	قسط تأمين اضافي
Additive property	caractère additif	صفة الانجماع
Adjusted figures	chiffres ajustés – données ajustées	أرقام معدلة – بيانات معدلة
Adjustment assistance	aide à la reconversion	معونة التحول
Adjustment mechanism	mécanisme d'ajustement	جهاز ضبط – جهاز تعديل جهاز موازنة – جهاز توفيق
Administered prices	prix imposés	أسعار مفروضة – أثمان مفروضة
Administrative budget	budget administratif	موازنة ادارية
Administrative costs Administrative expenses	frais d'administration frais administratifs	نفقات ادارية
Administrative machinery	appareil administratif	جهاز اداري
Administrative organisation	organisation administrative	تنظيم اداري – نظام اداري
Administrative planning	planification bureaucratique	تخطيط بيروقراطي – تخطيط اداري
Administrative provisions	mesures administratives	اجراءات ادارية – تدابير ادارية

Administrative services	services administratifs	خدمات ادارية
Adult population	population adulte	البالغون – السكان البالغون
Advance	avance	سلفية – سلف – قرض
Advance by overdraft	avance à découvert	سلفة على حساب مكشوف
Advance contracting	engagement anticipé	تعاقد مسبق
Advance deposit	dépôt préalable	وديعة مسبقة
Advance deposit requirements	obligation de dépôt préalable	التزام الايداع المسبق
Advance financing	financement anticipé	تمويل مسبق
Advance on current account	avances en compte courant	سلفيات حساب جار – سلف حساب جار
Advance payment	paiement anticipé	دفع مسبق – دفع مقدم
Advance repayment	remboursement anticipé	سداد مبتسر – سداد قبل الأجل
Advance upon collateral	avance sur titres	سلفة بضمان أوراق مالية
Advanced capitalism	capitalisme avancé	رسمالية متقدمة – رسمالية ناضجة
Advanced country	pays avancé	دولة متقدمة
Adverse balance of trade	balance commerciale défavorable	ميزان تجاري سالب – ميزان تجاري في غير صالح الدولة
Advertising	publicité – réclame	دعاية تجارية – اعلان
Advertising campaign	campagne de publicité	حملة دعائية -- حملة دعاية تجارية
Affidavit	affidavit	اقرار
Affiliate	filiale	تابعة – شركة تابعة
Affiliated company	filiale – société filiale	شركة تابعة
Affluence	affluence – abondance	رغد – رفاهية – فناق
Affluent society	société d'abondance société d'opulence	مجتمع الرفهنية – مجتمع الفناق
Afforestation	boisement – afforestation	تشجير
Affreightment	affrètement – frètement	تأجير سفينة – تأجير شاحنة
After-hours prices	prix après-bourse	أسعار بعد الاقفال
After-sale service	service après-vente	خدمات بعد البيع – خدمات لاحقة
After-tax yield	rendement net d'impôts	العائد بعد الضرائب – العائد الصافي
Age distribution	distribution des âges	توزيع الأعمار
Age group	groupe d'âge	فئة العمر
Age pyramid	pyramide des âges	هرم الأعمار
Age structure	structure par âges	هيكل الأعمار
Ageing of the population	vieillissement de la population	تكهل السكان
Agency	agence – bureau – cabinet	وكالة – مكتب
Agency contract	contrat de représentation	عقد وكالة
Agency transactions	opérations pour le compte d'autrui opérations d'agence	عمليات بالوكالة
Agent	agent – commissionaire	وكيل – وكيل بالعمولة
Agent of production	agent de production	عامل انتاج

Aggregate	agrégat – total	كل – مجمل – مجموع
Aggregate demand	demande globale	طلب كلي
Aggregate demand function	fonction de la demande globale	دالة الطلب الكلي
Aggregate employment	emploi global	اجمالي العمالة – العمالة الكلية
Aggregate supply	offre globale	عرض كلي
Aggregate supply function	fonction de l'offre globale	دالة العرض الكلي
Aggregate value	valeur globale	قيمة اجمالية – قيمة كلية
Aggregation problem	problème de l'agrégation	مشكلة التجميع
Aggregative growth model	modèle agrégatif de croissance	نموذج نمو كلي
Agio	agio	علاوة – فرق
Agiotage	agiotage	مضاربة
Agrarian economy	économie agraire	اقتصاد زراعي
Agrarian reform	réforme agraire	اصلاح زراعي
Agrarian socialism	socialisme agraire	الاشتراكية الزراعية
Agrarian structure	structure agraire	هيكل زراعي
Agrarian system	système agraire	نظام زراعي – نظام فلاحي
Agreed price	prix convenu – prix forfaitaire	الثمن المتفق عليه – ثمن جزافي
Agreement to reimburse	garantie de remboursement	تعهد بتغطية السداد
	engagement de remboursement	تعهد بتغطية الدفع
Agriculture	agriculture	زراعة – فلاحة
Agricultural area	zone agricole	منطقة زراعية
Agricultural bank	banque agricole	بنك زراعي – مصرف زراعي
Agricultural census	recensement agricole	مسح زراعي – احصاء زراعي
Agricultural commodities	produits agricoles	منتجات زراعية – سلع زراعية
	denrées agricoles	
Agricultural cooperative	coopérative agricole	تعاونية زراعية
Agricultural credit	crédit agricole	ائتمان زراعي
Agricultural credit cooperative	coopérative de crédit agricole	تعاونية للائتمان الزراعي
Agricultural development	développement agricole	تنمية زراعية – انماء زراعي
Agricultural economics	économie agricole	الاقتصاد الزراعي – علم الاقتصاد الزراعي
	agro-économie	اقتصاديات الزراعة
Agricultural economy	économie agraire	اقتصاد زراعي
Agricultural engineer	ingénieur agronome	مهندس زراعي
	agronome	
Agricultural engineering	génie rural	هندسة زراعية
Agricultural equipment	matériel agricole –	أجهزة فلاحية – آلات زراعية
	équipement agricole	
Agricultural extension centre	centre de vulgarisation agricole	مركز ارشاد زراعي – مركز خدمات زراعية
		مركز ارشاد فلاحي
Agricultural holdings	exploitations agricoles	حيازات زراعية – استغلالات زراعية
Agricultural labour	main d'oeuvre agricole	عمال الزراعة – عمال زراعيون
Agricultural machinery	matériel agricole	آلات زراعية – آلات فلاحية

Agricultural markets	marchés agricoles	أسواق زراعية
Agricultural mechanisation	mécanisation agricole	ميكنة الزراعة – ميكنة زراعية
Agricultural planning	planification agricole	تخطيط زراعي
Agricultural policy	politique agricole politique agraire	سياسة زراعية
Agricultural prices	prix agricoles	أسعار زراعية – أثمان زراعية
Agricultural products	produits agricoles	منتجات زراعية – منتجات فلاحية
Agricultural production	production agricole	انتاج زراعي – انتاج فلاحي
Agricultural processing industry	industrie de transformation de produits agricoles	صناعة تحويل المنتجات الزراعية
Agricultural project	projet agricole	مشروع زراعي
Agricultural sector	secteur agricole	قطاع زراعي – قطاع فلاحي
Agricultural support policy	politique de soutien agricole	سياسة مساندة الزراعة
Agricultural surplus	excédent agricole	فائض الانتاج الزراعي – فائض زراعي
Agricultural taxation	fiscalité agricole	ضرائب زراعية – نظام الضرائب الزراعية
Agricultural training	formation agricole	تدريب فلاحي – تدريب زراعي
Agricultural unit	unité culturale – unité agricole	وحدة زراعية – وحدة فلاحية
Agricultural waste	déchets agricoles	فضلات زراعية
Agri-product processing	traitement des produits agricoles transformation des produits agricoles	تصنيع المنتجات الزراعية
Agrogorod (USSR)	agrogorod (URSS) agroville	مدينة زراعية (الاتحاد السوفييتي)
Agro-industries	agro-industries industries agricoles	صناعات زراعية
Agro-industrial complex	complexe agro-industriel	مركب زراعي صناعي
Agronomic research	recherche agronomique	أبحاث زراعية – أبحاث فلاحية
Agronomist	agronome	مهندس زراعي
Agronomy	agronomie	علم الزراعة – علم الفلاحة
Aid	aide – assistance	معونة – مساعدة – اعانة
Aid agency	organisme d'aide	هيئة معونات – هيئة مساعدات جهاز معونات
Aid channels	volets de l'aide	مسالك المعونة
Aid commitments	engagements d'aide	تعهدات اعانية
Aid consortium	consortium d'aide	دارة اعانية
Aid coordination	coordination de l'aide	تنسيق المعونات – تنسيق المساعدات
Aid-donor country	pays donneur d'aide	دولة عاطية
Aid evaluation	évaluation de l'aide	تقييم المعونات – تقييم المساعدات
Aid in kind	aide en nature	معونة عينية – مساعدة عينية
Aid institution	organisme d'aide	هيئة معونات – هيئة مساعدات
Aid package	ensemble de mèsures d'assistance	مجموعة تدابير اعانية
Aid performance	effort d'assistance – effort d'aide	أداء اعاني – جهد اعاني
Aid programme	programme d'assistance	برنامج معونات – برنامج مساعدات
Aid recipient country	pays récipiendaire d'aide pays bénéficiaire de l'aide	دولة معانة – دولة مستفيدة من المعونة

Aid statistics	statistiques de l'aide	احصاءات المعونة
Aid users	usagers de l'aide	مستخدمي المعونة
Air cargo	fret aérien	شحن جوي
Air freight		
Aircraft industry	industrie aéronautique	صناعة الطائرات
Airline network	réseau aérien	شبكة الخطوط الجوية
Air route	ligne aérienne	خط جوي
Air traffic	trafic aérien	حركة النقل الجوي
Air transportation	transport aérien	نقل جوي
Alien labour	travailleurs immigrés – main d'oeuvre immigrée	عمال وافدون
Alien property	biens étrangers	ملكية الأجانب – أملاك الأجانب
Alimentary aid	aide alimentaire	معونة غذائية – مساعدة غذائية – اعانة غذائية
Alimentation	alimentation	غذاء – تغذية
All risks insurance	assurance tous risques	تأمين شامل
Allocate, to	allouer – attribuer – répartir	خصص – وزع
Allocations and allotments	allocation et déblocage des crédits	تخصيص الاعتمادات
Allocation of aid	répartition de l'aide	تخصيص المساعدات – تخصيص المعونات
Allocation of loan proceeds	affectation des fonds empruntés	تخصيص حصيلة القرض
Allocation of net income	affectation du revenu net	تخصيص صافي الدخل
Allocation of profit	répartition des profits	تخصيص الأرباح
Allocation of resources	affectation des ressources répartition des ressources	تخصيص الموارد – توزيع الموارد
Allocation of traffic	répartition du trafic	توزيع حركة النقل
Allocative efficiency	efficacité de l'affectation des ressources efficacité allocative	فاعلية تخصيص الموارد
Allotment	somme affectée – attribution – lotissement	قطعة أرض – مبلغ مخصص – نصيب
Allotment of shares	attribution d'actions	توزيع أسهم
Allowance	provision – rabais – tolérance allocation – remise – déduction	مخصص – حطيطة – خصم – سماح
Allowance for exchange depreciation	provision pour dépréciation des changes	مخصص انخفاض الصرف
Alloy	alliage	مزيج
Alternate	suppléant	مناوب – نائب
Alternative	variante	بديل
Alternative cost	coût alternatif	تكلفة الخيار – نفقة الخيار – تكلفة بديلة
Alternative use cost	coût d'opportunité	
Alternative growth paths	sentiers alternatifs de croissance	مسالك نمو بديلة
Alternative maturity deposits	dépôts à maturité optionelle	ودائع مع خيار الأجل
Alternative projects	contre-projets	مشاريع بديلة
Alternative source of energy	source alternative d'énergie	مصدر بديل للطاقة

Alternative technology	variante technologique technologie alternative	فن انتاجي بديل-تكنية بديلة-تكنولجية بديلة
Amalgamation	fusion	اندماج – دمج
Amortisation of a loan	amortissement d'un prêt	استهلاك قرض – سداد قرض
Amortisation of an asset	amortissement d'un bien	استهلاك اصل
Amortisation schedule **Amortisation table**	calendrier d'amortissement tableau d'amortissement	جدول استهلاك – جدول سداد
Amortisation procedure	modalités d'amortissement	أحكام الاستهلاك
Amount	montant – somme	مبلغ
Amount drawn	montant prélevé – montant déboursé montant utilisé	مبلغ مسحوب – مبلغ مستخدم
Amount of money invested	somme d'argent placée – mise de fonds	مبلغ مستثمر
Amounts past due	montants échus	مبالغ مستحقة-مبالغ حل استحقاقها-مبالغ حالة
Amount repaid	montant remboursé	مبلغ مسدد
Analysis column	colonne de ventilation	عمود الفرز
Analytical approach	approche analytique	منهج تحليلي – اسلوب تحليلي
Anarchism	anarchisme	الفوضوية-المذهب الفوضوي
Anarchy of production	anarchie de la production	فوضى الانتاج
Anchorage charges	droits d'amarrage	رسوم الرسو
Ancillary equipment	appareillage annexe équipement ancillaire	أجهزة تكميلية – معدات تكميلية
Ancillary facilities	installations ancillaires	منشآت تكميلية
Ancillary government enterprises	entreprises publiques auxiliaires	مشروعات خدمة الحكومة
Ancillary works	travaux accessoires	أعمال تكميلية – أشغال تبعية
Animal and vegetable oils and fats	huiles et graisses animales et végétales	زيوت وشحوم حيوانية ونباتية
Animal breeding	élevage sélection animale	تربية الحيوان – تحسين السلالات الحيوانية
Animal fats	graisses animales	شحوم حيوانية – دهون حيوانية
Animal husbandry	élevage	تربية الحيوان
Animal manure	engrais animal	سماد حيواني
Animal nutrition	nutrition animale	تغذية الحيوان
Animal production	production animale	انتاج حيواني
Animal resources	ressources animales	موارد حيوانية
Annual budget	budget annuel	موازنة سنوية – ميزانية سنوية
Annual consultation	consultations annuelles	دورة التشاور السنوي
Annual cost	coût annuel	تكلفة سنوية – نفقة سنوية
Annual instalment	annuité versement annuel	قسط سنوي
Annuity	annuité	قسط سنوي – ربع سنوي – سناهية
Anti-cyclical policy	politique anticyclique politique conjoncturelle	سياسة مواجهة الدورات – سياسة مكافحة الدورات
Anti-dumping duties	droits antidumping	رسوم مكافحة الاغراق

Anti-dumping measures	mesures antidumping	تدابير مكافحة الاغراق – اجراءات مكافحة الاغراق
Anti-inflationary policy	politique anti-inflationniste	سياسة مكافحة التضخم
Anti-protectionist policy	politique anti-protectionniste	سياسة مكافحة الحماية التجارية
Anti-trust laws	lois antitrusts	قوانين مكافحة الاحتكار
Anticipated demand	demande prévue	طلب متوقع – طلب مرتقب
Anticipated payment	paiement anticipé	دفع مسبق – دفع قبل الأجل – دفع مبتسر
Anticipated profit	bénéfice escompté	ربح متوقع – ربح مرتقب
Anticipated redemption	rachat anticipé	سداد مبتسر – سداد قبل الأجل
	remboursement anticipé	
apartheid	apartheid	فصل عنصري – تمييز عنصري – عزل عنصري
	ségrégation raciale	
Apiculture	apiculture	تربية النحل – النحالة
Applicant	demandeur – postulant	طالب – مكتتب
	requérant – souscripteur	
Application	demande – souscription	طلب – اكتتاب – تخصيص
	affectation	
Application for reimbursement	demande de remboursement	طلب سداد نفقات – طلب تغطية دفع
Application of funds	emplois des fonds	أوجه استخدام الأموال – استخدام الموارد المالية
Application rights	droits de souscription	حقوق اكتتاب
Applied economics	économie appliquée	الاقتصاد التطبيقي
Apportion expenses, to	ventiler les frais	صنّف النفقات – وزع النفقات
Appraisal	évaluation – évaluation *ex ante*	تقييم – تقدير
Appraisal methodology	méthodologie de l'évaluation	منهج التقييم – منهجية التقييم
Appraisal mission	mission d'évaluation	بعثة التقييم
Appraisal objectivity	objectivité de l'évaluation	موضوعية التقييم
Appraisal value	valeur estimative	قيمة مقدرة
Appraised value		
Appraiser	évaluateur – priseur	مثمّن – مقيّم – مقدّر
	estimateur – commissaire-priseur	
Appreciation	accroissement de valeur	ارتفاع القيمة – زيادة القيمة – نماء
	plus-value – appréciation	
Apprentice	apprenti – novice	صبي – متدرب
Apprenticeship	apprentissage – noviciat	تدرّب
Appropriate funds, to	affecter des fonds	خصص مبالغ – خصص أموالا
Appropriate technology	technologie appropriée	تكنولوجية مناسبة
Appropriations (*budgetary*)	crédits (*budgétaires*)	اعتمادات (موازنة)
Appropriation account	compte d'affectation	حساب التخصيص
Appropriations-in-aid	recettes non fiscales	ايرادات غير ضريبية
Approval of a loan	octroi d'un prêt – approbation d'un prêt	اعتماد قرض – منح قرض
Approximation error	erreur d'approximation	خطأ التقريب
Arable land	terres arables	اراض فليحة – اراض قابلة للفلاحة
	terres labourables	اراض قابلة للزراعة
	terres cultivables	

Arbitrage **Arbitration** (*exchange, markets*)	arbitrage (*devises, marchés*)	موازنة (الصرف ، الأسواق)
Arbitrager **Arbitrageur**	arbitragiste	موازن
Arbitration (*law*)	arbitrage (*droit*)	تحكيم (قانون)
Arbitrage award	sentence arbitrale	قرار التحكيم
Arbitration clause	clause compromissoire	شرط التحكيم – نص التحكيم
Arbitrator	arbitre	محكم
Arboriculture	arboriculture	زراعة الأشجار
Arc elasticity	élasticité d'arc	مرونة قوسية
Area	région zone périmètre	منطقة
Arid zone	zone aride	منطقة جافة
Arithmetic mean	moyenne arithmétique	وسط حسابي – متوسط حسابي
Arithmetic progression	progression arithmétique	متوالية حسابية
Arm's length price	prix acheteur non affilié	سعر الغرباء
Arrears	impayés arriérés	متأخرات
Artel (USRR)	*artel* (URSS)	آرتل (الاتحاد السوفيتي) – تعاونية زراعية
Artifical insemination	insémination artificielle	تلقيح صناعي
Asiatic mode of production	mode de production asiatique	نظام الانتاج الآسيوي
Asked price	cours-vendeur	سعر البيع – سعر البائع
Assembly costs	coûts de montage	تكاليف التجميع
Assembly industry	industrie de montage	صناعة تجميع
Assembly line	chaîne – tapis roulant	بساط تجميع
Assembly plant	usine d'assemblage – usine de montage	مصنع تجميع
Assembly workshop	atelier de montage	ورشة تجميع
Assessable income **Assessed income**	revenu imposable	دخل خاضع للضريبة
Assessable value	valeur imposable	قيمة خاضعة للضريبة
Assessed value	valeur estimée	قيمة مقدرة – قيمة تقديرية
Assessment (*taxation*)	imposition – cote (*impôts*)	فرض الضريبة – اخضاع للضريبة – ضريبة تقدير الضريبة
Assets	actif – avoirs	اصول
Assets and liabilities	actif et passif	اصول وخصوم
Asset management	gestion de l'actif – gestion d'actif	ادارة الاصول -- تدبير الاصول
Assignment of a claim	cession d'une créance	تحويل دين – تحويل حق
Assistance	assistance – aide	معونة – مساعدة – اعانة
Assistant manager	sous-directeur – directeur adjoint	مدير مساعد
Associated costs (*projects*)	coûts adjoints (*projects*)	تكاليف ملحقة – تكاليف جانبية (مشاريع)
Association	association	مشاركة – تشارك – جمعية – رابطة

Association agreement	traité d'association	اتفاق مشاركة – اتفاق انتساب
	accord d'association	
Association coefficient	coefficient d'association	معامل الاقتران
Assurance	assurance	تأمين
Assurance company	compagnie d'assurance	شركة تأمين
Assurance policy	police d'assurance	صك تأمين
Asymmetrical distribution	distribution asymétrique	توزيع غير متماثل
Atomic power	énergie atomique	طاقة ذرية
Attachment	saisie	حجز
Auction	enchères – encan	مزاد – حراج – مناداة
Auction room	salle de vente aux enchères	صالة مزاد
Auction sale	vente aux enchères	بيع بالمزاد
Auctioneer	commissaire-priseur	دلال
Audio-visual teaching aids	auxiliaires d'instruction audio-visuels	أجهزة تعليم سمعية بصرية
Audit committee	comité de vérification des comptes	لجنة تدقيق الحسابات
Audit report	rapport de verification	تقرير التدقيق – تقرير التقييم – تقرير التقييم اللاحق
	rapport d'évaluation	
	rapport de post-verification	
Audited financial statements	comptes certifiés	بيانات مالية مدققة – حسابات مدققة
	comptes vérifiés	
Auditing	vérification des comptes	تدقيق الحسابات
Auditing agency	organe vérificateur	جهاز تدقيق الحسابات – جهاز تدقيق
	organisme de vérification comptable	مكتب تدقيق
Auditor	vérificateur de comptes	مدقق حسابات – مدقق
	réviseur comptable	
Austerity	austérité	تقشف
Austerity measures	mesures d'austérité	اجراءات تقشف
Autarky	autarcie	اكتفاء ذاتي
Author's rights	droits d'auteur	حقوق المؤلف
Authorised bank	banque agréée	بنك معتمد
Authorised capital	capital autorisé – capital social	رسمال مصرح
Authorised signatures	signataires habilités	توقيعات معتمدة – أصحاب الحق في التوقيع
	signatures autorisées	
Auto-correlation	auto-corrélation	ارتباط ذاتي
Automate, to	automatiser	اتمت – وتمت
Automated plant	usine automatisée	مصنع مؤتمت – مصنع موتمت
Automated production	production automatisée	انتاج مؤتمت – انتاج موتمت
Automation	automation	أتمتة – وتمتة
	automatisation	
Automotive industry	industrie automobile	صناعة السيارات
Autonomous capital movement	mouvement autonome de capital	حركة رسمال مستقلة
Autonomous investment	investissement autonome	استثمار مستقل
Autonomous transactions	opérations autonomes	عملية ذاتية – عمليات مستقلة
Autonomy	autonomie	استقلال ذاتي
Auto-regression	auto-régression	ارتداد ذاتي
Available funds	disponibilités	مبالغ متاحة – أموال متاحة
	fonds disponibles	

Available resources	ressources disponibles	موارد متاحة
Average	moyenne	وسط – متوسط
Average (*maritime law*)	avaries (*droit maritime*)	خسائر بحرية (قانون بحري)
Average cost	coût moyen	متوسط التكلفة – التكلفة الوسط – التكلفة المتوسطة
Average life (*bonds*)	maturité moyenne (*obligations*)	متوسط الأجل (سندات)
Average price	prix moyen	متوسط الثمن – الثمن الوسط – متوسط السعر الثمن المتوسط
Average return	rendement moyen	متوسط العائد – العائد الوسط – العائد المتوسط
Average revenue	revenu moyen	متوسط الدخل – الدخل الوسط متوسط الايراد – الدخل المتوسط
Average value	valeur moyenne	متوسط القيمة – القيمة الوسطى القيمة الوسط – القيمة المتوسطة
Averaging	faire la moyenne péréquation	توسيط – حساب الوسط – أخذ المتوسط
Averaging operations (*stock exchange*)	opérations de péréquation (*bourse*)	عمليات توسيط (بورصة)
Aviculture	aviculture	تربية الدجاج
Award	décision jugement montant adjugé	قرار – حكم – مبلغ محكوم به
Award of contracts	octroi de marchés	ارساء التعاقد – اختيار المتعاقدين ارساء العطاءات

B

Baby bonds	mini-obligations	سنيدات
Back a bill, to	endosser un effet	ظهر ورقة تجارية
Back interest	arrérages d'intérêts	فوائد متأخرة – فوائد سابقة
Back-to-back guarantee	garantie réciproque garantie croisée	ضمان متبادل – كفالة متبادلة
Back-to-back joint ventures	entreprises conjointes réciproques entreprises conjointes croisées	مشاريع مشتركة متبادلة
Backward areas	régions arriérées	مناطق متخلفة
Backward economy	économie arriérée	اقتصاد متخلف – اقتصاد متأخر
Backward integration	intégration vers l'amont	تكامل خلفي – تكامل إلى الخلف
Backward linkages	liens à l'amont liaisons – amont	روابط خلفية
Backward sloping supply curve	courbe d'offre renversée	منحنى العرض الملتوي
Backwardisation Backwardation	déport	علاوة تأجيل – ترحيل – تأجيل
"Bads"	nuisances – biens négatifs	اضرار – منتجات سالبة

Bad claims	mauvaises créances	ديون معدومة – ديون مشبوهة
Bad debts	créances amorties	
Balance	balance	ميزان – رصيد – توازن
	solde	
	équilibre	
Balance, to	balancer	وازن
	solder	
Balance brought forward	solde de l'exercice précédent	رصيد مرحل من الفترة السابقة
	solde à reporter	
Balance of capital	balance des capitaux	ميزان الرسمال – ميزان حركات الرسمال
Balance of external payments	balance des comptes extérieurs	ميزان المدفوعات الخارجية
Balance of payments	balance des paiements	ميزان المدفوعات
Balance of payments deficit	déficit de la balance des paiements	عجز ميزان المدفوعات
Balance of payments gap	écart dans la balance des paiements	فجوة ميزان المدفوعات–عجز ميزان المدفوعات
Balance of payments on current account	balance des paiements courants	ميزان المدفوعات الجارية
Balance of payments position	état de la balance des paiements	وضع ميزان المدفوعات
Balance of payments support	soutien à la balance des paiements	مساندة ميزان المدفوعات–دعم ميزان المدفوعات
Balance of payments surplus	excédent de la balance des paiements	فائض ميزان المدفوعات
Balance of trade	balance commerciale	ميزان التجارة
Balance sheet	bilan	ميزانية
Balance sheet item	poste du bilan	بند الميزانية
Balanced budget	budget équilibré	موازنة متكافئة – ميزانية متوازنة
Balanced budget multiplier	multiplicateur du budget équilibré	مضاعف الموازنة المتكافئة–مضاعف الميزانية المتوازنة
Balanced growth	croissance équilibrée	نمو متوازن – نمو متكافىء
Balancing item	élément de contrepartie	بند موازن
	poste de contrepartie	
Band of foreign exchange fluctuation	bande de fluctuation des changes	هامش تغير الصرف
Bank	banque	بنك – مصرف
Bank acceptance	acceptation bancaire	قبول مصرفي – قبالة مصرفية
Bank account	compte bancaire	حساب مصرفي
Bank balances	soldes bancaires – comptes bancaires	أرصدة مصرفية
Bank charges	frais bancaires	رسوم مصرفية
	frais de banque	
Bank clearing	compensation bancaire	مقاصة مصرفية
Bank commission	commission bancaire	عمولة مصرفية
Bank credit	crédit bancaire	ائتمان مصرفي
Bank deposits	dépôts bancaires	ودائع مصرفية
Bank discount	escompte bancaire	خصم مصرفي – حسم مصرفي
	escompte commercial	
Bank guarantee	caution bancaire	كفالة مصرفية
Bank holiday	jour férié	يوم أجازة– عطلة
Bank liquidity	liquidité des banques	سيولة البنوك – سيولة المصارف سيولة مصرفية
	liquidité bancaire	

Bank liquidity ratio	ratio de liquidité bancaire	نسبة السيولة المصرفية
Bank loan	prêt bancaire	قرض مصرفي
Bank manager	directeur de banque	مدير مصرف
Bank money	monnaie scripturale monnaie bancaire	نقود مصرفية – نقود كتابية
Bank-note	billet de banque	ورقة نقدية – بنكنوت
Bank-notes in circulation	billets de banque en circulation	الأوراق النقدية المتداولة
Bank of issue	banque d'émission institut d'émission	بنك الاصدار – مصرف الاصدار
Bank rate	taux officiel d'escompte	سعر الخصم الرسمي–سعر الحسم الرسمي
Bank shares	valeurs bancaires	أسهم مصرفية
Bank statement	relevé de compte bancaire	كشف حساب مصرفي
Bank transfer	virement bancaire	تحويل مصرفي
Bankable loan	emprunt conforme aux normes bancaires – prêt bancable	قرض صالح مصرفياً قرض موافق للمعايير المصرفية
Bankable paper	effet bancable	سند قابل للخصم – سند صالح مصرفياً
Bankable project	projet bancable	مشروع صالح لاقراض مصرفي–مشروع صالح مصرفيا
Banker	banquier	صاحب مصرف – بنكير
Banker's draft	chèque bancaire	حوالة مصرفية – شيك مصرفي
Banking circles	milieux bancaires – la banque	دوائر مصرفية
Banking house **Banking institution**	établissement bancaire	مؤسسة مصرفية
Banking laws	législation bancaire	تشريعات مصرفية
Banking network	réseau bancaire	شبكة مصرفية
Banking operations	opérations bancaires	عمليات مصرفية
Banking organisation	organisation bancaire	تنظيم مصرفي
Banking policy	politique bancaire	سياسة مصرفية
Banking practice	usage bancaire	عرف مصرفي
Banking secret	secret bancaire	السرية المصرفية – الكتمان المصرفي
Banking structure	structure bancaire	هيكل مصرفي
Banking syndicate	syndicat de banques consortium bancaire	جمعية مصارف–جمعية مصرفية دارة مصرفية
Banking system	système bancaire	نظام مصرفي
Bankruptcy	faillite – banqueroute	افلاس
Bar gold	or en barres	سبائك ذهبية – سبائك ذهب
Bargain	affaire - négociation marché	معاملة – عملية تجارية – صفقة – تفاوض
Bargain, to	marchander	ساوم
Bargain prices	prix de solde – prix soldés	أسعار مخفضة – أثمان تصفية

Bargaining	marchandage	مساومة – مماكسة – مكاس
	négociation	
Bargaining power	pouvoir de négociation	قوة المساومة – طاقة المساومة
Barter	troc – échange	مقايضة – مبادلة عينية
Barter agreement	accord de troc	اتفاقات مقايضة
Barter arrangement		
Barter economy	économie de troc	اقتصاد مقايضة
Barter terms of trade	termes réels de l'échange	المعدل السلعي للتبادل
Barter trade	troc –	مقايضة – تجارة مقايضة
	commerce de troc	
Barter transactions	opérations de troc	عملية مقايضة
Base period	période de base	فترة الاساس
	période de référence	
Base portfolio	portefeuille-type	حافظة نموذجية
Base price	prix de base	سعر الأساس – ثمن أساسي
Basic price		
Base reversal test	test d'inversion de la base	اختبار عكس الأساس – معيار عكس الأساس
Base year	année de base	سنة الأساس
	année de référence	
Basic commodities	produits de base	سلع أساسية – سلع رئيسية
Basic consumption items	biens de consommation de base	سلع الاستهلاك الأساسي
Basic crops	cultures de base	محاصيل أساسية – حاصلات أساسية
Basic data	données de base	بيانات أساسية
Basic industry	industrie de base	صناعة أساسية
Basic needs	besoins essentiels	حاجات اساسية
Basic tariff	tarif de base	تعرفة أساسية
Basic wage	salaire de base	اجر أساسي
Basic works	travaux de base	أعمال أساسية – أشغال أساسية
Basin irrigation	irrigation par bassins	ري الحياض
Basing point system	système du prix de référence	نظام التسعير الجغرافي
	géographique	نظام نقطة الأساس
	système du point de base	
Bear	baissier – spéculateur à la baisse	مضارب انخفاضي – دب
Bear market	marché à la baisse	سوق متشائم – سوق حادر
Bear sale	vente à découvert	بيع على المكشوف
Bearer	porteur	حامل (سند)
Bearer bond	obligation au porteur	سند لحامله – اذن لحامله
	bon au porteur	
Bearer check	chèque au porteur	شيك لحامله
Bearer securities	titres au porteur	صكوك لحاملها – سندات لحاملها
Bearer share	action au porteur	سهم لحامله
Bearish market	marché orienté à la baisse	سوق متشائم

Bearing interest	portant intérêts productif d'intérêts	مدر لفوائد
Bedouin population	bédouins – population bédouine	البدو – سكان البادية
Before-and-after test (*projects*)	test "avant-après" (*projets*)	اختبار الواقع والمتوقع (مشاريع)
Beggar-my-neighbour policy	politique de bataille	سياسة افقار الجار
Behaviour	comportement attitude	سلوك – اتجاه
Behaviour equations **Behavioural equations**	équations de comportement	معادلات سلوكية
Bell-shaped curve	courbe à forme de cloche	منحنى جرسي الشكل
Below the line	hors bilan	خارج الميزانية
Benchmark data	données de référence	بيانات أساسية – بيانات اسنادية
Beneficiary	bénéficiaire	مستفيد
Beneficiary country	pays bénéficiaire	دولة مستفيدة
Beneficial interest **Beneficial ownership**	droit d'usufruit	حق انتفاع
Benefits	avantages – bénéfices	منافع – فوائد
Benefit plan	système de prévoyance	نظام تأمين
Best fit	meilleur ajustement	أفضل مطابقة
Betterment tax	impôt sur la plus-value	ضريبة النماء – ضريبة على زيادة القيمة
Beverage industries	industries des boissons	صناعة المشروبات
Biased estimate	estimation partiale – estimation biaisée	تقدير منحاز
Biased sample	échantillon non neutre – échantillon biaisé	عينة غير عشوائية – عينة متحيزة
Biased test	test biaisé	اختبار متحيز – اختبار غير عشوائي
Bid	offre – soumission – mise – enchère	عرض – عطاء – طلب – مزايدة
Bid, to	miser – enchérir	زايد – عرض ثمنا
Bid analysis	vérification des offres	فحص العطاءات
Bid bond	caution de soumission	تأمين العطاء
Bid evaluation	évaluation des offres	تقييم العطاءات
Bid price	prix acheteur prix de soumission	سعر العطاء – ثمن الشراء ثمن المشترى
Bidder	soumissionnaire enchérisseur	صاحب عطاء – مزايد
Bidding conditions	bases de soumission	شروط العطاء
Bi-factorial terms of trade	termes de l'échange bifactoriel	معدل التبادل العواملي المزدوج
Big business	grand capital	كبار الرسماليين – الرسمال الكبير
Big-push theory	théorie de la grande poussée théorie de la propulsion	نظرية الدفرة القوية
Bilateral agreement	accord bilatéral	اتفاق ثنائي – اتفاقية ثنائية
Bilateral aid **Bilateral assistance**	aide bilatérale assistance bilatérale	مساعدة ثنائية – معونة ثنائية اعانة ثنائية
Bilateral concessional loans	prêts concessionnels bilatéraux	قروض ثنائية ميسرة

Bilateral monopoly	monopole bilatéral	احتكار ثنائي
Bilateral payments agreement	accord de paiements bilatéral	اتفاق ثنائي للمدفوعات – اتفاقية ثنائية للدفع
Bilateral trade	commerce bilatéral	تجارة ثنائية
Bilateralism	bilatéralisme	الثنائية
Bill	facture – effet	فاتورة – حسبونة –
	traite – bulletin	كمبيالة – سند اذني
	billet	ايصال – ورقة نقدية
Bill, to	facturer	فوتر – حسبن
Bill diary	échéancier	دفتر الاستحقاقات
Bill of exchange	traite – effet commercial	كمبيالة – ورقة تجارية
	effet de commerce – lettre de change	
Bill of lading	connaissement	شهادة شحن – صك شحن
Bills payable	effets à payer	أوراق تحت الدفع – سندات للدفع
Bills receivable	effets à recevoir	أوراق تحت القبض – سندات مستحقة
Bimetallism	bimétallisme	نظام المعدنين
Bimodal distribution	distribution bimodale	توزيع ذو منوالين
Binomial distribution	distribution binomiale	توزيع ذات الحدين
Birth control	contrôle des naissances	تنظيم النسل – تحديد النسل
	régulation des naissances	
Birth-rate	taux de natalité	معدل المواليد
Black list	liste noire	القائمة السوداء
Black market	marché noir	سوق سوداء
Blank cheque	chèque en blanc	شيك على بياض
Blank endorsement	endossement en blanc	تظهير على بياض
Blend lending	aide mixte – prêt panaché	اقراض خليط – اقراض مختلط
Block of securities	paquet de titres	رزمة أوراق مالية
Blockade	blocus	حصار
Blocked balances	avoirs bloqués – fonds bloqués	أرصدة مجمدة – أموال مجمدة
Blue chips	valeurs de premier ordre	أوراق مالية ممتازة
Blue-collar workers	travailleurs manuels – cols-bleus	عمال يدويون – عمال اليد – ذور الياقات الزرقاء
Blue-sky laws	lois sur l'émission et la vente de titres	قوانين اصدار وبيع الأوراق المالية
Body of creditors	masse des créanciers	مجموعة الدائنين
Bogus company	société fantôme – société fictive	شركة وهمية
bona fide **holder**	porteur de bonne foi	حامل حسن النية – حائز حسن النية
Bonanza	prospérité – abondance	ازدهار – رفاهية – يسار
Bond	bon – titre – obligation – garantie	سند – اذن – ضمان
Bond, in	entreposé – à l'entrepôt	مودع – مخزون
Bond issue	émission d'obligations	اصدار سندات
Bond market	marché des obligations	سوق السندات
	marché obligataire	
Bond rate	taux d'intérêt nominal	سعر الفائدة الاسمي
Bond yield	rendement des obligations	عائد السندات
Bondage	servage	رق

Bonded debt	dette garantie	دين مكفول – دين مضمون
Bonded goods	marchandises entreposées	سلع في المخزن – سلع في الجمرك
Bonded warehouse	entrepôt légal	مخزن رسمي – مخزن جمركي
	entrepôt de douane	
Bondholder	obligataire	حامل سند – صاحب سند
	détenteur d'obligations	
Bondholder community	association des obligataires – syndicat	جمعية حملة السندات
	des obligataires	
	masse des obligataires	
Bonding	entreposage	تخزين
Bondsman	garant	كفيل – ضامن
Bonus	prime – gratification –	علاوة – منحة – مكافأة
	bonus	
Bonus issue	émission d'actions gratuites	توزيع أسهم مجانية – اصدار أسهم مجانية
	distribution d'actions gratuites	
Bonus shares	actions gratuites	أسهم مجانية
Book entry	écriture comptable	قيد دفتري – قيد محاسبي
Book-keeping	comptabilité –	محاسبة – مسك دفاتر
	tenue des livres	
Book losses	pertes comptables	خسائر دفترية
Book profits	bénéfices comptables	أرباح دفترية
Book value	valeur comptable	قيمة دفترية
Books	livres – comptabilité	دفاتر – محاسبة
Boom	boom – hausse conjoncturelle	رخاء – فترة الرخاء
Booming economy	économie euphorique	اقتصاد منتعش – اقتصاد مزدهر
	économie en plein essor	
Border prices	prix frontaliers – prix à la frontière	أسعار الحدود
Border workers	travailleurs frontaliers	عمال الحدود
Borrow, to	emprunter	اقترض
Borrower	emprunteur	مقترض
Borrowing capacity	capacité d'endettement	طاقة الاقتراض – طاقة الاستدانة
Borrowing country	pays emprunteur	دولة مقترضة
Bottleneck	goulot d'étranglement – goulet	مأزم – مأزل – مختنق
	d'étranglement	
Bottom-up planning	planification à partir de la base	تخطيط من القاعدة
Bounty	prime	علاوة – منحة
Boycott	boycottage	مقاطعة
Brain drain	exode des cerveaux	هجرة الفنيين – هجرة العقول
	émigration des intellectuels	
Branch (*corporations*)	succursale (*sociétés*)	فرع (شركات)
Branch banking	système bancaire à succursales	نظام مصرفي متعدد الفروع
	multiples	

Branch of production	branche économique	فرع انتاج – قطاع انتاجي
	branche de production	
Brand	sorte – marque	نوع – علامة تجارية – سمة تجارية
	marque de fabrique	
Breakdown of costs	ventilation des coûts	فرز التكاليف – بيان التكاليف – توزيع التكاليف
Breakdown theory	théorie de l'effondrement	نظرية الانهيار
Break-even chart	diagramme du point mort	رسم الأربحية – رسم عتبة الأربحية
	graphique de rentabilité	
Break-even point	point mort	عتبة الأربحية – نقطة بدء الأربحية
	seuil de rentabilité	
Breeding	élevage	تربية الحيوان
Bridging agreement	accord de soudure	اتفاقية التحام
Brisk market	marché animé	سوق نشط
Broker	courtier	سمسار – عميل
Brokerage	courtage	سمسرة – عمولة
	commission	
Brokerage fee	courtage	رسم السمسرة – سمسرة – رسم عمالة
	commission	
Budget	budget	موازنة – ميزانية – ميزانية تقديرية
Budget accounts	comptes budgétaires	حسابات الموازنة – حسابات الميزانية
Budget allotments	allocations budgétaires	مخصصات الموازنة – اعتمادات مالية
Budget appropriations	crédits budgétaires	اعتمادات الموازنة – اعتمادات مالية
Budget constraint	contrainte budgétaire	قيد الموازنة – القيد المالي – الحد المالي
Budget control	contrôle budgétaire	رقابة الموازنة – الرقابة المالية
Budget deficit	déficit budgétaire	عجز الموازنة – عجز مالي
Budget equilibrium	équilibre budgétaire	تعادل الموازنة – تكافؤ الموازنة – توازن الميزانية
Budget estimates	prévisions budgétaires	تقديرات الموازنة – تقديرات الميزانية
	budget prévisionnel	
Budget expenditures	dépenses budgétaires	مصروفات الموازنة – مصروفات مالية
Budget items	articles de budget	بنود الموازنة – بنود الميزانية
	postes budgétaires	
Budget forecasts	prévisions budgétaires	تقديرات الموازنة – توقعات مالية
Budget line	ligne du budget	خط الانفاق
Budget management	gestion budgétaire	ادارة الموازنة – ادارة الميزانية
Budget policy	politique budgétaire	سياسة مالية
Budget practice	pratiques budgétaires	أساليب مالية
Budget proposal	projet de budget	مشروع الموازنة – مشروع الميزانية
Budget receipts	recettes budgétaires	ايرادات الموازنة – ايرادات الميزانية
Budget revenues		
Budget surplus	excédent budgétaire	فائض الموازنة – فائض مالي – فائض الميزانية
Budget support	aide budgétaire	مساندة الموازنة – مساندة الميزانية
Budget year	exercice budgétaire	سنة مالية
Budgetary aid	aide budgétaire	اعانة الموازنة – مساعدة الميزانية

Budgetary gap	déficit budgétaire	قدرة تجارية – مهارة تجارية
Budgetary pressures	difficultés budgétaires	صعوبات مالية
Budgetary resources	ressources budgétaires	موارد الموازنة – ايرادات الميزانية
Budgeted funds	fonds inscrits au budget	أموال مرصودة في الموازنة – اعتمادات الميزانية
Budgeting	établissement du budget budgétisation	موازنة – توزين
Buffer-stock	stock tampon stock régulateur	مصد سلعي
Buffer-stock agency	organisme chargé du stock régulateur gérant du stock régulateur	جهاز تسيير المصد السلعي
Building industry	industrie du bâtiment	صناعة البناء
Built-in stabiliser	stabilisateur automatique	مثبت ذاتي – ثبات ذاتي
Bulk carrier	transporteur en vrac	ناقلة أحجام
Bulk purchase	achat en gros – achat en vrac	شراء بالجملة – شراء أحجام
Bulk transactions	opérations en gros	عمليات جملة
Bull	haussier	مضارب على ارتفاع السوق – مضارب متفائل – ثور
Bull purchase	achat à découvert – achat à la hausse	شراء على المكشوف
Bullet issue	émission à maturité unique	اصدار طلقي
Bullion	barres – lingots	سبيكة – سبائك معدنية
Bullion trade	commerce des métaux précieux	تجارة المعادن النفيسة
Bullish market	marché orienté à la hausse	سوق متفائل – سوق صاعد
Bumper crop	récolte exceptionnelle	محصول استثنائي
Bunkering facilities	facilités d'approvisionnement	تسهيلات تزويد السفن – تسهيلات تموين السفن
Buoyant market	marché actif – marché animé	سوق نشط – سوق منتعش
Burden of aid	fardeau de l'aide	عبء المعونات – عبء المساعدات
Burden sharing	répartition des charges partage des charges	توزيع العبء – اقتسام العبء
Bureaucracy	bureaucratie	بيروقراطية
Bureaucratisation	bureaucratisation	برقطة
Business	les affaire – entreprise commerce – négoce	النشاط التجاري – المبادلات – التجارة – مشروع
Business administration	gestion industrielle	ادارة صناعية
Business climate	ambiance économique	مناخ الأعمال – جو الأعمال
Business community	milieux d'affaires	دوائر الأعمال
Business conditions	conjoncture	وضع الأسواق – حالة الأسواق
Business customs	usages commerciaux	عرف تجاري – أعراف تجارية
Business cycle	cycle économique	دورة اقتصادية
Business day	jour ouvrable	يوم من أيام العمل – يوم عمل
Business economics	économie de l'entreprise	اقتصاديات المشروع
Business failures	faillites commerciales	افلاس المؤسسات – مفالس – تفاليس
Business men	hommes d'affaires	رجال أعمال
Business origination	initiation d'affaires	خلق الأعمال
Business school	école de commerce	معهد تجاري – مدرسة تجارية

Business sense	flair commercial / talent commercial	عجز الموازنة – عجز الميزانية – عجز مالي
Buy, to	acheter	اشترى
Buy-back price	prix de rachat	سعر اعادة الشراء
Buy maturities, to	acheter des échéances	شراء استحقاقات – شراء شرائح قروض
Buyer	acheteur	مشترى
Buyers' credit	crédit-acheteur	ائتمان المشترين
Buyers market	marché acheteur	سوق المشترين
Buying power	pouvoir d'achat	قوة شرائية
Buying rate	cours acheteur	سعر الشراء
By-product	sous-produit	ناتج مشتق – ناتج فرعي
By-road	chemin de desserte	طريق جانبي – طريق فرعي

C

Cable transfer	virement télégraphique – transfert télégraphique	تحويل برق
Calculated risk	risque calculé	مخاطرة متعمدة
Calendar of issues	calendrier des émissions	برنامج الاصدار – برنامج الاصدارات
Call a loan, to	demander le remboursement d'un prêt	طلب سداد القرض
Call deposit	dépôt à vue	وديعة معجلة – حساب مصرفي معجل / وديعة تحت الطلب – حساب تحت الطلب
Call for capital	appel de fonds	طلب أداء الرسمال – دعوة الرسمال
Call loan	prêt au jour le jour / prêt exigible	قرض معجل – قرض مياوم
Call money	argent au jour le jour / argent à vue	ائتمان معجل – ائتمان مياوم / سلفية معجلة – سلفية تحت الطلب
Call of more	option du double	خيار الضعف
Call option	option d'achat / prime acheteur	خيار شراء – علاوة شراء
Call price	prix acheteur	سعر الشراء
Call receipt	récépissé de paiement sur appel de fonds	ايصال أداء
Callable bond	obligations remboursables / obligations révocables	سندات قابلة للسحب / سندات قابلة للسداد
Callable capital	capital exigible	رسمال ضامن – رسمال قابل للأداء
Callable loan	crédit révocable	قرض قابل للفسخ
Called bonds	obligations révoquées – obligations à rembourser	سندات مسحوبة
Called-up capital	capital appelé	رسمال مدعي
Cambist	cambiste	صراف – تاجر عملات
Cancellation of a debt	abrogation d'une dette / annulation d'une dette	الغاء دين

Canning industry	conserverie – industrie de conserves	صناعة التعليب
Canvassing	démarchage	تسويق – لفاف
Capacity for development	capacité de développement	قدرة على النمو – طاقة النمو
Capacity utilisation	utilisation de la capacité de production	استخدام طاقة الانتاج
Capita, per	per capita – par tête	للفرد الواحد-فردي-للفرد من السكان
Capital	capital – fonds – apport	رسمال – حصة
Capital account	compte de capital	حساب الرسمال
Capital accumulation	accumulation du capital	تراكم الرسمال
Capital appreciation	plus-value – appréciation du capital	نماء – زيادة الرسمال
Capital assets	biens de capital – capitaux fixes	أصول رسمالية
Capital budget	budget d'équipement budget d'investissement budget de capital	موازنة رسمالية – موازنة استثمارية
Capital budgeting	budgétisation du capital	برمجة الرسمال – توزين الرسمال
Capital consumption	consommation du capital	استهلاك الرسمال-استهلاك الأصول الرسمالية
Capital contribution	contribution en capital	اسهام في الموارد-اسهام في الرسمال
Capital costs	coûts d'investissement	تكاليف رسمالية – تكاليف استثمارية
Capital deepening	intensification du capital	تعميق الرسمال
Capital efficiency	productivité du capital efficacité du capital	انتاجية الرسمال – فاعلية الرسمال
Capital endowment	dotation en capital	التزويد بالرسمال – الزود الرسمالي
Capital equipment	capitaux matériels – équipement	أجهزة انتاجية
Capital erosion	érosion du capital	تآكل الرسمال – تداثر الرسمال
Capital expenditures	dépenses d'équipement dépenses d'investissement dépenses en capital	انفاق رسمالي – انفاق استثماري نفقات رسمالية – نفقات استثمارية
Capital export	exportation du capital	تصدير رسمال
Capital exports	exportations de capitaux	صادرات رسمالية
Capital exporting country	pays exportateur de capital	دولة مصدرة للرسمال
Capital flight	fuite de capitaux exode des capitaux	هروب الرسمال – هجرة الرسمال
Capital flow	flux de capitaux mouvement de capitaux apport de capitaux	تدفق الرسمال – فيض الرسمال حركة الرسمال
Capital formation	formation de capital	تكوين الرسمال – تراكم الرسمال
Capital gains	gains en capital plus-values	مكاسب رسمالية – أرباح رسمالية
Capital gain tax	impôt sur les plus-values	ضريبة النماء الرسمالي
Capital goods	biens de capital biens d'investissement biens d'équipement	سلع رسمالية – سلع استثمارية منتجات رسمالية

Capital goods industry	industrie de biens d'équipement	صناعة المنتجات الرسمالية – صناعة أجهزة الانتاج
Capital grant	don en capital donation en capital	منحة رسمالية – هبة مالية
Capital importing country	pays importateur de capital	دولة مستوردة للرسمال
Capital increase	augmentation de capital	زيادة الرسمال
Capital inflow	entrée de capitaux	دخول الرسمال
Capital intensity	intensité de capital intensité capitalistique	كثافة رسمالية – كثافة الرسمال
Capital-intensive project	projet capitalistique	مشروع كثيف الرسمال
Capital-intensive technology	technologie capitalistique	فن كثيف الرسمال – تكنولوجية رسمالية تكنية كثيفة الرسمال
Capital invested	capital investi – apport capital engagé	رسمال مستثمر – رسمال موظف
Capital issue	émissions de valeurs	اصدار أوراق مالية
Capital-labour ratio	rapport capital-travail	نسبة الرسمال للعمل
Capital-labour substitution	substitution capital-travail	استبدال الرسمال والعمل
Capital levy	prélèvement sur le capital	ضريبة على الرسمال
Capital liabilities	passif à long terme	خصوم طويلة الأجل
Capital losses	pertes en capital	خسائر رسمالية
Capital market	marché des capitaux	سوق مالي – سوق الرسمال
Capital movement	mouvement de capitaux	حركة رسمال
Capital outflow	sortie de capitaux	خروج الرسمال
Capital outlays	dépenses d'équipement	انفاق رسمالي – نفقات رسمالية
Capital-output ratio	coefficient de capital	معامل الرسمال – معامل انتاجية الرسمال
Capital recovery factor	coefficient d'amortissement	معامل السداد – معامل الاسترداد معامل الاستهلاك
Capital repairs	réparations majeures	اصلاحات أساسية – اصلاحات جوهرية
Capital requirements	besoins en capital	احتياجات رسمالية
Capital reserves	réserves-capital	احتياطيات رسمالية
Capital resources	ressources en capital	موارد رسمالية
Capital revenue	recettes de capital	ايرادات رسمالية
Capital rotation	rotation du capital	دورة الرسمال – تدوير الرسمال
Capital-saving technique	technique épargnant du capital	فن موفر للرسمال – تكنية خفيفة الرسمال
Capital shortage	pénurie de capital	ندرة الرسمال – شح الرسمال قصور الموارد الرسمالية
Capital stock	capital-actions capital national	رسمال سهمي – رسمال قومي
Capital structure	structure du capital structure financière	هيكل الرسمال – عناصر الرسمال – تركيب الرسمال
Capital subscription	souscription au capital	اكتتاب في الرسمال
Capital supply	offre de capitaux – disponibilité de capitaux	عرض الرسمال – توفر الرسمال
Capital transactions	opérations en capital	عملية رسمالية

Capital transfer	transfert de capital	تحويل رسمالي
Capital turnover	rotation du capital	تدوير الرسمال – دورة الرسمال
Capital value	valeur en capital	قيمة رسمالية
Capitalism	capitalisme	الرسمالية
Capitalist	capitaliste	رسمالي – صاحب رسمال
Capitalist economy	économie capitaliste	اقتصاد رسمالي
Capitalist world	monde capitaliste	العالم الرسمالي
Capitalistic production	production capitalistique	انتاج رسمالي – انتاج قائم على الرسمال انتاج كثيف الرسمال
Capitalization	capitalisation	رسملة – مجموع الرسمال
Capitalize interest, to	capitaliser les intérêts	رسمل الفوائد
Capitalized value	valeur capitalisée	قيمة الرسملة – قيمة مرسملة
Capitation tax	impôt de capitation	ضريبة الأشخاص – فردة
Captain of industry	capitaine d'industrie	رائد من رواد الصناعة
Cardinal utility	utilité cardinale	المنفعة الأصلية – المنفعة الذاتية
Cargo	cargaison	شحنة بضائع
Cargo aircraft	avion-cargo	طائرة بضاعة
Cargo capacity	capacité de chargement	طاقة الشحن
Cargo handling facilities	installations de manutention	منشآت نقل البضائع –منشآت الشحن
Cargo ship	navire cargo – cargo	باخرة شحن
Carrier	transporteur	ناقل – ناقلة
Carry forward Carry-over	report à nouveau	رصيد مرحل
Cartel	cartel	كارتل – اتفاق احتكاري
Cartelisation	cartellisation	كرتلة – تكوين كارتل
Case studies of development	études de cas de développement	دراسة حالات انمائية–دراسات انمائية تطبيقية
Cash	fonds liquides – encaisse au comptant – en espèces	نقد – رصيد الخزانة – نقدا
Cash account	compte de caisse	حساب الخزانة – حساب الصندوق
Cash accruals	accroissement des liquidités accroissement de l'encaisse	زيادة أرصدة الخزانة
Cash and carry	paiement comptant	الدفع نقداً – الدفع فور التسلم
Cash assets	encaisse – liquidités	أصول نقدية
Cash balance	solde de trésorerie encaisse	رصيد نقدي – رصيد الخزانة
Cash basis accounting	comptabilité de caisse	محاسبة على أساس الدفع – محاسبة الصندوق
Cash bonus	prime en espèces	علاوة نقدية
Cash cost	coût comptant	تكلفة نقدية
Cash crops	cultures marchandes cultures de rapport	حاصلات نقدية – حاصلات تجارية حاصلات سوقية
Cash deficit	déficit de trésorerie découvert de trésorerie	عجز الخزانة – عجز نقدي – عجز السيولة

Cash discount	escompte au comptant	خصم الدفع نقدا
Cash dividends	dividendes payés	أرباح موزعة
Cash flow	cash flow	صافي الإيراد النقدي
	recettes monétaires nettes	
	capacité bénéficiaire	
Cash flows	flux de liquidités	تدفقات نقدية
Cash holdings	avoirs liquides – encaisse	أرصدة سائلة
Cash income	revenu monétaire	دخل نقدي
Cash investments	investissements monétaires	استثمارات نقدية
Cash item	poste liquide	بند سائل – أصل سائل
Cash on delivery	paiement à la livraison	دفع عند التسليم
Cash on hand	argent disponible – caisse –	نقد حاضر – نقد سائل
	encaisse	
Cash market	marché du comptant	سوق العاجل
Cash payment	paiement comptant – paiement en	الدفع نقداً
	espèces	
	paiement au comptant	
Cash position	situation de caisse	وضع الخزانة – وضع السيولة
	situation des liquidités	
Cash projections	projections de trésorerie	توقعات السيولة – اسقاطات السيولة
Cash purchase	achat au comptant	الشراء نقداً
Cash ratio	ratio de liquidité	نسبة السيولة
Cash requirements	besoins de trésorerie	احتياجات الخزانة – احتياجات السيولة
Cash reserves	encaisse – réserves liquides	أرصدة نقدية–احتياطي نقدي
Cash sale	vente au comptant	البيع نقداً
Cash shares	actions de numéraire	أسهم نقدية
Cash with order	payable à la commande	الدفع عند أمر الشراء
Cashier	caissier	صراف – خازن
Caste system	système des castes	نظام الطوائف
Casual employment	emploi irrégulier –	عمالة عارضة – عمالة مؤقتة
	emploi intermittent	
Casual labour	travail temporaire –	عمل مؤقت
	travail intérimaire	
Casualty insurance	assurance-accidents	تأمين ضد الحوادث
Catalyst	catalyseur	حافز
Catchment basin	bassin versant	حوض الدفق
Cattle breeding	élevage bovin – élevage de bétail	تربية الماشية
Caution money	caution	ضمان – مبلغ ضمان
Caveat emptor	*caveat emptor*	على المشتري الحذر
Ceiling price	prix plafond – prix maximal	سعر أقصى – ثمن أعلى
Census	recensement	احصاء – تعداد
Centile	centile	مئين

Central bank	banque centrale	بنك مركزي – مصرف مركزي
Central government	administration publique centrale	الحكومة المركزية
Central monetrary authorities	autorités monétaires nationales	السلطات النقدية
Central planning	planification centralisée – planification centraliste	تخطيط مركزي
Central rate	taux pivot	سعر مركزي
Central tendency	tendance centrale	اتجاه مركزي – مركز الثقل
Central value	valeur centrale	قيمة مركزية
Centralisation of capital	centralisation du capital	تركيز الرسمال
Centralised economy	économie centralisée – économie centraliste	اقتصاد مركزي
Centralised planning	planification centralisée – planification centraliste	تخطيط مركزي
Centre-periphery system	système centre–périphérie	نظام المركز والهامش – نظام المركز والمحيط
Certainty	certitude	اليقين
Certificate of deposit (C.D.)	certificat de dépôt	شهادة ايداع
Certificate of indebtedness	titre de créance reconnaissance de dette	سند دين – صك مديونية
Certificate of origin	certificat d'origine	شهادة مصدر – شهادة منشأ
Certificate of shipment	certificat d'embarquement connaissement	شهادة الشحن
Certified cheque	chèque confirmé – chèque visé	شيك معتمد
ceteris paribus	*ceteris paribus*	بقاء الأشياء الأخرى على حالها
Chain index	indice-chaîne indice caténaire	مؤشر مسلسل
Chain stores	magasins à succursales multiples	متاجر متعددة الفروع
Chamber of commerce	chambre de commerce	غرفة تجارة – غرفة تجارية
Chance variable	variable aléatoire	متغير عشوائي
Channel funds, to	canaliser des fonds	وجه أموالا
Charge	charge taxe dépense	عبء – فرض – رسم – تكلفة
Charge, to	charger – imputer taxer – affecter	حمل – أسند – أخضع للضريبة – خصص
Charging what the traffic will bear	politique de prix discriminatoires maximums politique de prix maximums	سياسة التسعير التمييزي الأقصى سياسة التسعير الأقصى
Charitable contributions	contributions philantrophiques	مساهمات انسانية – صدقات
Chart	diagramme graphique contrat	رسم بياني – رسم – لوحة عقد – ميثاق
Chartered accountant	expert comptable agréé	محاسب قانوني
Chartering	affrètement – frètement	إيجار ناقلة – تأجير ناقلة
Chattels	biens mobiliers	منقولات
Cheap labour	main-d'œuvre bon marché	عمل رخيص –أيدي عاملة رخيصة– عمل بخس

Cheap money	argent à bon marché	ائتمان ميسر – نقد ميسر
Check (cheque)	chèque	شيك – صك
Check account	compte-chèques – compte à vue	حساب شيكات – حساب معجل حساب تحت الطلب
Check book	chéquier – carnet de chèque	دفتر شيكات
Check without funds	chèque sans provision	شيك بدون رصيد
Checking account Checking deposit	dépôt à vue	حساب مصرفي معجل – حساب شيكات حساب مصرفي تحت الطلب
Chemicals and chemical products industry	industries chimiques	صناعة الكيماويات والمنتجات الكيماوية
Chemical fertiliser	engrais chimique	سماد كيماوي – سماد صناعي
Child allowances	allocations pour enfants à charge	اعانات الأسرة – مخصصات الأسرة اعانات عائلية
Child care Child welfare	protection de l'enfance protection infantile	رعاية الطفولة
Child labour	travail infantile travail des mineurs	عمل الأطفال – تشغيل الأطفال
China and earthenware industry	industrie de la céramique et de la poterie	صناعة الصيني والفخار
Choice criterion	critère de choix	معيار الخيار – معيار الاختيار
Choice of location	localisation	توطين – اختيار الموقع
Choice of technology	choix de la technologie	إختيار الفن الانتاجي – اختيار التكنولوجية
Chronic malnutrition	malnutrition chronique	هزال مزمن – سوء تغذية مزمن
Chronic unemployment	chômage chronique	بطالة مزمنة – تعطل مزمن
Cif (cost, insurance, freight)	caf (coût, assurance, fret)	سيف (تكلفة ، تأمين ، شحن)
Cif price	prix caf	سعر «سيف»
Circular flow	circuit	دورة – حركة دائرية
Circulating capital	fonds de roulement	رسمال متداول – رسمال تشغيل
Circulation of money	circulation de la monnaie	تداول النقود
Circulation of capital	circulation du capital	دوران الرسمال – دورة الرسمال – تداول الرسمال
Civil engineering	génie civil	هندسة مدنية
Civil service	administration – fonction publique	الادارة الحكومية – جهاز الوظائف العامة
Claims	exigibilités – réclamations droits – créances	مستحقات – استحقاقات – حقوق – مطالبات
Class	classe	طبقة – فئة
Class consciousness	conscience de classe	وعي طبقي
Class intervals	intervalles de classe	مدى الفئات
Class limits	limites des classes	حدود الفئات
Class struggle	lutte de classes	صراع طبقي
Classical economics	économie classique	الاقتصاد التقليدي – النظرية الاقتصادية التقليدية
Classical school	école classique	المدرسة التقليدية
Classless society	société sans classes	مجتمع لا طبقي – مجتمع بلا طبقات

Clean draft	traite simple traite non-documentaire	كمبيالة بسيطة – كمبيالة لا مستندية
Clean floating (*of a currency*)	flottement pur (*d'une monnaie*) flottaison pure	تعويم كامل (لعملة)
Clearance sale	liquidation – soldes	تصفية – تنزيلات – بيع تصفية
Clearing agreement	accord de clearing accord de compensation	اتفاق مقاصة
Clearing bank	banque de clearing	مصرف عضو في غرفة المقاصة مصرف مقاصة – بنك مقاصة
Clearing facilities	facilités de clearing facilités de compensation	جهاز مقاصة – تسهيلات مقاصة
Clearing house	chambre de compensation	غرفة مقاصة
Clearing system	système de clearing	نظام مقاصة
Clientele	clientèle	عملاء
Climatic variations	variations climatiques	تغيرات مناخية
Cliometrics	cliométrie – historiométrie	التاريخ القياسي
Cliometricians	cliomètres – historiomètres	اخصائي التاريخ القياسي
Closed accounts	comptes définitifs	حسابات ختامية
Closed economy	économie fermée	اقتصاد مغلق

Close-end investment company
  Close-end investment trust
	société d'investissement fermée
	  société d'investissement à capital fixe
		شركة استثمار مغلقة
		شركة استثمار ذات رسمال محدد

Closing date	date de clôture – date limite jour de clôture	أجل الانتهاء – تاريخ الختم تاريخ الاقفال
Closing prices	cours de clôture	أسعار الاقفال
Co-borrower	co-emprunteur emprunteur conjoint	مقترض مشترك – مقترض مزامل
Co-debtor	co-débiteur débiteur conjoint	مدين متضامن – مدين مزامل
Co-financing	cofinancement	تمويل مشترك
Co-lender	co-prêteur	مقرض مشترك – مقرض مزامل
Co-lending	prêt conjoint	اقراض مشترك
Co-manager	co-manageur co-directeur	مدير مشارك – مدبر مشارك
Co-production agreement	accord de production	اتفاقية انتاج مشترك–اتفاق مشاركة الانتاج
Coal and steel industry	industrie du charbon et de l'acier	صناعة الفحم والصلب
Coastal country	pays littoral	دولة ساحلية – دولة سيفية
Coastal fishing	pêche littorale – pêche côtière	صيد ساحلي – صيد سيفي
Coastal traffic	traffic littoral – cabotage	حركة النقل الساحلي
Coastal trade **Coasting trade**	cabotage	تجارة ساحلية – تجارة سيفية
Cobweb theorem	théorie de la toile d'araignée	نظرية العنظل – نظرية نسيج العنكبوت

Code of conduct	code déontologique	مبادىء سلوكية – تقنين سلوكي
Code of investment	code d'investissement	مبادىء معاملة الاستثمار – تشريع الاستثمار
		تشريع معاملة الاستثمارات
Coding	codage	ترميز – تشفير
Coefficient of concordance	coefficient de concordance	معامل توافق – معامل وفاق
Coefficient of contingency	coefficient de contingence	معامل ائتلاف – معامل تآلف
Coefficient of determination	coefficient de détermination	معامل التحديد
Coefficient of elasticity	coefficient d'élasticité	معامل المرونة
Coefficient of multiple correlation	coefficient de corrélation multiple	معامل الارتباط المتعدد
Coefficient of partial correlation	coefficient de corrélation partielle	معامل الارتباط الجزئي
Coherence test	test de cohérence	معيار الالتئام – معيار التناسق
Coinage	monnayage – frappe de monnaie monnaies	سك النقود – سك العملة نقود
Coins	pièces de monnaie	مسكوكات – سكة
Cold storage facilities	installations frigorifiques	منشآت تثليج وتخزين
Collateral	nantissement	رهن – ضمان
Collateral loan	prêt garanti – prêt nanti – prêt sur gage	قرض برهن
Collecting agency	agence perceptrice	وكالة تحصيل – شركة تحصيل
Collecting company	société d'encaissement	
Collection items	effets à l'encaissement	أوراق تحت التحصيل
Collection of a debt	recouvrement d'une dette recouvrement d'une créance	استيفاء دين
Collection of data	collecte de données collecte d'informations	تجميع بيانات – جمع بيانات
Collective agreement	convention collective	اتفاق جماعي
Collective bargaining	négociation collective	تفاوض جماعي – مساومة جماعية
Collective consumption	consommation collective	استهلاك جماعي
Collective economy	économie collectiviste économie collective	اقتصاد جماعي
Collective farm	ferme collective	مزرعة جماعية
Collective goods	biens collectifs	منتجات جماعية – أموال جماعية
Collective investment institution	société d'investissement collectif	مؤسسة استثمار مشترك – مؤسسة استثمار جماعي
Collective property	propriété collective	ملكية جماعية
Collective reserve unit (cru)	unité collective de réserve	وحدة احتياط جماعية
Collective self-reliance	autonomie collective autodétermination collective	الاعتماد على النفس الجماعي – الجهود الذاتية الجماعية
Collectivisation	collectivisation	تأميم
Collectivism	collectivisme	النظام الجماعي – المذهب الجماعي
Collector	percepteur – receveur	مأمور ضرائب – محصل
Collusive tendering	collusion des soumissionnaires	تواطؤ مقدمي العطاءات
Colonial emancipation	émancipation coloniale	تحرر المستعمرات
Colonial liberation	libération coloniale	
Colonial structure	structure coloniale	نمط استعماري – هيكل استعماري

Colonial system	système colonial	نظام استعماري
Colonial pact	pacte colonial	الميثاق الاستعماري
Colonialism	colonialisme	الاستعمار
Colonization	colonisation	استعمار – استيطان
Combinat (USSR)	*combinat* (URSS)	مجمع صناعي (الاتحاد السوفييتي)
Combination export manager	directeur collectif d'exportation	مدير صادرات مشترك
Combination of the factors of production	combinaison des facteurs de production	تأليف عوامل الانتاج – توليف عناصر الانتاج
Combine	entente – cartel	اتفاق
Commerce	commerce	تجارة
Commercial agreement	accord commercial	اتفاق تجاري
Commercial aviation	aviation commerciale	الطيران التجاري
Commercial bank	banque commerciale	بنك تجاري – مصرف تجاري
Commercial bill	effet commercial	ورقة تجارية
Commercial channels	circuits commerciaux débouchés commerciaux	مسالك تجارية – أسواق تجارية
Commercial credit	crédit commercial	ائتمان تجاري
Commercial deficit	déficit commercial	عجز تجاري – عجز في ميزان التجارة
Commercial facilities	facilités commerciales	تسهيلات تجارية
Commercial invoice	facture commerciale	فاتورة تجارية – حسبونة تجارية
Commercial loan	prêt commercial	قرض تجاري
Commercial paper	effets commerciaux	أوراق تجارية
Commercial policy	politique commerciale	سياسة تجارية
Commercial port	port de commerce	ميناء تجاري
Commercial profitability	rentabilité commerciale	أربحية تجارية
Commercial profitability criterion	critère de la rentabilité commerciale	معيار الأربحية التجارية
Commercial prospects	perspectives commerciales	التوقعات التجارية–الأوضاع التجارية المرتقبة
Commercial relations	relations commerciales	علاقات تجارية
Commercial risks	risques commerciaux	مخاطر تجارية
Commercial terms	conditions commerciales conditions du marché	شروط تجارية – شروط سوقية شروط السوق
Commercial tourism	tourisme commercial	سياحة تجارية
Commercialisation	commercialisation	تسويق – تصريف
Commission	commission – courtage	سمسرة – عمولة – رسم
Commission agent	commissionnaire	وكيل بالعمولة
Committed assets	actifs engagés	اصول مخصصة – أصول موظفة
Commitment	engagement	التزام – تعهد – ارتباط
Commitment authority	pouvoir d'engagement	سلطة الالتزام – صلاحية التعهد
Commitment charge Commitment fee	commission d'engagement	رسم التزام
Commitment limit	limite d'engagement	حد الالتزام–حد التعهد
Commitment period	période d'engagement	فترة الالتزام–فترة التعهد

Commodities	marchandises – denrées	سلع – منتجات – بياعات
Commodity agreement	accord sur les produits de base	اتفاقية سلعية
Commodity aid	aide en nature	مساعدات عينية – معونات عينية
Commodity exchange	bourse de commerce bourse de marchandises	بورصة سلعية
Commodity futures	opérations à terme sur marchandises	عمليات سلعية آجلة
Commodity group	groupe de produits	مجموعة سلعية
Commodity loan	prêt-marchandises – prêt en nature	قرض عيني – قرض سلعي
Commodity markets	marchés des produits	أسواق سلعية – أسواق المنتجات
Commodity money	monnaie-marchandise	نقود سلعية
Commodity prices	prix des produits primaires prix des produits	أسعار المنتجات الأولية – أثمان السلع
Commodity reserves	réserves de produits	احتياطيات سلعية – مخزون سلعي كداس سلعي – بئيرة
Commodity resources	ressources-marchandises	موارد سلعية
Commodity terms of trade	termes de l'échange matériel	معدل التبادل السلعي
Commodity trade	commerce des produits	تجارة المنتجات – تجارة السلع
Common currency	monnaie commune monnaie collective	عملة مشتركة – عملة جماعية
Common external tariff	tarif externe commun	تعرفة خارجية جماعية – تعرفة خارجية مشتركة
Common market	marché commun	سوق مشتركة – سوق مشترك
Common shares Common stock	actions ordinaires	أسهم عادية
Common tariff	tarif commun	تعرفة مشتركة – تعرفة موحدة
Commonweal economy	économie d'intérêt général	اقتصاد المصلحة العامة
Commune	commune populaire	جمعة شعبية – جمعة
Communications	communications	مواصلات
Communism	communisme	الشيوعية
Community development	développement des communautés locales aménagement des collectivités locales	تنمية الجماعات المحلية – تنمية قروية
Comparative advantages	avantages comparés avantages comparatifs	مزايا نسبية – مزايا مقارنة
Comparative costs	coûts comparés coûts comparatifs	تكاليف نسبية – تكاليف مقارنة
Comparative statics	statique comparative	منهج السكون المقارن
Compensation	indemnisation	تعويض – مكافأة
Compensation of employees	rémunération des employés	مكافأة العاملين
Compensatory duty	droit compensatoire	رسم عائض – رسم معوض
Compensatory financing	financement compensatoire	تمويل موازن
Compensatory financing of export fluctuations	financement compensatoire des fluctuations des exportations	تمويل موازن لتقلب الصادرات
Compensatory spending	politique du déficit budgétaire systématique	سياسة الأنفاق العائض

Competing firms	entreprises concurrentielles	مؤسسات متنافسة – مشروعات متنافسة
Competing industries	industries concurrentes	صناعات متنافسة
Competing products	produits concurrentiels	سلع متنافسة
Competing projects	projets concurrentiels	مشاريع متنافسة
Competition	concurrence	منافسة – تنافس
Competitive bidding	adjudication publique	مناقصة عامة
Competitive devaluation	dévaluation compétitive	تخفيض تنافسي (للعملة)
Competitive economy	économie concurrentielle	اقتصاد تنافسي
Competitive equilibrium	équilibre concurrentiel	توازن تنافسي
Competitive goods	biens concurrentiels	سلع تنافسية – سلع متنافسة
Competitive market	marché concurrentiel	سوق تنافسي
Competitive position	position concurrentielle	وضع تنافسي – قدرة تنافسية
Competitive power	capacité concurrentielle	قوة تنافسية – قدرة تنافسية
Competitive price	prix concurrentiel	سعر تنافسي – ثمن تنافسي
Competitive protectionism	protectionnisme concurrentiel	حماية تنافسية
Competitive socialism	socialisme concurrentiel	اشتراكية تنافسية
Competitiveness	compétitivité capacité concurrentielle	قدرة المنافسة – قدرة تنافسية تنافسية
Competitors	concurrents	منافسون – متنافسون
Complementarity agreement	accord de complémentarité	اتفاقية تكامل
Complementary financing	financement complémentaire	تمويل تكميلي
Complementary goods	produits complémentaires	سلع متكاملة
Completion guarantee	garantie de bonne fin – garantie d'achèvement	ضمان الانجاز
Completion of a project	achèvement d'un projet	انجاز مشروع – اتمام مشروع
Completion time	délai d'exécution période d'exécution	فترة الانجاز – فترة التنفيذ
Composite index	indice composé indice composite	مؤشر مركب
Composite products	produits composites	منتجات مركبة
Composite unit of account	unité de compte composite	وحدة حساب مركبة
Compound growth	croissance exponentielle	نمو مركب – نمو أسي
Compound interest	intérêts composés	فوائد مركبة
Comprador class	classe des compradors	طبقة العملاء – طبقة الوسطاء
Comprehensive insurance	assurance multirisque assurance tous risques	تأمين شامل – تأمين متعدد
Comprehensive planning	planification intégrale planification globale	تخطيط شامل
Comptroller	vérificateur de comptes – contrôleur de comptes	مراقب حسابات
Compulsory deposits	dépôts obligatoires	ودائع اجبارية – ودائع جبرية
Compulsory fees	taxes obligatoires charges obligatoires	رسوم اجبارية – رسوم جبرية

Compulsory investments	investissements nécessaires investissements de nécessité	استثمارات ضرورية – استثمارات لازمة
Compulsory liquidation	liquidation forcée	تصفية جبرية
Compulsory loan	emprunt forcé	قرض جبري – قرض اجباري
Compulsory saving	épargne forcée	ادخار اجباري – ادخار جبري
Computed value	valeur calculée	قيمة محتسبة
Computer	ordinateur	حاسبة
Concentration	concentration	تركز
Concentration of capital	concentration du capital	تركز الرسمال
Concentration of trade	concentration du commerce centralisation du commerce	تركز التجارة – تركيز التجارة
Concentration ratios	indices de concentration	نسب التركز – مؤشرات التركز
Concern	entreprise – firme	مشروع – مؤسسة
Concession	concession	حق امتياز – امتياز
Concessionaire Concessionary	concessionnaire	صاحب امتياز
Concessional aid Concessional assistance Concessionary aid	aide concessionnelle aide à des conditions libérales	معونة ميسرة مساعدة ميسرة الشروط
Concessional element Concessionary element	élément de subvention élément concessionnel élément de libéralité	عنصر التيسير
Concessional terms Concessionary terms	conditions concessionnelles conditions de faveur – conditions libérales	شروط ميسرة
Conditional aid Conditional assistance	aide conditionnelle assistance conditionnelle	معونة مشروطة – مساعدة شرطية
Conditions of contract	cahier des charges clauses du contrat	شروط العقد
Confidence interval	intervalle de fiabilité intervalle de confiance	مجال الوثوق – مجال الثقة
Confidence level	niveau de fiabilité niveau de confiance	مستوى الوثوق – مستوى الثقة
Confidence limit	seuil de fiabilité – seuil de confiance	حد الوثوق
Confirmed credit	crédit confirmé	ائتمان مؤكد
Confiscation	confiscation	مصادرة
Conflict of interest	conflit d'intérêt	تضارب مصالح – تناقض مصالح
Conglomerate(s)	conglomérat(s)	قضة (قضاض)
Conquest of markets	conquête des marchés	غزو الأسواق – فتح الأسواق
Conservation	conservation – économie des ressources	حفظ الموارد – اقتصاد الموارد
Conservationism	conservationnisme	مذهب حفظ الموارد – الحفاظية
Conservationist	conservationniste	حفاظي

Consideration	rémunération – contre-partie indemnité	مقابل – تعويض
Consignment	consignation – expédition	ابداع – ارسال – شحن
Consistent growth	croissance cohérente	نمو متناسق – نمو نسيق
Consistency analysis	analyse de cohérence	تحليل التناسق – تحليل النسق
Consistency test	test de cohérence	اختبار التناسق – معيار النسق
Consolidated accounts	comptes consolidés	حسابات مجمعة
Consolidated balance sheet	bilan consolidé	ميزانية مجمعة
Consolidation of a debt	consolidation d'une dette	تثبيت دين
Consolidation (*corporations*)	fusion (*sociétés*)	اندماج – دمج (شركات)
Consolidation process	processus de consolidation	مجرى التثبيت – مجرى الاستقرار
Consortium	consortium – syndicat	دارة – حلقة – جميعة
Conspicuous consumption	consommation ostentatoire	اراءة – استهلاك ارائي
Constant capital	capital constant	رسمال ثابت
Constant costs	coûts constants	تكاليف ثابتة
Constant elasticity of substitution	élasticité de substitution constante	مرونة استبدال ثابتة – مرونة احلال ثابتة
Constant income hypothesis	hypothèse de revenu constant	فرض الدخل الثابت
Constant outlay curve	courbe de dépense constante	منحنى الانفاق الثابت
Constant prices	prix constants	أسعار ثابتة – أثمان ثابتة
Constant returns	rendements constants	غلة ثابتة – اناء ثابت – انتاجية ثابتة – عائد ثابت
Constant returns to scale	rendements constants à l'échelle	انتاجية ثابتة بتغير الحجم
Constrained optimisation	optimation conditionnelle	إمثال شرطي – إمثال مقيد
Constrained optimum	optimum conditionnel	حد أمثل مقيد – أمثل مقيد حد أمثل شرطي – أمثل محصر
Constraint	contrainte	قيد – حد – شرط
Construction contract	marché de construction	عقد بناء – عقد تشييد
Construction industry	industrie du bâtiment	صناعة البناء
Construction period	période d'exécution	فترة التنفيذ – فترة الانجاز
Construction progress chart	graphe d'exécution des travaux	بيان تقدم التنفيذ – لوحة تقدم العمل
Construction sequence	agencement temporel des travaux séquence des travaux	تتابع عناصر التنفيذ
Consular fees	droits consulaires	رسوم قنصلية
Consular invoice	facture consulaire	فاتورة قنصلية – حسبونة قنصلية
Consultant	consultant – ingénieur-conseil	مستشار – شيّر
Consultants' report	rapport des consultants	تقرير المستشارين
Consultant services **Consulting services**	conseils services-conseils	خدمات الاستشارة – خدمات استشارية
Consultative group	groupe consultatif	مجموعة استشارية
Consulting firm	bureau d'études	بيت استشاري – مؤسسة استشارية
Consulting engineer	ingénieur-conseil	مهندس استشاري
Consume, to	consommer	استهلك

Consumer	consommateur	مستهلك
Consumer behaviour	attitude du consommateur	سلوك المستهلك
Consumer choice	choix du consommateur	خيار المستهلك
Consumer credit	crédit à la consommation	ائتمان استهلاكي
Consumer demand	demande de consommation	طلب استهلاكي
Consumer durables	biens de consommation durables	سلع استهلاك معمرة – سلع استهلاكية معمرة
Consumer expenditure	dépenses des consommateurs	انفاق استهلاكي
Consumer goods **Consumption goods**	biens de consommation	سلع استهلاك – سلع استهلاكية
Consumer goods industry	industrie de biens de consommation	صناعة سلع استهلاكية
Consumer price	prix à la consommation	سعر المستهلك – ثمن المستهلك سعر الاستهلاك
Consumer price index	indice des prix à la consommation	رقم قياسي لأسعار الاستهلاك
Consumer protection	défense des consommateurs	حماية المستهلك
Consumer sovereignty	souveraineté du consommateur	سيادة المستهلك
Consumer spending	dépenses des consommateurs	انفاق المستهلكين – انفاق استهلاكي
Consumer surplus	rente de consommateur	فائض المستهلك
Consumers' cooperative	coopérative de consommation	تعاونية استهلاكية
Consumers' preference	préférence des consommateurs	تفضيل المستهلكين
Consumers' tastes	goûts des consommateurs	أذواق المستهلكين
Consumerism	consommatisme – consommaction	حركة حماية المستهلك الافراط الاستهلاكي
Consumption	consommation	استهلاك
Consumption account	compte de la consommation	حساب الاستهلاك
Consumption credit **Consumptive credit**	crédit à la consommation	ائتمان استهلاكي
Consumption function	fonction de consommation	دالة الاستهلاك
Consumption economy	économie de consommation	اقتصاد استهلاكي
Consumption needs	besoins de consommation	حاجات الاستهلاك
Consumption-possibility line	ligne de consommation possible	خط الاستهلاك المتاح
Consumption tax	taxe de consommation impôt sur la consommation	ضريبة على الاستهلاك – ضريبة استهلاكية
Container	conteneur emballage	وعاء – عبوة – غلاف
Container ship	navire-conteneur porte-conteneur	سفينة وعائية – حاملة وعائية
Contango	report – prix du report	ترحيل – تأجيل – ثمن التأجيل
Contingencies	imprévus – aléas	طوارئ
Contingency allowance	provisions pour imprévus	مخصص طوارئ
Contingency fund	fonds de prévoyance fonds de secours	صندوق طوارئ – صندوق اعانة
Contingency plan	plan de prévoyance	خطة طوارئ – خطة احتياطية
Contingency reserve	réserve de prévoyance provision pour imprévus	مخصص طوارئ – احتياطي طوارئ

Contingency table	table de contingence	جدول تآلف – جدول توافق
Contingent commitment	engagement conditionnel	تعهد شرطي – التزام شرطي
Contingent expenses	dépenses imprévues	نفقات طارئة – نفقات غير متوقعة
Contingent liabilities	passif éventuel dettes éventuelles	ديون احتمالية – التزامات احتمالية
Contingent order	ordre lié	أمر مشروط – أمر مزاوج
Contingent reserve	provision pour imprévus	احتياطي طوارئ – مخصص طوارئ
Continental shelf.	plateforme continentale	الرصيف القاري – الجرف القاري
Continuous irrigation	irrigation permanente	ري دائم
Continuous variable	variable continue	متغير متواصل
Contour lines	lignes de niveau	خطوط المستوى
Contra-accounts	comptes d'ordre comptes de contre-partie	حسابات نظامية – حسابات مقابلة
Contra-entry	contre-écriture	قيد مقابل
Contraband	contrebande	تهريب
Contraception	contraception	منع الحمل
Contract price	prix contractuel	ثمن العقد – ثمن تعاقدي
Contract value	valeur contractuelle	قيمة عقدية – قيمة تعاقدية
Contractionary pressures	tensions déflationnistes	ضغوط انكماشية – عوامل انكماشية
Contractive measures	mesures de déflation	اجراءات انكماشية – تدابير انكماشية
Contractor	maître d'œuvre – entrepreneur	مقاول
Contractual payments	paiements contractuels	مدفوعات تعاقدية
Contractual saving	épargne contractuelle	ادخار تعاقدي
Contra-cyclical policy	politique anti-cyclique politique conjoncturelle	سياسة مواجهة الدورة–سياسة مكافحة الدورة
Contradiction	contradiction	تناقض
Contributing country	pays contributeur – pays participant	دولة مساهمة – دولة مشاركة
Contributory capacity	capacité contributive	قدرة اسهامية–طاقة اسهامية
Contribution	contribution – cotisation	مساهمة – اسهام
Control	contrôle	رقابة – اشراف – تحكم
Control chart	tableau de contrôle graphique de contrôle	لوحة المتابعة – لوحة المراقبة
Controlled economy	économie dirigée	اقتصاد موجه
Controlled market	marché réglementé	سوق موجه – سوق منظم
Controlled prices	prix taxés	أسعار محددة – أثمان محددة
Controlling interest	part prépondérante	حصة سائدة–مصلحة سائدة–حصة غالبة
Conventional economics	pensée économique courante	الفكر الاقتصادي السائد–الفكر الاقتصادي الدارج
Conventional tariff	tarif conventionnel	تعرفة اتفاقية
Conventional terms	conditions du marché conditions usuelles	شروط السوق – شروط عادية
Conversion	conversion	تحويل
Conversion factor	facteur de conversion	معامل تحويل – معامل ابدال
Conversion loan	emprunt de conversion	قرض استبدالي

Conversion of a debt	conversion d'une dette	استبدال دين
Conversion premium	prime de conversion	علاوة الاستبدال – علاوة الابدال
Conversion price	prix de conversion	ثمن الابدال – سعر الابدال
Convertibility	convertibilité	قابلية للتحويل
Convertible bonds Convertible debentures	obligations convertibles	سندات قابلة للابدال – سندات ابدالية
Convertible currency	monnaie convertible	عملة قابلة للتحويل – عملة حرة
Convertible equipment	installations transformables	منشآت قابلة للتحويل–أجهزة قابلة للتحويل
Conveyance	transport – mutation – cession	نقل – تحويل
Conveyer	transporteur – convoyeur	ناقل
Cooperating country	pays coopérant	دولة معاونة – دولة متعاونة
Cooperation programme	programme de coopération	برنامج تعاون
Cooperative bank	banque coopérative coopérative de crédit	بنك تعاوني – مصرف تعاوني
Cooperative farming	culture coopérative	زراعة تعاونية
Cooperative movement	mouvement coopératif	الحركة التعاونية
Cooperative ownership	propriété coopérative	ملكية تعاونية
Cooperative society	coopérative – société coopérative	شركة تعاونية – تعاونية
Coordination	coordination	تنسيق
Copartnership	société en nom collectif	شركة تضامن
Copyright	droits d'auteur – propriété littéraire	حقوق التأليف – حقوق المؤلف
Core technology	technologie médullaire	جوهر التكنولجية – التكنولجية الجوهرية
Corn exchange	bourse de céréales	سوق الحبوب – بورصة الحبوب
Corner	accapparement – spéculation	احتكار – مضاربة
Corner the market, to	accaparer le marché	احتكر السوق
Corporate assets	actif social	اصول الشركة
Corporate bonds	obligations de sociétés	سندات الشركات
Corporate hierarchy	hiérarchie sociétaire	مراتب العاملين بالشركة–هرم العاملين بالشركة
Corporate image	image de la société	سمعة الشركة – اسم الشركة
Corporate income tax	impôt sur le revenu des sociétés	ضريبة أرباح الشركات
Corporate profits	bénéfices sociaux bénéfices des sociétés	أرباح الشركات
Corporate saving	épargne des sociétés	ادخار الشركات
Corporate state	état corporatif	دولة حرفية
Corporate stocks	actions de sociétés	أسهم شركات
Corporate structure	structure de l'entreprise	هيكل المؤسسة – هيكل الشركة
Corporate tax	impôt sur les sociétés	ضريبة الشركات
Corporation	société	شركة
Corporatism	corporatisme	المذهب الحرفي – الحرفية
Correlation coefficient	coefficient de corrélation	معامل الارتباط
Correspondent bank	banque correspondante – correspondant	بنك مراسل

Cost	coût – prix de revient	تكلفة – نفقة – كلفة
Cost, at	au prix coûtant	بسعر التكلفة
Cost accounting	comptabilité analytique comptabilité des prix de revient	محاسبة التكاليف
Cost analysis	analyse des coûts	تحليل التكاليف
Cost averaging	péréquation des coûts	توسيط التكاليف
Cost-benefit analysis	analyse avantages-coûts analyse coûts-rendements	تحليل المنافع والتكاليف
Cost-benefit ratio	rapport avantages-coûts	نسبة المنافع للتكاليف
Cost control	contrôle des coûts	رقابة التكاليف – مراقبة التكاليف
Cost differentials	différences de coût	فروق التكلفة
Cost-effectiveness analysis	analyse coûts-efficacité	تحليل فاعلية التكاليف
Cost element	élément du coût	عنصر تكلفة
Cost escalation clause	clause d'escalation des coûts	شرط تزايد التكاليف – شرط تصاعدي
Cost estimates	devis	تكاليف مقدرة
Cost estimation	évaluation des coûts estimation des coûts	تقدير التكاليف
Cost inflation	inflation-coûts	تضخم التكاليف – تضخم ناجم عن التكاليف
Cost item	élément du coût	عنصر تكلفة
Cost minimisation	minimisation des coûts	تضئيل التكاليف – تنزير التكاليف – ادناء التكاليف
Cost of acquisition	prix d'achat	تكلفة الشراء
Cost of capital	coût du capital	تكلفة الرسمال – كلفة الرسمال
Cost of living	coût de la vie	تكاليف المعيشة
Cost of living allowance	indemnité de vie chère	علاوة غلاء المعيشة
Cost of living index	indice du coût de la vie	مؤشر تكاليف المعيشة
Cost of production	coûts de production – frais de production	تكاليف الانتاج – نفقات الانتاج
Cost overruns	dépassement des coûts dépassement des devis	تعدي التكاليف – زيادة التكاليف المقدرة
Cost-plus pricing	détermination des prix par marge bénéficiaire	تسعير هامشي
Cost price	prix coûtant	سعر التكلفة
Cost-push inflation	inflation-coûts	تضخم تكاليف
Cost structure	structure des coûts	هيكل التكاليف – عناصر التكلفة
Cost trends	évolution des coûts – tendance des coûts	اتجاه التكاليف
Costing	établissement des coûts – estimation des coûts calcul des coûts	تقدير التكلفة – تحديد التكلفة
Costing sheet	table des coûts	جدول التكاليف
Cottage industry	industrie à domicile industrie familiale	صناعة منزلية

Counter bid	offre concurrentielle	عرض منافس
Counter cheque	chèque de guichet	شيك بنكي – شيك صرف
Counterfeit money	fausse monnaie	نقود مزيفة
Counterpart funds	fonds de contrepartie	أموال مقابلة
Counterpart personnel	homologues personnel homologue	نظراء
Countervailing duty	droit compensatoire	رسم عائض – رسم معوض
Countervailing power	force compensatoire force équilibrante	قوة عائضة – قوة موازنة – قوة معوضة
Counter-value	contre-valeur	قيمة مقابلة – مقابل
Country of destination	pays destinataire pays de destination	الدولة المرسل إليها
Country of emigration	pays d'émigration	دولة المهجر
Country of immigration	pays d'immigration	دولة الهجرة
Country of origin	pays d'origine	دولة المصدر – دولة الأصل
Country performance	performance du pays	أداء الدولة
Country planning	aménagement du territoire	التخطيط الاقليمي
Coupon	coupon	كعب – قسيمة
Coupon bonds	valeurs à revenu fixe	سندات دخل ثابت
Coupon rate	taux d'intérêt nominal	سعر القسيمة – سعر الفائدة الاسمي
Coupon rationing	rationnement par les tickets	فرض البطاقات – تقنين بطاقي – احصاص بطاقي
Coupon tax	impôt sur les coupons	ضريبة على العائد – ضريبة القسائم
Covariance	covariance	التغير المتكافئ
Cover	couverture – acompte provision	غطاء – تغطية – عربون
Craft guild	corporation – corps de métier	نقابة حرفية – طائفة حرفية
Crafts	artisanat	حرف
Craftsman Craft-worker	artisan ouvrier artisanal	عامل حرفي – حرفي
Craft organisation	coopérative d'artisans	تعاونية حرفية
Craft-union	corps de métier – corporation	نقابة حرفية – طائفة حرفية
Crash	krach – débâcle financière	انهيار – تداعي
Crawling peg system	régime des parités mobiles régime de parités à crémaillère	نظام الصرف المتحرك
Creation of money	création de monnaie	خلق النقود
Creation of international reserves	création de réserves internationales	خلق أرصدة دولية
Credit	crédit – avoir	ائتمان – رصيد مصرفي – اعتماد
Credit (accounting)	crédit (comptabilité)	دائن – له (محاسبة)
Credit, to	créditer – bonifier – porter au crédit	قيّد لصالح – قيّد بالدائن
Credit advice	avis de crédit	اشعار بقيد دائن

Credit and debit	crédit et débit — doit et avoir	له وعليه – دائن ومدين
Credit balance	solde créditeur — solde actif	رصيد دائن
Credit bank	banque de crédit	بنك ائتمان
Credit buying	achat à crédit	شراء بالتقسيط
Credit card	carte de crédit	بطاقة مصرفية
Credit ceiling	plafond de crédit	حد أقصى للائتمان
Credit contraction	resserrement du crédit	تضييق الائتمان
Credit cooperative	coopérative de crédit	تعاونية ائتمانية
Credit creation	création de crédit	خلق ائتمان
Credit economy	économie de crédit	اقتصاد ائتماني
Credit entry	écriture portée au crédit	قيد بالدائن – قيد دائن
Credit expansion	expansion du crédit	بسط الائتمان – تيسير الائتمان
Credit extension	prorogation de crédit	مد الائتمان – تمديد الاعتماد
Credit facilities	facilités de crédit	تسهيلات ائتمانية
Credit guarantee	garantie de crédit	ضمان الائتمان
Credit inflation	inflation du crédit	تضخم الائتمان – تضخم ائتماني
Credit in kind	crédit en nature	ائتمان عيني
Credit institution	établissement de crédit	مؤسسة ائتمانية
Credit instruments	instruments de crédit	أدوات ائتمان
Credit insurance	assurance-crédit	تأمين الائتمان – ضمان الائتمان
Credit item	poste créditeur	بند دائن
Credit limit	plafond de crédit	حد الائتمان
Credit money	monnaie scripturale	نقود مصرفية-نقد مصرفي-نقود كتابية
Credit operation Credit transaction	opération de crédit	عملية ائتمانية
Credit policy	politique du crédit	سياسة الائتمان – السياسة الائتمانية
Credit rating	cote de crédit	درجة الملاءة – تقدير الملاءة
Credit requirements	besoins de crédit	حاجات التمويل – احتياجات التمويل
Credit reserves	crédits non-utilisés	رصيد الائتمان
Credit restrictions	restrictions du crédit	قيود الائتمان
Credit risks	risques de crédit risque(s) de défaillance	مخاطر الائتمان – مخاطر الاعسار
Credit sale	vente à crédit	بيع بالتقسيط – نسيئة
Credit slip	bordereau de versement	ايصال دفع
Credit squeeze	resserrement du crédit	تضييق الائتمان
Credit standing	cote de crédit – degré de solvabilité	درجة الملاءة – الوضع الائتماني
Credit system	système du crédit	نظام الائتمان
Credit terms	conditions du crédit	شروط الائتمان
Credit transaction	opération de crédit	عملية ائتمان – عملية ائتمانية
Credit tightening	resserrement du crédit	تضييق الائتمان
Credit tranche	tranche de crédit	شريحة ائتمانية

Credit union	coopérative de crédit	تعاونية ائتمانية
Credit voucher	fiche de crédit	سند قيد دائن
Creditor	créancier	دائن
	créditeur	
Creditor country	pays créancier	دولة دائنة
Credit-worthiness	solvabilité –	ملاءة – ملاءة مالية
	crédit	
Credit-worthy	solvable	ملىء
Creeping expropriation	expropriation insidieuse	نزع ملكية دالف – مصادرة دالفة
Creeping inflation	inflation latente – inflation larvée	تضخم دالف – تضخم كامن
	inflation rampante	تضخم زاحف
Criterium	critère	معيار
Critical path analysis	analyse du chemin critique	تحليل المسار الحاسم
Critical value	valeur critique	قيمة حاسمة
Crop acreage	surface cuturelle	مساحة محصولية
Crop diversification	diversification des cultures	تنويع المحاصيل – تنويع الحاصلات
Crop failure	mauvaise récolte	عجز في المحصول
Crop grading	classement des produits agricoles	تصنيف الحاصلات
Crop protection	protection des cultures	حماية الحاصلات – حماية المحاصيل
Crop rotation	assolement	دورة فلاحية – دورة زراعية
Crop sharing	métayage	مزارعة – مؤاكرة
Crop year	année agricole –	سنة محصولية – سنة فلاحية
	campagne agricole	
Crop yield	rendement des cultures	غلة – محصول
Cropping intensity	intensité des cultures	كثافة الاستغلال الزراعي – كثافة الفلاحة
Cropping plan	programme de culture	خطة الزرع – برنامج فلاحي
Cross-breeding	croisement –	تهجين
	hybridation	
Cross classification	classification matricielle	تصنيف – ترتيب مصفوفي
Cross-country comparison	comparaison inter-pays	مقارنة بين دولية – مقارنة دول
Cross-default provision	clause de défaillance croisée	شرط الاعسار المنعكس
Cross elasticity	élasticité croisée	مرونة متبادلة
Cross rates	taux croisés	أسعار مشتقة
Cross-section analysis	analyse transversale	تحليل مستعرض
	analyse par coupes instantanées	
Crossed check	chèque barré	شيك مسطر
Crude oil	pétrole brut	نفط خام – بترول خام
Crude petroleum		
Cultivated area	zone cultivée	منطقة مزروعة – مساحة مزروعة
Cultivated land	terre cultivée	أرض مزروعة
Cultivation techniques	méthodes de culture	أساليب الفلاحة
Cultural development	développement culturel	تنمية ثقافية
Cultural tourism	tourisme culturel	سياحة ثقافية
cum **coupon**	coupon attaché	بالأرباح
cum **dividend**		

Current ratio	ratio de liquidité	نسبة الاصول الجارية – النسبة الجارية
Current repairs	réparations courantes	اصلاحات جارية
Current transactions	opérations courantes	عمليات جارية
Current yield	rendement courant	عائد جار – عائد جاري
Curriculum	*curriculum*	برنامج دراسة – مقرر دراسي
Curve fitting	ajustement de courbe	توفيق منحنيات
Curvilinear regression	régression curvilinéaire	ارتداد غير خطي – ارتداد قوسي
Curvilinear trend	tendance curvilinéaire	اتجاه غير خطي – اتجاه قوسي
Custody of securities	garde de titres	حفظ الأوراق المالية
Customers	clients – clientèle	عملاء
Customer's man	remisier	وكيل حافظة
Customer's position	position du client	مركز العميل
Customs	douanes	جمارك
Customs agency	agence en douance	وكالة جمركية – مخلص – مكتب تخليص
Customs area	territoire douanier	منطقة جمركية
Customs authorities	autorités douanières	سلطات جمركية
Customs bills	traites douanières	اذون جمركية
Customs clearance	dédouanement	جمركة – تخليص
Customs control	contrôle douanier	اشراف جمركي – رقابة جمركية
Customs declaration	déclaration de douane	اقرار جمركي
Customs duties	droits de douane	رسوم جمركية
Customs formalities	formalités douanières procédures douanières	اجراءات جمركية
Customs frontier	frontière douanière	حدود جمركية
Customs inspection	visite douanière	تفتيش جمركي
Customs invoice	facture douanière	فاتورة جمركية – حسبونة جمركية
Customs protection	protection douanière	حماية جمركية
Customs receipts **Customs revenues**	recettes douanières	ايرادات جمركية – ايرادات الجمارك
Customs regulations	règlements douaniers	لوائح جمركية
Customs release	dédouanement	افراج جمركي – جمركة
Customs system	régime douanier	نظام جمركي
Customs tariff	tarif douanier	تعرفة جمركية
Customs valuation	évaluation douanière estimation douanière	تقديرات جمركية – تقييم جمركي
Customs value	valeur douanière valeur en douane	قيمة جمركية
Customs union	union douanière	اتحاد جمركي
Cut-off rate	taux éliminatoire – taux limite	معدل فاصل
Cut-throat competition	concurrence ruineuse – concurrence acharnée	منافسة حادة

Cum warrant	warrant attaché	بحق الشراء – بخيار الشراء
Cumulative diagram	diagramme cumulatif	رسم بياني مجمع
Cumulative frequency distribution	distribution de fréquence cumulative	توزيع تكراري مجمع
Cumulative interest	intérêts cumulatifs	فوائد مجمعة – فوائد مركبة
Cumulative preference shares	actions privilégiées cumulatives	أسهم امتياز مجمعة
Currency	monnaie – devise	عملة – نقد
Currency appreciation	appréciation de la monnaie amélioration du change	ارتفاع العملة –- تحسن العملة
Currency area	zone monétaire	منطقة نقدية
Currency arbitrage	arbitrage monétaire	موازنة أسعار العملات–موازنة أسعار الصرف
Currency board	conseil monétaire conseil de la monnaie	مجلس نقد
Currency clause	clause d'option de change	نص خيار العملة
Currency conversion rates	taux de conversion monétaire	معدلات التحويل النقدي
Currency depreciation	dépréciation de la monnaie	انخفاض العملة – انخفاض الصرف
Currency devaluation	dévaluation de la monnaie	تخفيض العملة
Currency holdings	encaisses monétaires	أرصدة نقدية
Currency issued	émission monétaire numéraire mis en circulation	عملة مصدرة
Currency of payment	monnaie de paiement	عملة الدفع
Currency option	option de change	خيار العملة – خيار الصرف
Currency reform	réforme monétaire	اصلاح نقدي
Currency reserves	réserves monétaires	أرصدة نقدية
Currency union	union monétaire	اتحاد نقدي
Currency unit	unité monétaire	وحدة نقدية
Current account	compte courant	حساب جاري – حساب العمليات الجارية
Current account budget	budget ordinaire	موازنة عادية – ميزانية جارية
Current assets	actif réalisable actif liquide	اصول متداولة – اصول جارية – اصول سائلة
Current balance of payments	balance des paiements courants	ميزان المدفوعات الجارية
Current budget	budget de fonctionnement	موازنة جارية–موازنة التسيير–ميزانية عادية
Current expenditures	dépenses de fonctionnement	انفاق جاري – نفقات تشغيل
Current income	revenu courant	دخل جاري –
Current international payments	paiements internationaux courants	مدفوعات دولية جارية
Current international transactions	transactions internationales courantes	عمليات دولية جارية
Current liabilities	passif exigible passif à court terme	التزامات جارية – خصوم جارية
Current operating expenses	frais courants d'exploitation	نفقات استغلال جارية
Current operating profit	bénéfice courant d'exploitation	ربح الاستغلال الجاري
Current payments	paiements courants	مدفوعات جارية
Current price	prix courant prix du marché	سعر جاري – ثمن السوق

Cybernetics	cybernétique	الدفافة
Cycle	cycle	دورة
Cyclical behaviour	comportement cyclique	سلوك دوري
Cyclical component	composante cyclique	عنصر دوري – عنصر الدورة
Cyclical downturn	phase cyclique descendante	فترة التراجع – فترة الانكماش
Cyclical fluctuations	fluctuations cycliques	تقلبات دورية
Cyclical swings	oscillations cycliques	
Cyclical unemployment	chômage cyclique	بطالة دورية
Cyclical upturn	reprise cyclique	فترة الانتعاش – الانتعاش الدوري
Cyclical variations	variations cycliques	تغيرات دورية

Daily money	argent au jour le jour	قرض مياوم
Dairy industry	industrie laitière	صناعة الألبان
Damaged goods	marchandises avariées	بضائع تالفة
Damages	dommages – dommages-intérêts	خسائر – تعويضات
Data	données	معطيات – بيانات
Data bank	banque de données	مركز بيانات – مركز احصائي
Data collection	collecte des données	جمع البيانات
Data interpretation	interprétation des données	تفسير البيانات
Data processing	traitement des données	تجهيز البيانات – معالجة البيانات
	exploitation des données	
Day-to-day money	argent au jour le jour	قرض مياوم-قرض يومي
Days of grace	différé de paiement	فترة امهال
De-regulation of prices	déblocage des prix	تحرير الأسعار
Dead assets	actif improductif – avoirs stériles	اصول غير منتجة – اصول عقيمة
Dead money	capital inactif	رسمال غير عامل – رسمال مشلول
Dead season	morte-saison	موسم الركود – موسم الكساد
Deadweight tonnage	tonnage réel – port en lourd	حمولة حقيقية – حمولة فعلية
Dealer	marchand – négociant	تاجر – متعامل
Dear money	argent cher	غلاء الائتمان
Death duties	droits de succession	ضريبة تركات – ضريبة ارث
Death rate	taux de mortalité	معدل الوفيات
Debenture	obligation	سند
Debenture bond	obligation sans garantie	سند بلا ضمان
Debenture capital	capital-obligations	رسمال مقترض
Debenture holder	obligataire – porteur d'obligations	حامل سند – صاحب سند
Debenture loan	emprunt obligataire	قرض سندي
Debenture stocks	obligations sans garantie	سندات بلا ضمان – أسهم امتياز
	actions privilégiées	

Debit (*accounting*)	débit (*comptabilité*)	عليه – مدين
Debit, to	débiter	قيّد بالمدين
	porter au débit	
Debit account	compte débiteur	حساب مدين
Debit advice	avis de débit	اشعار بقيد مدين
Debit note		
Debit and credit	doit et avoir	له وعليه – دائن ومدين
	débit et crédit	
Debit balance	solde débiteur	رصيد مدين
Debit entry	écriture portée au débit	قيد بالمدين
	inscription au débit	
Debit item	poste débiteur	بند مدين
Debit voucher	fiche de débit	سند قيد مدين
Deblocking of funds	déblocage de fonds	افراج عن أموال
Debt ceiling	plafond de la dette	حد أقصى للمديونية – حد المديونية
Debt consolidation	consolidation de la dette	تثبيت الدين
Debit costs	coûts de la dette	تكاليف المديونية – تكاليف الدين
	coûts d'endettement	
Debt-equity ratio	ratio d'endettement	نسبة الملاءة – نسبة المديونية
	ratio de solvabilité	
Debt financing	financement de la dette	تمويل الدين
Debt-holder	détenteur d'instruments de dette	حامل سند مديونية – دائن
Debt instrument	instrument de dette	سند مديونية – اداة مديونية
Debt load	charge de la dette	عبء المديونية
Debt management	gestion de la dette	ادارة المديونية – تدبير الديون
Debt monetisation	monétisation de la dette	تسييل الدين
Debt problems	problèmes d'endettement	مشاكل المديونية
Debt redemption	amortissement d'une dette	استهلاك دين – سداد دين
Debt refinancing	refinancement de la dette	اعادة تمويل دين
Debt relief	allègement de la dette	تخفيف الدين
Debt renegotiation	renégociation de la dette	اعادة التفاوض على الدين
Debt rescheduling	révision de l'échéancier de la dette	تعديل جدول سداد الدين
	révision du tableau d'amortissement	اعادة جدولة الدين
Debt retirement	retrait d'une dette	سداد الدين – قضاء الدين
	remboursement d'une dette	
Debt securities	titres de dette	سندات مديونية
Debt service	service de la dette	خدمة الدين
Debt-service ratio	coefficient du service de la dette	مؤشر خدمة الدين
Debt-servicing capacity	aptitude à assurer le service de la dette	القدرة على خدمة الدين
Debtor	débiteur	مدين
Debtor country	pays débiteur	دولة مدينة
Deceleration of growth	ralentissement de la croissance	تباطؤ النمو
Deceleration of prices	ralentissement de la hausse des prix	تباطؤ ارتفاع الأسعار
Decentralisation	décentralisation	لا مركزية

Decentralised decision-making	prise de décision décentralisée	بت لا مركزي – ادارة لا مركزية
Decentralised planning	planification décentralisée	تخطيط لا مركزي
Decile	décile	عشير
Decision criteria	critères de décision	معايير البت
Decision function	fonction de décision	دالة البت – دالة التقرير
Decision-maker	décideur décisionnaire	صاحب البت – المبت
Decision-making **Decision-taking**	prise de décision	البت – اتخاذ القرارات
Decision-making centre	centre de décision	مركز البت
Decision model	modèle de décision	نموذج بني – نموذج بت
Decision table	table de décision	جدول بت
Decision tree	arbre de décision	شجرة بت
Declared value	valeur déclarée	قيمة معلنة – قيمة مقررة
Declining balance method (*depreciation*)	amortissement dégressif amortissement décroissant	اسلوب الاستهلاك المتناقص
Decolonisation	décolonisation	تصفية الاستعمار
Decontrol of prices	libération des prix	تحرير الأسعار
Decreasing cost	coût décroissant	تكلفة متناقصة
Decreasing returns	rendements décroissants	غلة متناقصة – عائد متناقص
Deepening of capital	intensification du capital	تكثيف الرسمال
de-facto **convertibility**	convertibilité de fait	قابلية فعلية للتحويل
Default	défaillance – manquement	اعسار – عجز
Default on payment	défaut de paiement	اعسار – عجز عن الدفع
Default price	cours de résiliation	سعر الفسخ
Default risk	risque de défaillance	خطر الاعسار
Defaulting country	pays défaillant	دولة معسرة – دولة متوقفة عن الدفع
Defaulting party	défaillant	معسر – طرف معسر – طرف متخلف
Defaulting underwriter	garant défaillant	ضامن متخلف
Defence expenditures	dépenses de défense nationale dépenses militaires	نفقات الدفاع – نفقات عسكرية
Deferred interest	intérêt différé	فائدة مؤجلة
Deferred payment	paiement différé	دفع مؤجل
Deferment period	différé – franchise	فترة تأجيل – فترة امهال – فترة انظار
Deficit	déficit	عجز
Deficit country	pays déficitaire	دولة ذات عجز
Deficit finance	financement par déficit budgétaire	تمويل بعجز الموازنة – تمويل بالعجز
Deficit spending	dépenses alimentées par le déficit budgétaire	انفاق بالعجز
Definitional equations	équations de définition équations définitionnelles	معادلات تعريف – معادلات تعريفية
Deflate prices, to	exprimer en prix constants	أطر الأسعار

		الأطر
Deflation (*price adjustment*)	déflation (*ajustement de prix*)	
Deflation (*business cycle*)	déflation (*cycles*)	انكماش (دورة اقتصادية)
Deflationary gap	écart déflationniste	فجوة انكماشية – ثغرة انكماشية
Deflator(s)	déflateur(s)	آطر (أواطر)
Deforestation	déboisement	تعرية من الأشجار
Degrees of freedom	degrés de liberté	درجات الحرية
Degressive tax	impôt dégressif	ضريبة متناقصة المعدل الحدى
De-growth	décroissance	نمو سالب
Delayed payment	paiement différé	دفع مؤجل
del credere **commission**	commission ducroire	عمولة ضمان الوفاء
Delinquent taxes	arriérés d'impôts	متأخرات ضريبية
Deliveries	livraisons	توريدات
Delivery date	date de livraison	تاريخ التسليم – تاريخ التوريد
	date de délivrance (*titres*)	
Delivery order	bon de livraison	أمر التسليم – أمر التوريد
Delivery period	période de livraison	فترة التسليم – فترة التوريد
Delivery price	prix de livraison	سعر التسليم – ثمن التسليم
	prix franco à la livraison	
Demand	demande	طلب
Demand deposit	dépôt à vue	وديعة معجلة – وديعة جارية
		وديعة تحت الطلب
Demand loan	prêt à vue	قرض معجل
Demand curve	courbe de la demande	منحنى الطلب
Demand elasticity	élasticité de la demande	مرونة الطلب
Demand function	fonction de la demande	دالة الطلب
Demand inflation	inflation-demande	تضخم انفاقي – تضخم ناجم عن الطلب
Demand-pull inflation	inflation due à la demande	
Demand liabilities	engagements à vue	التزامات معجلة
Demand management	politique de la demande	سياسة الطلب – ادارة الطلب
	gestion de la demande	
Demand price	prix-acheteur	ثمن الطلب – ثمن المشترين
Demand rate	cours à vue	سعر العاجل
Demand schedule	tableau de la demande	جدول الطلب
Democracy	démocratie	الديمقراطية
Democratic centralism	centralisme démocratique	المركزية الديمقراطية
Democratic socialism	socialisme démocratique	الاشتراكية الديمقراطية
Democratisation	démocratisation	دمقرطة
Demonetisation	démonétisation	إبطال الصفة النقدية
Demographic explosion	explosion démographique	انفجار سكاني
Demographic increase	accroissement démographique	زيادة سكانية
Demographic indicators	indicateurs démographiques	مؤشرات سكانية
Demographic pressure	pression démographique	ضغط سكاني
Demography	démographie	علم السكان

Demonstration effect	effet d'imitation	أثر التقليد – عامل التراسل – عامل المهايرة
	effet d'émulation	
Demonstration plot	parcelle témoin	حقل نموذجي
Demurrage	surestaries – frais de stationnement	تأخير – رسوم تأخير – رسوم انتظار
	droits d'attente	
Denationalisation	dénationalisation	أبطال التأميم – الغاء التأميم
Denominated in . . .	libellé en . . .	مقوم بـ ...
Density of population	densité démographique	كثافة السكان – كثافة سكانية
Dependence indicators	indices de dépendance	مؤشرات التبعية
Dependency economics	économique de la dépendance	اقتصاديات التبعية
Dependency ratio	taux de dépendance	معدل الاعالة
Depletion	épuisement	استنفاد – نفاد
Depletion allowance	provision pour épuisement	مخصص نفاد – مخصص استنفاد
Depletion charge		
Depletion factor	facteur d'épuisement	عامل الاستنفاد – معامل النفاد
	coefficient d'épuisement	
Depopulation	dépeuplement	تناقص السكان
	dépopulation	
Deposit	dépôt – versement – consignation	وديعة – دفع – ايداع
Deposits (*minerals*)	gisements (*minéraux*)	رواسب (معادن)
Deposit account	compte de dépôt	حساب ايداع
Deposit bank	banque de dépôt	بنك ايداع – مصرف ايداع – بنك ودائع
Deposit book	livret de dépôt	دفتر ايداع
Deposit currency	instruments de crédit	أدوات ائتمان
Deposits department	service des dépôts	قسم الودائع
Deposit insurance	assurance des dépôts bancaires	تأمين الودائع المصرفية
Deposit money	monnaie scripturale	نقود مصرفية – نقود كتابية
Deposit slip	récépissé de dépôt	ايصال ايداع
	fiche de versement	
Deposit turnover	rotation des dépôts	دورة الودائع – درجة استخدام الودائع
Depositor	déposant	مودع
Depository	dépositaire	جهة الايداع – أمين
Depositary		
Depository bank	banque dépositaire	بنك الايداع – مصرف الايداع
Depository receipt	récépissé de dépôt	ايصال ايداع – وصل ايداع
Depreciation (*money*)	dépréciation (*monnaie*)	انخفاض العملة
Depreciation (*assets*)	dépréciation (*biens*)	استهلاك (اصول)
	amortissement	
Depreciation allowance	provision d'amortissement	مخصص استهلاك
Depreciation rate	taux d'amortissement	معدل استهلاك
Depreciation reserve	réserve d'amortissement	مخصص استهلاك – احتياطي استهلاك
Depreciable assets	actif amortissable	اصول قابلة للاستهلاك
Depressed areas	régions touchées par la crise	مناطق كاسدة

Depressed market	marché déprimé	سوق كاسد – سوق راكد
Depression	dépression	كساد
Depression pole	pôle de dépression	قطب كساد
Derived demand	demande induite – demande dérivée	طلب مشتق
Desalination plant	usine de dessalement	مصنع تكرير مياه البحر
	usine de désalination	
Desallorism	*désallorisme*	التنموية – المذهب التنموي
Descriptive approach	approche descriptive	منهج وصفي
Desert creep	désertification	تصحر
Desertification	désertisation	
Design of a project	conception d'un projet	تصميم المشروع
	plan d'un projet	
Despotism	despotisme	استبداد – استبدادية
Destabiliser	déstabiliseur	عامل اختلال – مخل
	facteur de déséquilibre	
Destocking	déstockage	تصفية المخزون – تصفية الكداس
Deterioration	dégradation	تدهور – تفاقم
Deterioration of the terms of trade	détérioration des termes de l'échange	تدهور معدل التبادل
	dégradation des termes de l'échange	
Determinant	déterminant	محدد
Determinants of growth	facteurs de croissance	عوامل النمو – محددات النمو
Determination	détermination – résiliation	تحديد – تكوين – انهاء
Determination of prices	formation des prix	تكوين الأسعار – تكوين الأثمان
Determinism	déterminisme	الحتمية
Deterministic model	modèle déterministe	نموذج حتمي
Devalorisation	dévalorisation	انخفاض القيمة – خفض القيمة – نقصان القيمة
Devaluate, to	dévaluer	خفّض (العملة)
Devaluation of the currency	dévaluation de la monnaie	تخفيض العملة
	dévaluation monétaire	
Develop, to	développer	نمّى – طوّر
Developing country	pays en voie de développement	دولة نامية
	pays en développement	
Developing nation	nation en voie de développement	أمة نامية
	nation en développement	
Development	développement	انماء – تنمية – توسع – نمو – تطور
Development agency	organisme de développement	هيئة تنمية – وكالة تنمية
Development agent	agent de développement	عامل انمائي
Development aid	aide au développement	معونة انمائية – مساعدة انمائية – اعانة انمائية
Development assistance	assistance au développement	
Development area	zone de développement	منطقة تنمية
Development aspirations	aspirations des pays en voie de	آمال انمائية – تطلعات انمائية
	développement	
Development assistance targets	objectifs de l'aide au développement	أهداف المعونة الانمائية
	objectifs quantitatifs de l'aide au	مستهدفات المعونة الانمائية
	développement	

Development bank	banque de développement	بنك انماء – مصرف تنمية
Development board	conseil de développement	مجلس انماء
Development bottlenecks	obstacles au développement blocages du développement	مآزم النمو– مآزل الانماء–مخانق النمو
Development budget	budget de développement	ميزانية انماء – موازنة انمائية
Development committee	comité de développement	لجنة التنمية
Development company	société de développement	شركة تنمية – شركة انمائية
Development cooperation	coopération au développement	تعاون انمائي
Development credit	crédit de développement	قرض انمائي
Development decade	décennie du développement	عقد التنمية
Development economics	économie du développement	اقتصاديات التنمية
Development efforts	efforts de développement	جهود التنمية – جهود انمائية
Development factor	facteur de développement	عامل انمائي
Development finance company	société financière de développement	شركة تمويل انمائي
Development financing	financement du développement	تمويل انمائي
Development goals	objectifs du développement	أهداف التنمية – أهداف الانماء
Development ideology	idéologie du développement	مذهب انمائي – مذهبية الانماء
Development indicators	indicateurs de développement	مؤشرات الانماء – مؤشرات انمائية
Development impact	incidence sur le développement	أثر انمائي – تأثير انمائي
Development needs	besoins de développement	حاجات التنمية
Development opportunities	possibilités de développement	فرص الانماء–امكانيات التنمية
Development performance	performance dans le domaine du développement	أداء انمائي
Development priorities	priorités du développement	أولويات النمو – أولويات الانماء
Development plan	plan de développement	خطة تنمية – خطة انمائية
Development planning	planification du développement	تخطيط انمائي – تخطيط التنمية
Development policy	politique de développement	سياسة انمائية – سياسة التنمية
Development potential	potentiel de développement capacité de développement	طاقة انمائية – قدرة انمائية
Development process	processus de développement	مجرى التنمية – مجرى النمو
Development programme	programme de développement	برنامج انمائي
Development programming	programmation du développement	برمجة انمائية
Development project	projet de développement	مشروع انمائي
Development requirements	exigences du développement	احتياجات الانماء – احتياجات التنمية
Development research	recherche de développement recherche sur le développement	دراسات انمائية – بحوث انمائية
Development strategy	stratégie du développement	استراتيجية الانماء – منهج التنمية سياسة التنمية
Development trends	tendances de développement	اتجاهات التنمية
Developmentism	développementisme	مذهب التنموية – التنموية
Deviation	déviation – écart	انحراف

Deviation from par	écart avec la parité	انحراف عن سعر التعادل
Diagnosis	diagnostic	تشخيص
Diagram	diagramme	رسم بياني – رسم
Dialectical materialism	matérialisme dialectique	المادية الجدلية
Dictatorship of the proletariate	dictature du prolétariat	دكتاتورية العمال – دكتاتورية البروليتزية
Diet problem	problème diététique	مشكلة النظام الغذائي
Difference equations	équations de différence	معادلات فرقية
Differential cost	coût différentiel	تكلفة فرقية
Differential duties	droits différentiels	رسوم فرقية – رسوم تمييزية
Differential equations	équations différentielles	معادلات تفاضلية
Differential tariff	tarif différentiel	تعرفة تمييزية
Digital computer	ordinateur digital	حاسبة رقمية
Dilution of capital	dilution du capital	تذويب الرسمال
Diminishing costs	coûts décroissants	تكاليف متناقصة – نفقات متناقصة
Diminishing marginal utility	utilité marginale décroissante	منفعة حدية متناقصة
Diminishing returns	rendements décroissants	عائد متناقص – غلة متناقصة
Direct correlation	corrélation directe	ارتباط مباشر
Direct cost	coût direct	تكلفة مباشرة
Direct farming	faire-valoir direct	استغلال مباشر (زراعة)
Direct investment	investissement direct	استثمار مباشر
Direct issuance	émission directe	اصدار مباشر
Direct tax	impôt direct	ضريبة مباشرة
Dirty floating (*of a currency*)	flottaison impure (*d'une monnaie*) flottement impur	تعويم ناقص–تعويم غير كامل (لعملة)
Disaggregated model	modèle désagrégé	نموذج مفضوض – نموذج فضيض
Disaggregation	désagrégation	فض – افضاض – تفضيض
Disbursements	débours déboursements décaissements	مدفوعات – سحوبات
Disbursement period	période de déboursement	فترة السحب – فترة الدفع
Disbursement procedures	procédure de déboursement	اجراءات السحب – اجراءات الدفع
Disbursement rate	taux de déboursement	معدل السحب – معدل الدفع
Discharge of a debt	acquittement d'une dette	قضاء دين – أداء دين
Disclosure	divulgation	أعلان بيانات – كشف – افصاح
Disclosure of bids	divulgation des offres	اعلان العطاءات
Disclosure rules	normes de divulgation	قواعد الاعلان – قواعد الافصاح
Discount (*trade*)	rabais – remise – escompte	حطيطة – وضيعة – خصم،
Discount (*banking*)	escompte	خصم – حسم
Discount bank **Discount house**	banque d'escompte	بنك خصم – مصرف خصم
Discount bonds	obligations sous-paritaires	سندات دون التعادل
Discount rate	taux d'escompte taux d'actualisation	سعر الخصم – سعر الحسم معدل الاحطاط – معدل الخصم

Discountable paper	effets escomptables	أوراق قابلة للخصم-أوراق قابلة للحسم
Discounted cash-flow	recettes monétaires nettes actualisées	صافي الايراد النقدي المستحط
Discounted cash-flow method	méthode des recettes monétaires nettes actualisées	منهج احطاط صافي الايراد النقدي
Discounted value	valeur actualisée	قيمة مستحطة
Discounting	escompte actualisation	خصم – حسم – احطاط
Discounting period	période d'actualisation	فترة الاحطاط
Discreet variable	variable non-continue	متغير متقطع
Discrepancy	écart – différence	فرق – بند فرقي
Discrimination	discrimination	تمييز
Discriminatory duty	droit discriminatoire impôt discriminatoire	رسم تمييزي
Discriminatory practices	pratiques discriminatoires	اجراءات تمييزية – تدابير تمييزية
Diseconomies	déséconomies	وفورات سالبة-اضرار
Disembodied technology	technologie désincarnée technologie désincorporée	فن انتاجي غير مجسم-تكنولوجية غير مجسمة
Disequilibrating factor	facteur de déséquilibre facteur déséquilibrant	عامل اختلال – مخل
Disequilibrium	déséquilibre	اختلال
Disguised unemployment	chômage déguisé – chômage occulte	بطالة مقنعة – تعطل مقنع
Dishoarding	déthésaurisation	اطلاق المكتنز – انفاق المكتنز
Dishonoured cheque	chèque impayé	شيك مرتجع -- شيك غير مدفوع
Disincentive	anti-stimulant	مثبط
Disinflation	désinflation	علاج التضخم
Disinflationary policy	politique désinflationniste politique de désinflation	سياسة مضادة للتضخم – سياسة انكماشية
Disintermediation	désintermédiation démédiatisation	استغناء عن الوسطاء الماليين – سحب الودائع
Disinvestment	désinvestissement	استثمار سالب – سحب الاستثمار – تصفية الاستثمار
Dismantling of tariff barriers	suppression des barrières douanières	الغاء الحواجز الجمركية
Dispatching	expédition – envoi	ارسال
Dispersion	dispersion	تشتت
Dispersion coefficient	coefficient de dispersion	معامل التشتت
Disposable income	revenu disponible	دخل متاح
Disproportionality theory	théorie de la disproportionalité	نظرية اللاتناسق
Dispute	litige conflit	نزاع
Dissaving	désépargne épargne négative	ادخار سالب
Distorted prices	prix faussés	اسعار معوجة – اثمان معوجة

Distress sale	liquidation forcée	تصفية جبرية
Distressed areas	régions déprimées	مناطق كاسدة
Distribution	distribution – répartition	توزيع
Distribution channels	circuits de distribution	مسالك التوزيع
Distribution costs	coûts de la distribution	تكاليف التوزيع
Distribution facilities	installations de distribution	منشآت التوزيع – تجهيزات التوزيع
Distribution network	réseau de distribution	شبكة التوزيع
Distribution of wealth	répartition de la richesse	توزيع الثروة
Distributional effects	effets distributifs	آثار توزيعية
Distributional weights	coefficients de distribution – coefficients distributifs	أوزان توزيعية
Distributive equity	justice distributive	العدالة التوزيعية
Disturbances	perturbations	معكرات
Disutility	désutilité utilité négative	منفعة سالبة
Diversification	diversification	تنويع
Diversified economy	économie diversifiée	اقتصاد متنوع القطاعات –اقتصاد متنوع
Diversified firm	entreprise diversifiée	مشروع متنوع الانتاج – مشروع متنوع
Divestment	désinvestissement – dévestissement	تخلص من الاستثمار – تصفية الاستثمار
Dividends	dividendes	ارباح موزعة – ارباح
Dividend coupon	coupon de dividendes	قسيمة الربح – قسيمة الارباح
Dividend distribution	distribution des dividendes	توزيع الارباح
Dividend share	action de jouissance	سهم تمتع
Division of labour	division du travail	تقسيم العمل
Documentary bill	traite documentaire	كمبيالة مستندية – سند مستندي
Documentary credit	crédit documentaire	اعتماد مستندي
Dogmatism	dogmatisme	فرض – جمود الرأي
Dollar crisis	crise du dollar	ازمة الدولار
Dollar glut	pléthore du dollar	وفرة الدولار
Dollar shortage	pénurie du dollar rareté du dollar	ندرة الدولار – شح الدولار
Domestic assets	avoirs internes	اصول محلية
Domestic bills	traites locales	كمبيالات محلية
Domestic demand	demande locale	طلب محلي – طلب داخلي
Domestic consumption	consommation intérieure	استهلاك محلي – استهلاك داخلي
Domestic currency	monnaie nationale	عملة محلية – نقد محلي
Domestic economy	économie nationale	اقتصاد قومي – اقتصاد محلي
Domestic financing	financement intérieur	تمويل محلي
Domestic industry	industrie à domicile	صناعة منزلية
Domestic market	marché intérieur	سوق محلية – سوق داخلي
Domestic prices	prix internes – prix intérieurs	أسعار محلية
Domestic product	produit domestique	الناتج المحلي

Domestic resources	ressources locales	موارد محلية
Domestic resource cost	coût en ressources locales	تكلفة بالموارد المحلية
Domestic savings	épargne intérieure – épargne locale	ادخار محلي
Domestic services	services domestiques	خدمات منزلية
Domestic suppliers	fournisseurs locaux	موردون محليون
Domestic tourist trade Domestic tourism	tourisme intérieur	سياحة داخلية
Domestic trade	commerce intérieur	تجارة داخلية
Domestic traffic	trafic intérieur	حركة النقل الداخلي
Dominant economy	économie dominante	اقتصاد مسيطر
Dominant firm	firme dominante	مشروع مسيطر – مؤسسة مسيطرة
Donation	donation	هبة – منحة – عطاء – نحلان
Donor	donateur – donneur	عاطي
Donor country	pays donateur pays donneur	دولة عاطية
Door-to-door sales	vente de porte à porte démarchage	بيع لدى الزبائن – لفاف
Dormant assets	avoirs inactifs	اصول عقيمة – اصول عاطلة
Dormant debt	dette inactive dette passive	دين موقوف – دين مكبول
Dot chart	diagramme de points	رسم نقطي
Double counting	duplication double emploi	ازدواج – ازدواج الحساب
Double currency option	option de change double	خيار صرف مزدوج
Double entry accounting	comptabilité en partie double	محاسبة بالقيد المزدوج
Double factorical terms of trade	termes de l'échange bifactoriel	معدل التبادل العواملي المزدوج
Double taxation	double imposition	ازدواج ضريبي
Doubtful debts	créances douteuses	ديون مشبوهة
Downgrading	rabaissement	خفض – ادناء
Down-payment	acompte arrhes	عربون
Downstream operations	opérations à l'aval	عمليات أمامية
Downswing Down-turn	baisse phase descendante du cycle	فترة انكماشية – نكوص – حدور
Downward trend	tendance à la baisse	اتجاه انخفاضي – اتجاه هبوطي – اتجاه حدوري
Draft	traite	كمبيالة – سند اذني
Draft (law)	projet – version préliminaire	مسودة – مشروع
Draft budget	projet de budget	مشروع الموازنة – مشروع الميزانية
Draft prospectus	prospectus provisoire – prospectus préliminaire projet de prospectus	نشرة مبدئية – نشرة اصدار مبدئية مسودة نشرة
Draining of resources	épuisement des ressources drainage des ressources	استنفاذ الموارد – امتصاص الموارد

Drainage	drainage assainissement	صرف
Drawback	remboursement des droits – d'importation prime	رد رسوم الاستيراد – علاوة
Drawee	tiré	مسحوب عليه
Drawer	tireur	ساحب
Drawing	tirage utilisation	سحب
Drawing account	dépôt à vue	حساب معجل – حساب تحت الطلب
Drawing facilities	facilités de tirage	تسهيلات سحب
Drawing rights	droits de tirage	حقوق سحب
Drop-out rate	taux de déchet scolaire	معدل ترك الدراسة
Drought	sécheresse	قحط
Drugs and medicines industries	industrie des drogues et médicaments	صناعة العقاقير والأدوية
Drug trade	commerce des stupéfiants	تجارة المخدرات
Dry dock	cale sèche	حوض جاف
Dry farming	culture sèche culture à sec	زراعة جافة
Dual (*linear programming*)	dual (*programmation linéaire*)	صنو (برمجة خطية)
Dual economy	économie dualiste	اقتصاد مثنوى
Dual programme	programme dual	برنامج صنوى
Dual exchange rate system	système de change double	نظام صرف مزدوج
Dual trust	fonds d'investissement à deux volets fonds d'investissement bivalent	صندوق استثمار مزدوج
Dualism	dualisme	مثنوية – ازدواجية
Dualist economy	économie dualiste	اقتصاد مثنوي – اقتصاد مزدوج
Dualistic structure	structure dualiste	هيكل مثنوي – هيكل مزدوج – هيكل ازدواجي
Due date	échéance – date de l'échéance	تاريخ الاستحقاق
Dues	droits	رسوم
Dull market	marché indécis marché alourdi	سوق متقاعس
Dull season	morte-saison	موسم الركود
Dummy variable	variable symbolique	متغير رمزي
Dumping	dumping	اغراق
Duopoly	duopole	احتكار مثنوي (بيع)
Duopsony	duopsone	احتكار مثنوي (شراء)
Duplication	double emploi	ازدواج
Durable goods	biens durables biens non périssables	سلع معمرة
Dutch auction	enchères au rabais	مزاد عكسي
Dutiable goods	marchandises imposables marchandises taxables	سلع خاضعة للرسوم

Duties	droits – taxes – impôts	رسوم – ضرائب – مكوس
Duty-free goods	marchandises hors-taxe	سلع معفاة من الرسوم
Duty-free market	marché hors-taxe	سوق حر
Dyestuffs industry	industrie des colorants	صناعة الصباغ
Dynamics	dynamique	حركة – ديناميكية
Dynamic analysis	analyse dynamique	تحليل حركي
Dynamic equilibrium	équilibre dynamique	توازن حركي
Dynamic model	modèle dynamique	نموذج حركي
Dynamic planning	planification dynamique	تخطيط حركي
Dynamic stochastic programming	programmation stochastique dynamique	تخطيط احتمالي حركي

Early warning system	système de clignotants système d'indicateurs d'alerte	نظام انذار – نظام تحذير مبكر
Earmark, to	affecter – réserver	خصص – رصد
Earmarked funds	fonds alloués – fonds affectés	أموال مخصصة – أموال مرصودة
Earmarking	affectation – allocation	تخصيص – رصد
Earnest money	arrhes – acompte	عربون
Earnings	bénéfices – gains	مكاسب – ارباح
Earning assets	actifs productifs actifs lucratifs	اصول مربحة – اصول كاسبة – اصول مدرة
Earning power	capacité bénéficiaire rentabilité	أرحية–قدرة الكسب
Easing of credit	détente du crédit	تيسير الائتمان
Easy credit	argent facile	ائتمان يسر – ائتمان ميسر
Easy money	argent facile	ائتمان يسر – ائتمان ميسر
Easy terms	conditions favorables conditions libérales	شروط ميسرة – شروط سهلة
Ecological balance	équilibre écologique	توازن البيئة – توازن بيئي
Ecological conservation	conservation écologique défense écologique	حفظ البيئة – الدفاع عن البيئة
Ecology	écologie	دراسة البيئة – ميزان البيئة
Ecomanagement	écogestion	إدارة البيئة – تدبير شئون البيئة
Ecosystem	écosystème	النظام البيئي
Econometrics	économétrie	الاقتصاد القياسي
Econometric model	modèle économétrique	نموذج قياسي

Econometrician	économètre	اقتصادي قياسي
Economic accounts	comptes économiques	حسابات اقتصادية
Economic activity	activité économique	نشاط اقتصادي
Economic agent	agent économique	عامل اقتصادي – خلية اقتصادية
Economic agreement	accord économique	اتفاق اقتصادي – اتفاقية اقتصادية
Economic backwardness	arriération économique retard économique	تأخر اقتصادي – تخلف اقتصادي
Economic behaviour	comportement économique	سلوك اقتصادي
Economic benefits	avantages économiques	منافع اقتصادية – فوائد اقتصادية
Economic bloc	bloc économique	كتلة اقتصادية – تكتل اقتصادي
Economic calculus	calcul économique	حساب اقتصادي – تحليل اقتصادي
Economic capacity	potentiel économique	طاقة اقتصادية
Economic centres	centres économiques	مراكز اقتصادية
Economic choice	choix économique calcul économique	خيار اقتصادي – حساب اقتصادي
Economic concentration	concentration économique	تركز اقتصادي
Economic cooperation	coopération économique	تعاون اقتصادي
Economic cost	coût économique	تكلفة اقتصادية
Economic crisis	crise économique	ازمة اقتصادية
Economic dependence	dépendance économique	تبعية اقتصادية – خضوع اقتصادي
Economic determinism	déterminisme économique	مذهب الحتمية-الاقتصادية-الحتمية الاقتصادية
Economic development	développement économique	تنمية اقتصادية – انماء اقتصادي
Economic diplomacy	diplomatie économique	دبلوماسية اقتصادية
Economic doctrine	doctrine économique	مذهب اقتصادي
Economic dominance Economic domination	domination économique dominance économique	سيطرة اقتصادية
Economic dualism	dualisme économique	ثنوية اقتصادية – ازدواجية اقتصادية
Economic dynamics	dynamique économique	حركية اقتصادية
Economic environment	milieu économique	بيئة اقتصادية
Economic evaluation	évaluation économique	تقييم اقتصادي
Economic equilibrium	équilibre économique	توازن اقتصادي
Economic expansion	expansion économique	توسع اقتصادي – نمو اقتصادي
Economic factor	facteur économique	عامل اقتصادي
Economic flows	flux économiques	تيارات اقتصادية – تدفقات اقتصادية
Economic fluctuations	fluctuations économiques	تقلبات اقتصادية
Economic forces	forces économiques	عوامل اقتصادية – قوى اقتصادية
Economic forecast	prévision économique	تنبؤ اقتصادي – ابشار اقتصادي استنباء اقتصادي
Economic framework	cadre économique	اطار اقتصادي
Economic geography	géographie économique	الجغرافية الاقتصادية
Economic growth	croissance économique	نمو اقتصادي
Economic history	histoire économique	التاريخ الاقتصادي
Economic ideology	idéologie économique	مذهبية اقتصادية

Economic impact	effet économique	اثر اقتصادي ــ تأثير اقتصادي
	impact économique	
Economic imperialism	impérialisme économique	استعمار اقتصادي
Economic indicator	indicateur économique	مؤشر اقتصادي
	indice économique	
Economic intelligence service	service d'information économique	مركز اعلام اقتصادي
	service de renseignements économiques	
Economic instability	instabilité économique	عدم استقرار اقتصادي ــ لا استقرار اقتصادي
Economic institutions	institutions économiques	نظم اقتصادية
Economic integration	intégration économique	تكامل اقتصادي
Economic interpretation of history	interprétation économique de l'histoire	التفسير الاقتصادي للتاريخ
Economic laws	lois économiques	قوانين اقتصادية
Economic legislation	législation économique	تشريعات اقتصادية
Economic life (of an equipment)	durée utile (d'un équipement)	فترة الاستخدام (أجهزة)
Economic literature	littérature économique	مراجع اقتصادية ــ أدب اقتصادي
Economic losses	pertes économiques	خسائر اقتصادية
Economic man	homo economicus	الإنسان الاقتصادي
	homme économique	
Economic management	gestion économique	إدارة اقتصادية ــ تسيير اقتصادي
Economic maturity	maturité économique	نضج اقتصادي ــ نضوج اقتصادي
Economic miracle	miracle économique	معجزة اقتصادية
Economic model	modèle économique	نموذج اقتصادي
Economic nationalism	nationalisme économique	القومية الاقتصادية
Economic order	ordre économique	نظام اقتصادي
	système économique	
Economic outlook	perspectives économiques	الطالع الاقتصادي
Economic penetration	pénétration économique	توغل اقتصادي ــ غزو اقتصادي
Economic performance	performance économique	اداء اقتصادي
Economic phenomena	phénomènes économiques	ظواهر اقتصادية
Economic philosophy	philosophie économique	فلسفة اقتصادية
Economic planning	planification économique	تخطيط اقتصادي
Economic policy	politique économique	سياسة اقتصادية
Economic potential	potentiel économique	طاقة اقتصادية ــ امكانيات اقتصادية
Economic problem	problème économique	مشكلة اقتصادية ــ قضية اقتصادية
Economic progress	progrès économique	تقدم اقتصادي ــ تطور اقتصادي
Economic projection	projection économique	توقع اقتصادي ــ اسقاط اقتصادي
Economic prospects	perspectives économiques	التوقعات الاقتصادية ــ الطالع الاقتصادي
Economic rate of return	taux de rentabilité économique	معدل العائد الاقتصادي
Economic rationality	rationalité économique	الرشد الاقتصادي
Economic recovery	redressement économique	انعاش اقتصادي
	reprise économique	
Economic relations	rapports économiques	علاقات اقتصادية
	relations économiques	

Economic rent	rente économique	ربع اقتصادي
Economic research	recherche économique	بحث اقتصادي
Economic resources	ressources économiques	موارد اقتصادية
Economic revival	redressement économique	انتعاش اقتصادي
Economic sanctions	sanctions économiques	عقوبات اقتصادية
Economic science	science économique	علم الاقتصاد – الاقتصاد
Economic sector	secteur économique	قطاع اقتصادي
Economic security	sécurité économique	أمن اقتصادي
Economic semantics	sémantique économique	دراسة المصطلحات الاقتصادية
Economic setting	contexte économique	وضع اقتصادي – اطار اقتصادي
Economic situation	situation économique	حالة اقتصادية – احوال اقتصادية
Economic space	espace économique	مجال اقتصادي
Economic stability	stabilité économique	استقرار اقتصادي
Economic stimulants	stimulants économiques	حوافز اقتصادية
Economic strategy	stratégie économique	سياسة اقتصادية – استراتيجية اقتصادية
Economic structure	structure économique	هيكل اقتصادي
Economic study	étude économique	دراسة اقتصادية
Economic survey	enquête économique	مسح اقتصادي
Economic system	système économique	نظام اقتصادي
Economic test	test économique	اختبار اقتصادي
Economic theory	théorie économique	نظرية اقتصادية
Economic thought	pensée économique	فكر اقتصادي
Economic trends	conjoncture économique	اتجاه اقتصادي
	orientation de l'activité économique	
Economic union	union économique	اتحاد اقتصادي
Economic unit	unité économique – agent économique	وحدة اقتصادية
Economic warfare	guerre économique	حرب اقتصادية
Economic welfare	bien-être économique	رفاهية اقتصادية – رفاهة اقتصادية
Economics	science économique – économique	الاقتصاد – علم الاقتصاد – اقتصاديات
	économie	
Economics of development	économie du développement	اقتصاديات النمو
Economics of education	économie de l'éducation	اقتصاديات التعليم
Economics of energy	économie de l'énergie	اقتصاديات الطاقة
Economics of health	économie des services de la santé	اقتصاديات الخدمات الصحية
Economics of welfare	économie du bien-être	اقتصاديات الرفاهية
Economies of mass production	économies d'échelle	وفورات الإنتاج الكبير
	économies de la grande production	
Economies of scale	économies d'échelle	وفورات الحجم
Economism	économisme	النزعة الاقتصادية – الانحراف الاقتصادي
Economist	économiste	اقتصادي – رجل اقتصاد
Economy	économie	اقتصاد – اقتصاد قومي
Educational planning	planification de l'enseignement	تخطيط التعليم

Educational pyramid	pyramide de la population scolaire	الهرم التعليمي
Educational reform	réforme de l'enseignement	أصلاح التعليم
Educational system	système scolaire	نظام التعليم
Effective agricultural area	surface agricole utilisée	الرقعة الزراعية الفعلية
Effective control	contrôle effectif	اشراف فعلي – هيمنة فعلية – سيطرة فعلية
Effective date	date d'entrée en vigueur	تاريخ النفاذ
Effective demand	demande effective	طلب فعال
Effective exchange rate	taux de change effectif – taux de change réel	سعر صرف فعلي
Effective interest rate	taux d'intérêt effectif taux d'intérêt réel	سعر فائدة فعلي
Effective protection	protection effective	حماية فعلية
Effective value	valeur réelle	قيمة فعلية – قيمة حقيقية
Effective yield	rendement effectif	عائد فعلي
Effectiveness of the loan agreement	entrée en vigueur de l'accord de prêt	نفاذ اتفاقية القرض
Efficiency criteria	critères d'efficacité critères d'efficience	معايير الفاعلية – معايير الفعالية
Efficiency index	indice d'efficacité indice d'efficience	مؤشر الفاعلية – مؤشر الفعالية
Efflux of capital	sortie de capitaux	خروج رسمال
Egalitarianism	égalitarianisme	مذهب المساواة
Elastic demand	demande élastique	طلب مرن
Elastic supply	offre élastique	عرض مرن
Elasticity	élasticité	مرونة
Elasticity of substitution	élasticité de la substitution	مرونة الاستبدال – مرونة الاحلال
Electrification	électrification	كهربة
Electronic computer	ordinateur électronique	حاسبة الكترونية
Electronic data processing	traitement électronique des données	معالجة الكترونية للبيانات
Electronic industry	industrie électronique	الصناعة الالكترونية
Eligible currency	monnaie agréée	عملة معتمدة
Eligible paper	effets éligibles effets escomptables effets réescomptables	أوراق قابلة للخصم معايير
Eligibility criteria	critères d'éligibilité	معايير الصلاحية
Embargo	embargo	حظر
Embodied technology	technologie incarnée technologie incorporée	فن انتاجي مجسم – تكنولجيا مجسمة
Emergency aid Emergency relief	secours d'urgence	معونة طوارىء – مساعدة طوارىء – إغاثة
Emergency food reserve	réserve alimentaire de secours	احتياطي إغاثة غذائية
Emergency programme	programme d'urgence	برنامج طوارىء – خطة طوارىء
Emigrant	émigrant	مهاجر – مغترب
Emigrants' remittances	remises d'émigrants – transferts d'émigrants	تحويلات المهاجرين – تحويلات المغتربين

Emigrant traffic	trafic d'émigrants	تجارة المهاجرين
Emigration	émigration	هجرة – اغتراب
Emoluments	émoluments	مرتب – اتعاب
Empirical analysis	analyse concrète – analyse empirique	تحليل واقعي – تحليل الوقائع
Employee	employé	موظف
Employer	employeur – patron	صاحب عمل – رب عمل
Employers' association	syndicat patronal	اتحاد اصحاب اعمال – اتحاد ارباب اعمال
Employer-employee relations	relations patron-ouvriers	علاقات رب العمل والعمال
Employment	emploi	عمالة –تشغيل
Employment agency	agence de placement	مكتب تشغيل – مكتب توظيف
Employment discrimination	discrimination dans l'emploi	تمييز وظيفي – تمييز في التشغيل
Employment function	fonction de l'emploi	دالة العمالة
Employment opportunities	possibilités d'emploi	فرص العمالة – امكانيات التشغيل
Employment policy	politique de l'emploi politique de l'embauche	سياسة العمالة – سياسة التشغيل
End-product	produit final	ناتج نهائي – منتج نهائي
End-use	utilisation finale	استخدام نهائي – استعمال نهائي
Endogenous factor	facteur endogène	عامل داخلي – عامل ذاتي
Endogenous variable	variable endogène	متغير ذاتي – متغير داخلي
Endorse, to	endosser	ظهّر
Endorsement	endossement	تظهير
Endowment fund	fonds à dotation-fondation	صندوق اتهاب – وقفية
Endowment insurance	assurance à capital différé assurance-épargne	تأمين ادخاري
Energy capital	capital énergétique	رسمال طاقي
Energy crisis	crise de l'énergie	ازمة الطاقة
Energy income	revenu énergétique	دخل طاقي
Energy policy	politique énergétique	سياسة الطاقة
Energy requirements	besoins en énergie – besoins énergétiques	حاجات الطاقة – احتياجات الطاقة
Energy resources	ressources énergétiques	موارد الطاقة
Engineering consultant	ingénieur-conseil	مستشار هندسي
Engineering economics	économie technique	اقتصاد هندسي
Engineering functions	fonctions techniques	دالات فنية – دالات هندسية
Engineering industry	industrie mécanique	صناعة ميكانيكية
Engineering studies	études techniques études d'ingénierie	دراسات فنية – دراسات هندسية
Enrolment	inscription - embauche	قيد – تشغيل
Enterprise	entreprise	مشروع – مؤسسة
Entertainment industry	industrie des spectacles	صناعة الترفيه
Entertainment tax	taxe sur les spectacles	ضريبة ملاهي

Entrepot market	marché intermédiaire	سوق وسيط
Entrepot trade	commerce d'entrepôt	تجارة الخزن – التجارة الوسيطة
	commerce d'entreposage	
Entrepreneur	entrepreneur – exploitant	منظم – صاحب مشروع
Entrepreneurial income	revenu des entrepreneurs	دخل المنظمين – دخل اصحاب المشروعات
Entrepreneurial risk	risque de l'entrepreneur	مخاطر المنظم
Entrepreneurship	esprit d'entreprise	روح المبادرة – المبادرة
Entry in an account	écriture comptable	قيد محاسبي
Envelope curve	courbe-enveloppe	منحنى الادراج
Environment	environnement	بيئة
Environment economics	économie de l'environnement	اقتصاديات البيئة
Environmental costs	coûts d'environnement	تكاليف بيئية – تكاليف بيئوية
Environmental crisis	crise de l'environnement	أزمة البيئة
	crise écologique	
Environmental project	projet d'environnement	مشروع بيئي – مشروع بيئوي
Environmental resources	ressources environnementales	موارد بيئية – موارد بيئوية
Environmental quality	qualité de l'environnement	جودة البيئة –نوعية البيئة
Environmentalist	écologiste	متخصص في شئون البيئة – اخصائي البيئة
Equal instalment amortisation	amortissement par annuités	استهلاك متعادل الاقساط
	constantes	
Equal opportunity	égalité des chances	تكافؤ الفرص – تساوي الفرص – فرصة متكافئة
Equal pay for equal work	salaire égal à travail égal	اجر واحد للعمل الواحد
Equal-product curve	courbe d'iso-produits	منحنى الناتج المتكافىء – منحنى الناتج المتساوي
Equal treatment principle	principe du traitement égal	مبدأ المعاملة المتكافئة–مبدأ المعاملة المتساوية
Equal-utility lines	lignes d'utilité équivalente	خطوط المنفعة المتكافئة– خطوط المنفعة المتساوية
Equalisation fund	caisse de péréquation	صندوق معادلة
Equalisation of factor prices	égalisation du prix des facteurs	تعادل سعر عوامل الانتاج
Equilibrating capital flow	flux de capitaux compensatoire	حركة رسمال موازنة
	mouvement compensatoire de	حركة رسمالية موازنة
	capitaux	
Equilibrium	équilibre	توازن
Equilibrium conditions	conditions d'équilibre	شروط التوازن – مقتضيات التوازن
Equilibrium distribution	répartition d'équilibre	توزيع التوازن – توزيع توازني
Equilibrium of supply and demand	équilibre de l'offre et de la demande	توازن العرض والطلب
Equilibrium price	prix d'équilibre	ثمن التوازن – سعر التوازن
Equimarginal principle	principe équimarginal	مبدأ التساوي الحدي – مبدأ التعادل الحدي
Equipment	équipement –	أجهزة – تجهيز – معدات
	matériel	
Equity	justice	رسمال سهمي – رسمال ذاتي – عدالة
	capital-actions	
	capital propre	
Equity capital	capital propre	رسمال المساهمين – رسمال ذاتي
	fonds propres	
	capital-actions	

Equity investment	participation au capital	مساهمة في الرسمال
Equity market	marché des actions	سوق الأسهم
Equity participation	participation au capital	مشاركة في الرسمال
Equity sharing		مساهمة في الرسمال
Equivalent exchange	échange égal – échange équivalent	تبادل متكافىء – تبادل متعادل
Ergonomics	ergonomie	علم العمل – دراسة العمل
Erosion	érosion	تعرية – تآكل
Erosion control	lutte contre l'érosion	مكافحة التعرية
Erosive crops	cultures érosives	حاصلات اعرائية
Errors and omissions	erreurs et omissions	السهو والخطأ
Error curve	courbe d'erreur	منحنى الخطأ
Errors of observation	erreurs d'observation	اخطاء المشاهدة
Errors of estimation	erreurs d'estimation	اخطاء التقدير
Escalation clause	clause d'échelle mobile clause d'escalation clause de révision	نص التصعيد – نص التأشير
Escalator	escalateur coefficient de révision	مؤشر تصعيد
Escrow account	compte de garantie bloqué	حساب ضمان مجمد – وديعة ضمان مجمدة
Essential goods	biens de première nécessité	سلع اساسية
Estate agent	agent immobilier – administrateur foncier	سمسار عقاري – وكيل عقاري
Estate duty	droits de succession	ضريبة تركات – ضريبة ارث
Estimated costs	coûts estimatifs	تكاليف تقديرية – تكاليف مقدرة
Estimated price	prix estimatif	ثمن تقديري – سعر مقدر
Estimated value	valeur estimative	قيمة تقديرية – قيمة مقدرة
Estimation	estimation	تقدير
Estimator	estimateur	مقدر
Etatism	étatisme	الحكومية (مذهب أو سياسة)
Ethics	éthique	اخلاقيات – علم الاخلاق
Ethics of competition	éthique de la concurrence	اخلاقيات المنافسة
Ethnic factor	facteur ethnique	عامل عنصري
Ethnic group	groupe ethnique	مجموعة عنصرية – فئة عنصرية
Eugenics	eugénisme	تحسين النسل – علم تحسين النسل
Euro-bank	euro-banque	بنك يوردولي – بنك دولي
Euro-bonds	euro-obligations	سندات دولية أوربية – سندات دولية – سندات يوردولية
Euro-bond loans	emprunts euro-obligataires	قروض سندات يوردولية
Euro-cheque	euro-chèque	شيك يوردولي – شيك دولي
Euro-communism	euro-communisme	الشيوعية الاوربية
Euro-credits	euro-crédits	قروض يوردولية – سلفيات يوردولية – سلفيات دولية
Euro-currencies	euro-monnaies – euro-devises	عملات دولية أوروبية – عملات دولية – عملات يوردولية
Euro-deposit	euro-dépôt	وديعة دولية أوربية – وديعة يوردولية – وديعة دولية

64

Euro-dollars	euro-dollars	دولارات اوربية – دولارات يوردولية – دولارات دولية
Euro-issues	euro-émissions	اصدارات دولية اوربية – اصدارات دولية – اصدارات يوردولية
Euro-markets	euro-marchés	أسواق النقد الدولية الاوربية – اسواق يوردولية
Evaluation	évaluation	تقييم – تقدير القيمة
	évaluation à *posteriori*	تقييم لاحق
	évaluation *ex-post* – évaluation rétrospective	
Evaluation process	processus d'évaluation	مجرى التقييم
Evaluation system	système d'évaluation	منهج التقييم
Evolutionism	évolutionnisme	مذهب التطور – التطورية
ex ante investment	investissement *ex ante*	استثمار مرغوب – استثمار مرتقب
ex ante saving	épargne *ex ante*	ادخار مرغوب – ادخار مرتقب
ex coupon	coupon détaché	بلا كعب – بلا قسيمة
	ex-coupon	
ex dividend	ex dividende	بلا ربح
ex factory price	prix départ usine	ثمن تسليم المصنع – سعر المصنع
ex interest	sans intérêts	بلا فوائد
ex plantation	départ plantation	عند المزرعة
ex post investment	investissement *ex post*	استثمار متحقق
ex post saving	épargne *ex post*	ادخار متحقق
ex quay	à quai	على رصيف الميناء – على الرصيف
ex ship	au débarquement	خارج السفينة
ex warehouse	ex magasin	من المخزن
ex warrant	sans option	بلا خيار – بلا حق خيار
ex works	départ usine	تسليم المصنع
Examination of bids	examen des offres	فحص العطاءات – فحص العروض
Excess capacity	capacité excédentaire capacité inutilisée	طاقة فائضة – طاقة زائدة – فائض الطاقة
Excess demand	demande excédentaire excès de la demande	طلب فائض
Excess liquidity	surplus de liquidités liquidités excédentaires	فائض السيولة – سيولة فائضة
Excess profits	superbénéfices bénéfices exceptionnels	ارباح استثنائية
Exchange	échange – cours du change change – bourse	صرف – مبادلة – تبادل – سعر الصرف بورصة
Exchange adjustment	ajustement du change	تعديل سعر الصرف
Exchange allocation	allocation de devises	تخصيص الصرف – تخصيص النقد الأجنبي
Exchange arbitrage	arbitrage de change	موازنة الصرف – موازنة صرفية
Exchange broker	agent de change	صراف
Exchange budget	budget de devises	ميزانية صرفية – موازنة النقد الأجنبي
Exchange contract	contrat de change	عقد صرف – عقد صرفي

Exchange control	contrôle des changes	رقابة الصرف – رقابة النقد
Exchange control authorities	office des changes	إدارة رقابة الصرف
Exchange control regulations	réglementation des changes	لائحة الصرف – احكام رقابة الصرف
Exchange costs	coûts en devises	تكاليف بالعملة الأجنبية
Exchange equalisation account	fonds de stabilisation des changes	صندوق تثبيت الصرف–صندوق موازنة الصرف
Exchange losses	pertes au change	خسائر الصرف – خسائر صرفية
Exchange market	marché des devises	سوق الصرف – سوق العملات الأجنبية
Exchange office	bureau de change	صراف – مكتب صرف
Exchange parity	parité du change	سعر تعادل الصرف
Exchange pegging	stabilisation du change	تثبيت الصرف
Exchange premium	prime de change – agio	علاوة صرفية
Exchange profits	bénéfices de change bénéfices cambiaires	ارباح صرفية
Exchange rate	cours du change	سعر الصرف
Exchange rate adjustment	ajustement des taux de change	تعديل أسعار الصرف
Exchange rate differentials	différentiels des cours de change	فروق أسعار الصرف
Exchange regulations	règlement des changes	لائحة الصرف – قوانين الصرف
Exchange restrictions	restrictions de change	قيود الصرف
Exchange risk	risque de change risque cambiaire	مخاطر الصرف – خطر الصرف
Exchange stabilisation fund	fonds de stabilisation des changes	صندوق تثبيت الصرف
Exchange stability	stabilité des changes	ثبات أسعار الصرف – ثبات الصرف
Exchange taxes	impôts sur les opérations de change	رسوم على عمليات الصرف–رسوم صرفية
Exchange transactions	opérations de change opérations cambiaires	عمليات صرفية – تحويلات صرفية
Exchange value	valeur d'échange	قيمة المبادلة
Exchequer (U.K.)	Trésor public (R.U.)	بيت المال – الخزانة (المملكة المتحدة)
Excise duties **Excise taxes**	droits d'accise droits de consommation impôts indirects	رسوم استهلاك – ضرائب غير مباشرة
Executing agency	organe d'exécution	جهاز التنفيذ – هيئة مكلفة بالتنفيذ
Executive staff	cadres	كوادر – اطارات
Exemption	exonération exemption	اعفاء
Exemption from duties	franchise douanière	اعفاء جمركي
Exhaustion of the land	épuisement de la terre	انجاع الأرض–انهاك الأرض
Exhaustion of resources	épuisement des ressources	استنفاد الموارد – نفاد الموارد
Exhibition	exposition	معرض
Exit value	valeur réalisable	قيمة البيع
Exodus of capital	exode des capitaux	هجرة الرسمال – رحيل الرسمال
Exogenous factor	facteur exogène	عامل خارجي – عامل دخيل
Exogenous variable	variable exogène	متغير خارجي – متغير دخيل

Exoneration	exemption – exonération	اعفاء
Exotic shares	valeurs exotiques	اسهم ماوراء البحار
Expanded reproduction	reproduction élargie	اعادة الإنتاج الموسع – الإنتاج الموسع
Expansion of credit	gonflement du crédit	بسط الائتمان – توسيع الائتمان
Expansion of exports	expansion des exportations	زيادة الصادرات
Expansion path	trajet d'expansion	مسار التوسع
	sentier d'expansion	
Expansionary policy	politique d'expansion	سياسة توسعية – سياسة التوسع
Expatriate staff	employés expatriés	العاملون الأجانب – العاملون المغتربون
	employés étrangers	
Expectations	prévisions	تنبؤات – توقعات – تطلعات
	espérances	
Expected life of the plant	durée probable des équipements	الأجل المتوقع للمنشآت–الأجل المحتمل للمعدات
Expected price	prix prévu	ثمن متوقع – ثمن مرتقب
Expected value	valeur prévue	قيمة متوقعة – قيمة احتمالية
	valeur probable	
Expenditures	dépenses	نفقات – انفاق
Expense account	compte de dépenses	حساب نفقات
	compte de frais	
Expenses deducted	frais défalqués	بعد خصم المصاريف – مصاريف مخصومة
Experimental plot	parcelle d'essai	حقل تجارب
	lopin d'essai	
Experimental station	ferme pilote	مزرعة نموذجية – مزرعة تجريبية
Experimental technology	technologie expérimentale	فن انتاج تجريبي–تكنولجية تجريبية
Experimental test	test expérimental	اختبار تجريبي
Expiry date	date d'expiration – date d'échéance	تاريخ انتهاء الاجل – المئجال – الأجل
Explanatory variables	variables explicatives	متغيرات التفسير – متغيرات مفسرة
Exploitation	exploitation	استغلال
Exploitation of labour	exploitation du travail	استغلال العمال
	exploitation de la main – d'œuvre	
Exploitation of natural resources	exploitation des ressources naturelles	استغلال الموارد الطبيعية
Exploration economics	économie de la prospection	اقتصاديات التنقيب
Exponential growth	croissance exponentielle	نمو أسي
Export	exportation	تصدير
Export, to	exporter	صدّر
Exports	exportations	صادرات
Export agent	mandataire-exportateur	وكيل تصدير
	agent d'exportation	
Export ban	blocage des exportations	حظر التصدير
Export bonus	prime d'exportation	اعانة تصدير – علاوة تصدير
Export bounty		
Export cartel	cartel d'exportation	كارتل تصدير
Export control	contrôle de l'exportation	رقابة التصدير – قيود التصدير

Export credit	crédit à l'exportation	ائتمان تصدير
Export credit insurance	assurance-crédit à l'exportation	تأمين الائتمان التصديري–تأمين الاقراض للتصدير
Export crops	cultures d'exportation	حاصلات تصدير – حاصلات تصديرية
Export diversification	diversification des exportations	تنويع الصادرات
Export drive	campagne d'exportation	حملة تصدير
Export duty	droit d'exportation	رسم تصدير
Export earnings	recettes d'exportation	ايرادات التصدير
Export embargo	embargo sur l'exportation	حظر التصدير
Export finance	financement des exportations	تمويل الصادرات
Export goods	biens d'exportation	سلع تصدير
Export-import trade	commerce d'export-import	تجارة التصدير والاستيراد
Export industry	industrie d'exportation	صناعة تصدير
Export incentives	stimulants à l'exportation	حوافز تصدير
Export insurance	assurance-exportation	تأمين الصادرات
Export license **Export permit**	permis d'exportation	اذن تصدير
Export markets	marchés d'exportation	اسواق التصدير
Export marketing	commercialisation des exportations	تسويق الصادرات
Export marketing group	groupement d'exportation	حلقة تصدير – مجموعة تصدير
Export-oriented economy	économie orientée vers l'exportation	اقتصاد موجه للتصدير
Export-oriented industry	industrie orientée vers l'exportation	صناعة موجهة للتصدير
Export possibilities	possibilités d'exportation	فرص التصدير – امكانيات التصدير
Export premium	prime d'exportation	علاوة تصدير
Export price	prix à l'exportation	سعر التصدير
Export proceeds	recettes d'exportation produit des exportations	حصيلة الصادرات – حصيلة التصدير
Export products	produits d'exportation	منتجات التصدير
Export prohibition	embargo sur l'exportation	حظر التصدير – منع التصدير
Export prospects	perspectives d'exportation	توقعات التصدير – فرص التصدير
Export sales	ventes à l'exportation	مبيعات إلى الخارج
Export quota	contingent d'exportation	حصة تصدير
Export routes	circuits d'exportation	مسالك التصدير
Export subsidy	subvention à l'exportation prime à l'exportation	اعانة تصدير
Export surplus	excédent d'exportation	فائض تصدير
Export tax	taxe à l'exportation	ضريبة على الصادرات – ضريبة تصدير
Export trade	commerce d'exportation	تجارة التصدير
Export volume	volume des exportations	حجم الصادرات
Exportable surplus	excédent exportable	فائض قابل للتصدير
Exportation	exportation	تصدير
Exporter	exportateur	مصدّر
Exporting country	pays exportateur	دولة مصدرة
Expropriation	expropriation	نزع الملكية

Expropriation risks	risques d'expropriation	مخاطر نزع الملكية
Extend, to (*a loan, a credit*)	accorder (*un prêt, un crédit*)	قدم – منح (قرضاً أو ائتماناً)
	consentir	
	octroyer	
Extension of credit	octroi d'un crédit	تقديم ائتمان
Extension of maturity	prorogation d'échéance	مد الأجل – مد أجل الاستحقاق
Extension services	services de vulgarisation	خدمات الاعانة والارشاد
Extensive agriculture	agriculture extensive	زراعة خفيفة – زراعة رحبة
Extensive farming	culture extensive	فلاحة خفيفة – فلاحة رحبة
External aid	aide extérieure	معونة خارجية – مساعدة خارجية
External assistance	assistance extérieure	اعانة خارجية
External accounts	comptes extérieurs	حسابات خارجية
External assets	avoirs à l'étranger	اصول خارجية – اصول في الخارج
External commerce	commerce extérieur	تجارة خارجية
External component (*of a project*)	composante externe (*d'un projet*)	العنصر الخارجي – العنصر المستورد (للمشروع)
External debt	dette extérieure	دين خارجي
External debt outstanding	encours de la dette extérieure	الدين الخارجي القائم
External diseconomies	déséconomies externes	وفورات خارجية سالبة – اضرار خارجية
External economies	économies externes	وفورات خارجية
External financing	financement extérieur	تمويل خارجي
External indebtedness	endettement extérieur	مديونية خارجية
External loan	emprunt étranger	قرض خارجي
	emprunt extérieur	
External suppliers	fournisseurs étrangers	موردون خارجيون – موردون من الخارج
External trade	commerce extérieur	تجارة خارجية
Externalities	externalités –	اخارج – خارجيات – آثار خارجية
	effets externes	
Extinction of a debt	extinction d'une dette	سداد دين – زوال دين
Extra-budgetary accounts	comptes extra-budgétaires	حساب خارج الموازنة – حسابات خارج الميزانية
Extra-budgetary funds	fonds extra-budgétaires	موارد خارج الموازنة – موارد خارج الميزانية
Extra-budgetary investments	investissements extra-budgétaires	استثمارات خارج الموازنة
		استثمارات خارج الميزانية
Extra-cost	coût supplémentaire	كلفة اضافية
Extraction industries	industries extractives	صناعات استخراجية
Extractive industries		
Extraordinary budget	budget extraordinaire	موازنة استثنائية – ميزانية غير عادية
Extraordinary receipts	recettes extraordinaires	موارد غير عادية – موارد استثنائية
Extrapolation	extrapolation	استكمال – استمداد
Extreme values	valeurs extrêmes	النهايات – قيم النهاء – القيم القصوى
Extremum values	valeurs extrémales	

F

Fabian socialism	socialisme fabien	الاشتراكية الفابية
Fabianism	fabianisme	الفابيانية – الفابية
Face value	valeur nominale – valeur faciale	قيمة اسمية – قيمة صكية
Facilities	facilités	تسهيلات
Factor analysis	analyse factorielle	تحليل العوامل
Factor combination	combinaison des facteurs	تأليف عوامل الانتاج – تركيب عوامل الانتاج توليفة عوامل الانتاج
Factor cost	coût des facteurs	كلفة عوامل الانتاج – كلفة العوامل
Factor demand	demande de facteurs	طلب عوامل الانتاج – طلب العوامل
Factor endowment	dotation en facteurs	توفر عوامل الانتاج – وجود عوامل الانتاج
Factor immobility	immobilité des facteurs viscosité des facteurs	لزوجة عوامل الانتاج
Factor income	revenu des facteurs revenu factoriel	دخل عوامل الانتاج – دخل العوامل
Factor input ratio	ratio d'intrants factoriels	نسبة العوامل المستخدمة
Factor intensity criterion	critère de l'intensité factorielle	معيار كثافة العوامل
Factor market	marché des facteurs	سوق عوامل الانتاج
Factors of production	facteurs de production	عوامل الانتاج – عناصر الانتاج
Factor prices	prix des facteurs – prix factoriels	اسعار عوامل الانتاج – اثمان العوامل
Factor proportions	proportion des facteurs	نسب عوامل الانتاج – نسب العوامل
Factor services	services factoriels	خدمات العوامل
Factor substitution	substitution des facteurs substitution factorielle	استبدال عوامل الانتاج – استبدال العوامل
Factor terms of trade	termes de l'échange factoriel	معدل التبادل العواملي
Factoring	factoring affacturage	تعميل
Factory	fabrique usine atelier	مصنع
Factory system	système des ateliers de production	نظام ورش الانتاج
Fade-out arrangement	accord en fondu – accord de désistement progressif	اتفاق انسحابي – تدبير انسحابي
Failure	faillite échec	افلاس – فشل
Fair	foire	معرض

Fair price	prix raisonnable prix équitable	سعر عادل – سعر معقول
Fair return	rendement équitable	عائد معقول – عائد عادل
Fair trade practices	pratiques commerciales non-déloyales	اساليب تجارية مشروعة
Fair wage	salaire équitable	اجر عادل
Faked invoicing	facturation frauduleuse	تزييف الفواتير – حسبنة مزيفة
Fall due, to	échoir venir à échéance	استحق – حل اجله
Fall in prices	baisse des prix	انخفاض الاسعار – هبوط الاثمان
Fallow land	terre en jachère terre en friche	ارض مستحالة – ارض بور
Family allowances	allocations familiales	مخصصات عائلية – اعانات عائلية
Family budget	budget familial	موازنة الاسرة – ميزانية الاسرة
Family enterprise	entreprise familiale	مشروع عائلي
Family farm	exploitation agricole familiale	مزرعة عائلية
Family income	revenu familial	دخل الاسرة
Family planning	planning familial	تنظيم الاسرة
Famine	famine	مجاعة
Fare	tarif – prix du passage prix du transport	ثمن النقل – اجرة النقل
Farm	exploitation agricole – ferme	مزرعة
Farm administration **Farm management**	gestion des exploitations agricoles	ادارة المزارع – ادارة زراعية
Farm economics	économie agricole	اقتصاد فلاحي
Farm equipment	matériel agricole	آلات زراعية – معدات زراعية
Farm implements	outils agricoles	ادوات زراعية
Farm machinery	matériel agricole	آلات زراعية
Farm mechanisation	mécanisation agricole	ميكنة الفلاحة
Farm workers	ouvriers agricoles	عمال زراعيون
Farming	agriculture – culture	زراعة – فلاحة
Farming equipment	matériel agricole	اجهزة فلاحية – معدات زراعية
Farming methods	méthodes culturales	اساليب الفلاحة
Farming sector	secteur agricole	قطاع فلاحي
Farming system	système d'exploitation agricole	نظام فلاحي – نظام زراعي
"FAS" (*free alongside ship*)	franco quai	عند الرصيف
Fascism	fascisme	الفاشية – الفاشيستية
Fascist ideology	idéologie fasciste	المذهبية الفاشية
Fashion goods	articles de mode	سلع الموضة-سلع الزينة
Favourable balance	solde créditeur	رصيد دائن – ميزان موجب
Favourable trade balance	balance commerciale favorable	ميزان تجاري موجب
Feasibility	factibilité – viabilité faisabilité	امكان – امكانية – جدوى

Feasibility field	champ des solutions possibles	منطقة الامكان – منطقة الحلول الممكنة
Feasibility frontier		
Feasibility study	étude de factibilité	دراسة امكان – دراسة الامكانية – دراسة جدوى
	étude de faisabilité	
Feasible solution	solution possible	حل ممكن
Fecundity	fécondité	خصوبة
Fee	charge – taxe	رسم – مكافأة – اجر
	redevance – droits	
	honoraires	
Feedback	feedback	رجع – رجعان
	réaction	
	rétroaction	
Feedback effect	effet de réaction	عامل الرجعان – عامل الرجع – اثر الرجع
	effet de retour	
Feeder roads	voies de desserte	طرق روافد
	routes d'accès	
Fellaheen **society**	société de fellahs	مجتمع فلاحين
Female labour	main-d'œuvre féminine	عمل نسائي
Fertiliser factory	usine d'engrais	مصنع سماد
Fertiliser industry	industrie des engrais	صناعة الاسمدة – صناعة السماد
Fertility	fertilité	خصوبة
Fertility index	indice de fécondité	مؤشر الخصوبة
Fertility rate	taux de fécondité	معدل التناسل – معدل الخصوبة
Fetichism	fétichisme	تصنيم
Feudal system	système féodal	النظام الاقطاعي
Feudalism	féodalisme	الاقطاع – النظام الاقطاعي
Fiat money	papier-monnaie	نقود ورقية – نقود الزامية
	monnaie à cours forcé	
Fictitious assets	avoirs fictifs	اصول وهمية
Fictitious capital	capital fictif	رسمال وهمي
Fiduciary money	monnaie fiduciaire	نقود ورقية
Field appraisal	évaluation *in situ* – évaluation sur le	تقييم ميداني
	terrain	
Field data	données recueillies sur le terrain	بيانات ميدانية
Field mission	mission sur le terrain	بعثة ميدانية
Field work	travaux sur le terrain	عمل ميداني
Final account	compte final	حساب ختامي
Final consumer	consommateur final	مستهلك نهائي
Final consumer price	prix de consommation finale	سعر الاستهلاك النهائي–ثمن الاستهلاك النهائي
Final consumption	consommation finale	استهلاك نهائي
Final consumption expenditures	dépenses de consommation finale	نفقات الاستهلاك النهائي
Final demand	demande finale	طلب نهائي

Final design	projet définitif	تصميم نهائي
Final goods	biens terminaux	سلع نهائية
Final instalment	versement final	القسط الأخير
Final maturity	échéance finale	أجل الاستحقاق النهائي
Finance	finance	مال – مالية – تمويل
	financement	
Finance, to	financer	موّل
Finance act	loi des finances	القانون المالي – التشريع المالي
Finance company	banque d'affaires – société financière	شركة مالية – بنك استثمار
Finance house	établissement de crédit à la	مؤسسة لتمويل الاستهلاك
	consommation	مؤسسة تمويل استهلاكي
Financeable project	projet finançable	مشروع صالح للتمويل
Financial administration	administration financière	ادارة مالية
Financial aid	assistance financière	معونة مالية – مساعدة مالية – اعانة مالية
Financial assistance	aide financière	
Financial analysis	analyse financière	تحليل مالي
Financial aspects	aspects financiers	جوانب مالية
Financial balance sheet	bilan financier	ميزانية مالية
Financial burden	fardeau financier	عبء مالي
	charge financière	
Financial centre	place financière	مركز مالي
	centre financier	
Financial charges	charges financières	رسوم مالية – اعباء مالية
Financial circles	monde de la finance – milieux	دوائر المال – دوائر مالية
	financiers	
Financial claims	créances financières	حقوق مالية
Financial control	contrôle financier	رقابة مالية
Financial credit	crédit financier	ائتمان مالي–سلفية–سلفة مالية
Financial crisis	crise financière	ازمة مالية
Financial forecasting	prévision financière	تنبؤ مالي – توقعات مالية
Financial house	maison de banque	بيت مالي – مؤسسة مالية
	établissement financier	
Financial inducements	stimulants financiers	حوافز مالية
Financial institutions	institutions financières	مؤسسات مالية – نظم مالية
Financial intermediaries	intermédiaires financiers	وسطاء ماليون
Financial leverage	leviérage financier	مرابعة مالية – ارباح مالي
	greffage financier	
Financial loss	perte financière	خسارة مالية
Financial management	gestion financière	ادارة مالية
Financial market	marché financier	سوق مالية – سوق مالي
Financial means	moyens financiers	موارد مالية
Financial paper	effets financiers	اوراق مالية
Financial period	exercice financier	سنة مالية – فترة مالية

Financial plan	plan de financement	خطة تمويل – خطة تمويلية
Financing plan		
Financial planning	planification financière	تخطيط مالي
Financial policy	politique financière	سياسة مالية
Financial rate of return	taux de rentabilité financière	معدل العائد المالي
Financial reorganisation	assainissement financier	اصلاح مالي
Financial requirements	besoins financiers	احتياجات مالية
Financial resources	ressources financières	موارد مالية
Financial soundness	solidité financière	جدوى مالية – سلامة مالية
Financial stability	stabilité financière	استقرار مالي
Financial standing	surface financière	مركز مالي – وضع مالي
	situation financière	
Financial statement	état financier	بيان مالي
	compte	
Financial system	système financier	نظام مالي
Financial world	milieux financiers	عالم المال – دوائر مالية – دوائر المال
	monde de la finance	
Financial year	exercice financier	سنة مالية
Financier	financier – financeur	رجل مال – ممول – رب مال
	bailleur de fonds	
Financing	financement	تمويل
Financing costs	coûts de financement	تكاليف التمويل – كلفة التمويل
Financing methods	méthodes de financement	اساليب التمويل
Financing requirements	besoins de financement	احتياجات التمويل – حاجات التمويل احتياجات مالية
Financing sources	sources de financement	مصادر التمويل – مصادر مالية
Fine	amende	غرامة
Fine gold	or fin	ذهب خالص
Fineness (of gold)	titre (or)	عيار (الذهب)
Finished goods	produits finis	سلع تامة الصنع
Finished products		
Fire insurance	assurance-incendie	تأمين ضد الحريق
Firm	firme –	مؤسسة – مشروع – منشأة
	entreprise	
	maison commerciale	
Firm buyer	acheteur ferme	مشترى بات – مشترٍ بات
Firm evaluation	évaluation des entreprises	تقييم المؤسسات
Firm market	marché ferme	سوق ثابت
Firm offer	offre ferme	عرض بات
Firm purchase	achat ferme	شراء بات
Fiscal administration	administration fiscale	ادارة الضرائب
Fiscal agent	agent fiscal – agent financier	وكيل مالي

Fiscal economics	science financière – économie financière	الاقتصاد المالي
Fiscal equity	justice fiscale	عدالة ضريبية
Fiscal evasion	évasion fiscale fraude fiscale	تهرب ضريبي – تهرب من الضريبة
Fiscal haven	paradis fiscal havre fiscal	ملجأ ضريبي – مأوى ضريبي
Fiscal immunity	immunité fiscale	حصانة مالية – حصانة ضريبية
Fiscal incentives	incitations fiscales	حوافز مالية
Fiscal law	droit fiscal	تشريع مالي
Fiscal monopoly	monopole fiscal	احتكار مالي
Fiscal performance	effort fiscal	اداء ضريبي – مجهود ضريبي
Fiscal policy	politique fiscale politique budgétaire	سياسة مالية
Fiscal regime **Fiscal system**	régime fiscal	نظام ضريبي
Fiscal revenue	recettes financières recettes budgétaires	ايرادات مالية – موارد مالية
Fiscal theory	théorie de l'impôt science financière	نظرية الضريبة – المالية العامة
Fiscal transparency	transparence fiscale	شفافية ضريبية
Fiscal year	exercice budgétaire année budgétaire	سنة مالية
Fish-farming	pisciculture	تربية الأسماك
Fisheries	industrie de la pêche	صناعة صيد الأسماك
Fisheries development	développement des pêches	تنمية الموارد السمكية
Fishery resources	ressources halieutiques	موارد سمكية
Fishing fleet	flotille de pêche	اسطول صيد
Fishing port	port de pêche	ميناء صيد
Fitting of a curve	ajustement d'une courbe	ضبط منحنى – توفيق منحنى
Five-year plan	plan quinquennal	خطة خمسية
Fixed assets	immobilisations	اصول ثابتة
Fixed base index	indice à base fixe	مؤشر ثابت الأساس
Fixed capital	capital fixe	رسمال ثابت
Fixed capital formation	formation de capital fixe	تكوين رسمال ثابت
Fixed charges	charges fixes	نفقات ثابتة
Fixed-charge coverage	couverture des charges fixes rapport revenu-intérêts	تغطية الالتزامات الثابتة نسبة الدخل إلى الفوائد المستحقة
Fixed costs	coûts constants coûts fixes	تكاليف ثابتة
Fixed deposits	dépôts à terme dépôts fixes	ودائع لأجل – ودائع ثابتة
Fixed exchange rates	taux de change fixes changes fixes	اسعار صرف ثابتة

Fixed income	revenu fixe	دخل ثابت
Fixed income securities	valeurs à revenu fixe	سندات ثابتة الدخل
Fixed input	intrant fixe	مستخدم ثابت
Fixed instalment depreciation	amortissement par annuités constantes	استهلاك بالاقساط الثابتة
		استهلاك ثابت الاقساط
Fixed investment	investissement fixe	استثمار في رسمال ثابت
	investissement d'équipement	
Fixed liabilities	passif non courant – passif fixe	خصوم غير جارية
Fixed price	prix fixe	سعر محدد – ثمن محدد
Fixed property	biens immeubles	عقارات – أموال عقارية
Fixed rate loan	prêt à taux fixe	قرض بسعر ثابت
Fixed rate of exchange	taux de change fixe	سعر صرف محدد – سعر صرف ثابت
Flag of convenience	pavillon de complaisance	علم مجاملة
Flat price	prix ex coupon	سعر بلا عائد – ثمن بلا عائد
Flat rate	tarif uniforme	سعر موحد – ثمن جزافي
	taux forfaitaire	
Flat yield	rendement courant	عائد جاري – عائد جار
Flexibility of exchange rates	flexibilité des changes	مرونة اسعار الصرف
Flexible planning	planification souple	تخطيط مرن
Flight capital	capitaux fugitifs	رسمال هارب
Flight of capital	fuite des capitaux	هروب الرسمال – هجرة الرسمال
Float	float	أموال عابرة–أموال عائمة
	fonds en transit	أموال تحت التحصيل
Float a loan, to	émettre un emprunt	اصدر قرضاً – طرح قرضاً
	lancer un emprunt	
Floatation of an issue	lancement d'une émission	طرح اصدار
Floating capital	capital de roulement	رسمال متداول – رسمال عائم
	capital circulant	
	capitaux mobiles	
	capitaux flottants	
Floating charge	gage général	رهن عام
Floating rate notes	obligations à taux variable	سندات متغيرة الفائدة
Floating debt	dette flottante –	دين عائم – دين قائم
	impayés	
Floating exchange rates	taux de change flottants	اسعار صرف متغيرة – اسعار صرف عائمة
	changes flottants	
Floating of a currency	flottement d'une monnaie	تعويم عملة
	flottaison d'une monnaie	
Floating policy (*insurance*)	police ouverte (*assurance*)	تأمين مفتوح
Floating rate	taux fluctuant	سعر متغير – سعر غير ثابت
	taux flottant	
	taux ajustable	
Floating rate issue	émission à taux ajustable	اصدار بفائدة متغيرة
Flood control	lutte anti-inondation	ضبط الفيضان–مكافحة الفيضانات
	contrôle des eaux de crue	

Flood irrigation	irrigation par submersion	ري الفيضان – ري بالغمر
Floor price	prix plancher	سعر ادنى – ثمن ادنى
Floriculture	floriculture	زراعة الزهور
Flow chart	graphe de flux	رسم حركي – رسم الهيكل التنظيمي – لوحة تدفق
Flow diagram	organigramme	
Flow concept	concept de flux	مفهوم تدفقي
Flow of capital	mouvement de capital	تيار رسمال – حركة رسمال – تدفق رسمال
	flux de capitaux	
Flow-of-funds analysis	analyse des flux financiers	تحليل التدفقات المالية
Flow of resources	flux des ressources	حركة الموارد – تدفق الموارد
	mouvement des ressources	
Fluctuating rates	taux fluctuants	اسعار متغيرة – اسعار متحركة
	taux variables	اسعار غير ثابتة
	taux mobiles	
Fluctuation	fluctuation	تقلب – رقص – تذبذب
	oscillation	
"FOB" (free on board)	FOB	فوب – فوق السفينة
	franco bord	
FOB prices	prix FOB	اسعار فوب – اثمان فوب
Fodder crops	fourrages	اعلاف – حاصلات علفية
	cultures	
Follow-up	follow-up – suivi d'execution	متابعة
Follow-up project	projet complémentaire	مشروع تكميلي
Food	aliments	غذاء – اغذية – منتجات غذائية
Foodstuffs	denrées alimentaires	
Food aid	aide alimentaire	معونة غذائية – مساعدة غذائية – اعانة غذائية
Food allotments	attributions alimentaires	حصص غذائية – مخصصات غذائية
Food and live animals	produits alimentaires et animaux vivants	مواد غذائية وحيوانات حية
Food consumption	consommation alimentaire	استهلاك غذائي
Food crisis	crise de l'alimentation	ازمة الغذاء – ازمة غذائية
	crise alimentaire	
Food crops	cultures vivrières	حاصلات غذائية
Food industry	industries alimentaires	صناعات غذائية
Food processing industry		
Food needs	besoins alimentaires	حاجات غذائية – احتياجات غذائية
Food requirements		
Food policy	politique alimentaire	سياسة غذائية
Food processing	transformation de produits alimentaires	تصنيع المنتجات الغذائية
Food products	produits alimentaires	منتجات غذائية
Food production	production alimentaire	انتاج غذائي
	production vivrière	

Food security assistance	aide pour la sécurité alimentaire	معونة لتأمين الموارد الغذائية
Food security policy	politique de la sécurité alimentaire	سياسة تأمين الموارد الغذائية
Food shortage	pénurie des denrées alimentaires	عجز المواد الغذائية – عجز غذائي
	pénurie alimentaire	
Food supplies	provisions alimentaires	موارد غذائية
	disponibilités alimentaires	
	ressources alimentaires	
Food value	valeur nutritive	قيمة غذائية
Foot-loose industries	industries mobiles	صناعات قابلة للانتقال
Footwear industry	industrie de la chaussure	صناعة الاحذية
"FOR" (*free on rail*)	franco wagon	على القطار
Force majeure	force majeure	قوة قاهرة
Forced labour	travail forcé – corvée	سخرة – عمل جبري
Forced loan	emprunt forcé	قرض جبري – قرض اجباري
Forced sale	vente forcée	بيع جبري
Forced saving	épargne forcée	ادخار جبري – ادخار اجباري
Forecasts	prévisions	تنبؤات – توقعات
	prédictions	
Forecasting	prévision	استنباء – تنبؤ – توقع
	prédiction	
Forecasting errors	erreurs de prévision	أخطاء الاستنباء–أخطاء التنبؤ–أخطاء التوقع
Forecasting model	modèle prévisionnel	نموذج استنبائي – نموذج توقعي
Forecasting period	période de prévision	فترة التنبؤ – فترة الاستنباء – فترة التوقع
Forecasting technique	technique de prévision	اسلوب التنبؤ–اسلوب الاستنباء–اسلوب التوقع
Forces of progress	forces du progrès	عوامل التطور
Foreign aid	aide étrangère	معونة اجنبية – مساعدة خارجية
	aide extérieure	
Foreign assets	avoirs extérieurs	اصول خارجية
Foreign capital	capital étranger	رسمال اجنبي
Foreign control	contrôle étranger	سيطرة اجنبية
Foreign creditor	créancier étranger	دائن اجني
Foreign currency	devise	عملة اجنبية – نقد اجني
	monnaie étrangère	
Foreign currency account	compte en devises	حساب بالعملة الأجنبية–حساب بالنقد الأجنبي
Foreign currency issues	émissions en devises	اصدارات مقومة بعملة أجنبية–اصدارات بنقد اجني
Foreign currency reserves	réserves de devises	ارصدة العملة الأجنبية–أرصدة النقد الأجني
Foreign debt	dette extérieure	دين خارجي
	dette étrangère	
Foreign exchange	devises	عملات اجنبية – نقود اجنبية
	monnaies étrangères	
Foreign exchange allocation	allocation-devises	مخصص العملة الاجنبية
Foreign exchange component	composante-devises	عنصر النقد الاجني
Foreign exchange dealer	cambiste – agent de change	صراف – صيرفي

Foreign exchange expenditures	dépenses en devises	انفاق بالعملة الاجنبية – انفاق بالنقد الاجني
Foreign exchange holdings	avoirs en devises	ارصدة العملة الاجنبية – ارصدة النقد الاجني
Foreign exchange futures	opérations de change à terme	عمليات صرف آجلة
Foreign exchange liabilities	obligations en devises	التزامات بالعملة الاجنبية – التزامات بالنقد الاجني
Foreign exchange market	marché des changes	سوق الصرف
Foreign exchange permit	autorisation de change	اذن صرف
Foreign exchange policy	politique des changes politique cambiaire	سياسة الصرف
Foreign exchange position	situation des réserves extérieures	وضع العملات الاجنبية – وضع الارصدة الخارجية
Foreign exchange rationing	rationnement des devises	تقنين النقد الاجني – تقنين الصرف
Foreign exchange requirements	besoins en devises	احتياجات النقد الاجني
Foreign exchange reserves	réserves de change réserves en devises	ارصدة الصرف – ارصدة النقد الاجني
Foreign exchange resources	ressources en devises	موارد النقد الاجني
Foreign goods	produits étrangers – biens étrangers	منتجات اجنبية
Foreign grant	donation étrangère don étranger	منحة خارجية
Foreign indebtedness	endettement extérieur	مديونية خارجية
Foreign investments	investissements étrangers investissements extérieurs	استثمارات اجنبية – استثمارات خارجية
Foreign liabilities	engagements extérieurs	التزامات خارجية
Foreign loan	emprunt extérieur emprunt étranger	قرض خارجي
Foreign markets	marchés extérieurs	اسواق خارجية
Foreign military aid	aide militaire extérieure	مساعدة عسكرية خارجية
Foreign outlets	débouchés extérieurs	اسواق خارجية
Foreign property	biens étrangers	املاك اجنبية
Foreign reserves	avoirs extérieurs	ارصدة خارجية
Foreign trade	commerce extérieur	تجارة خارجية
Foreign trade bank	banque pour le commerce extérieur	بنك للتجارة الخارجية – مصرف للتجارة الخارجية
Foreign trade efficiency indexes	indices de l'efficacité du commerce extérieur	مؤشرات فاعلية التجارة الخارجية
Foreign trade multiplier	multiplicateur du commerce extérieur	مضاعف التجارة الخارجية
Foreign trade policy	politique du commerce extérieur politique commerciale	سياسة التجارة الخارجية – السياسة التجارية
Foreign transactions	opérations extérieures	عمليات خارجية
Foreign undertaking	entreprise étrangère	مشروع اجنبي
Foreman	contremaître	وهين
Forest engineering	génie forestier	هندسة حرشية
Forest lands	terres forestières	اراض حرشية
Forest policy	politique forestière	سياسة حرشية
Forest resources	ressources forestières	موارد حرشية
Forestation	boisement	تشجير – تحريش

Forestry	sylviculture	زراعة الاشجار – استغلال الاحراش
Forestry development	développement de la sylviculture	تنمية حرشية
Forestry economics	économie forestière	اقتصاديات الاحراش – اقتصاديات الغابات
Forestry planning	planification forestière	تخطيط حرشي
Forfaiting	affacturage à forfait	تعميل جزافي
Forfeiture	déchéance	سقوط الحق
Forfeiture of a patent	déchéance d'un brevet	سقوط حق اختراع – سقوط براءة اختراع
Formal sector	secteur organisé	القطاع المنظم
Formulation of projects	élaboration de projets	صياغة المشاريع – اعداد المشاريع
Forward and backward linkages	liaisons amont et aval – jonctions amont et aval	روابط امامية وخلفية
Forward exchange market	marché des changes à terme	سوق الصرف الآجل
Forward exchange operations	opérations de change à terme	عمليات صرف آجلة
Forward exchange rate	taux de change à terme	سعر الصرف الآجل
Forward integration	intégration vers l'aval	تكامل أمامي
Forward linkages	liens en aval – liaisons-aval – jonctions-aval	روابط أمامية
Forward markets	marchés à terme	أسواق آجلة
Forward purchase	achat à terme	شراء لأجل – شراء آجل
Forward rate	cours à terme	سعر آجل
Forward transaction	opération à terme	عملية آجلة
Forwarding agent	agent transitaire agent de transport	وكيل نقل
Founders' share Founders' stocks	part de fondateurs	حصص التأسيس – حصص المؤسسين
Four-year plan	plan quadriennal	خطة رباعية
Frame assistance agreement	accord-cadre d'assistance	اتفاق اطاري للاعانة
Franchise	licence concession franchisage	ترخيص – امتياز – حق تمثيل
Fraud	fraude	تدليس – غش – تهريب
Free competition	libre concurrence	منافسة حرة
Free customs admission Free entry	admission en franchise douanière	دخول مع اعفاء جمركي – دخول حر
Free enterprise	libre entreprise	حرية النشاط الاقتصادي – النشاط الاقتصادي الحر
Free enterprise economy Free market economy	économie de marché économie libérale	اقتصاد حر
Free goods	biens libres biens non-imposés biens exemptés	أموال حرة – سلع معفاة من الرسوم
Free imports	importations en franchise douanière	واردات حرة
Free limit loans	prêts d'approbation autonome	قروض حرة البت
Free market	marché libre	سوق حرة – سوق حر
Free port	port franc	ميناء حر
Free reserves	réserves disponibles réserves libres	ارصدة حرة

Free sample	échantillon gratuit	عينة بلا ثمن
Free trade	libre-échange	حرية التجارة – التجارة الحرة
Free trade area	zone de libre-échange	منطقة حرة – منطقة تجارية حرة
Free-traders	libre-échangistes	أنصار حرية التجارة
Free zone	zone franche	منطقة حرة
Freedom of association	liberté syndicale	حرية انشاء النقابات – الحرية النقابية
	liberté d'association	
Freedom of capital transfers	liberté du transfert des capitaux	حرية التحويلات الرسمالية
Freely convertible currency	monnaie librement convertible	عملة حرة التحويل – عملة حرة
Freezing of prices	blocage des prix	تجميد الاسعار
Freight	fret	شحن
Freight insurance	assurance-fret	تأمين الشحن
Freight market	marché des frets	سوق الشحن
Freight pre-paid	fret payé d'avance	شحن مدفوع مقدماً
Freight rate	cours du fret	سعر الشحن – أسعار الشحن
Freightage	affrètement –	إيجار سفينة شحن – عقد شحن
Freighting	nolisage	
Frequency	fréquence	تكرار
Frequency curve	courbe de fréquence	منحنى تكراري
Frequency distribution	distribution de fréquence	توزيع تكراري
Fresh funds	argent frais	أموال جديدة
Fresh money	capitaux frais	
Frictional unemployment	chômage frictionnel	بطالة احتكاكية – بطالة عارضة
Fringe benefits	indemnités accessoires – allocations	مزايا اضافية
	supplémentaires	
	avantages divers	
Frontier technology	technologie d'avant-garde	فن انتاجي رائد – تكنولوجية رائدة
	technologie de pointe	
Frozen assets	avoirs bloqués	اصول مجمدة
Frozen prices	prix bloqués	اسعار مجمدة
Full convertibility	convertibilité intégrale	قابلية كاملة للتحويل
Full employment	plein emploi	عمالة كاملة – تشغيل شامل
Full employment budget	budget de plein emploi	موازنة عمالة كاملة – ميزانية عمالة كاملة
Full employment equilibrium	équilibre de plein emploi	توازن العمالة الكاملة
Full employment policy	politique de plein emploi	سياسة العمالة الكاملة
Full fare	plein tarif	سعر كامل
Full-time employment	emploi à plein temps	عمل متفرغ
Fully paid capital	capital entièrement versé	رسمال كامل الدفع
Fully paid shares	actions entièrement libérées	اسهم كاملة الاداء
Fund	fonds – caisse	صندوق – مال
Funds	fonds – provision	أموال – ارصدة
Fund raising	mobilisation de fonds	جمع أموال

Fundamental disequilibrium	déséquilibre fondamental	اختلال اساسي
Funded capital	capital investi	رسمال مستثمر – رسمال موظف
Funded debt	dette consolidée	دين مثبت
Funding loan	prêt de consolidation	قرض تثبيت
	emprunt de consolidation	
Funding of a debt	consolidation d'une dette	تثبيت دين
Fungible goods	biens fongibles	اموال مثلية
Funk money	capitaux errants – argent fugueur	أموال رحّالة–أموال متنقلة
Furniture industry	industrie du meuble	صناعة الأثاث
Future delivery	livraison à terme	تسليم مؤجل
Futures	opérations à terme	عمليات آجلة
Futures market	marché du terme	سوق الآجل – سوق العمليات الآجلة
	marché des opérations à terme	
Futurology	futurologie	دراسة المستقبل

Gadget civilisation	civilisation des gadgets	حضارة الكماليات
Gain	gain	مكسب
Gains from trade	gains de l'échange	مكاسب التبادل
Gainfully occupied population	population active	السكان العاملون
Galloping inflation	inflation galopante	تضخم ضارم – تضخم راكض
Gambler	spéculateur	مضارب – مقامر
Gambling debt	dette de jeu	دين قمار – دين مقامرة
Game theory	théorie des jeux	نظرية التقارع – نظرية التباري
Gap	écart – fossé	فجوة – ثغرة
Garment industry	industrie du vêtement	صناعة الملابس
Gas pipeline	gazoduc	بيب غازي – خط أنابيب الغاز
Gathering of data	collecte des données	جمع البيانات
Gearing	greffage	مرابعة – ارباع
General equilibrium	équilibre général	توازن عام
General equilibrium analysis	analyse de l'équilibre général	تحليل التوازن العام
General government	administration publique	الادارة الحكومية – الحكومة
General price level	niveau général des prix	المستوى العام للاسعار
General strike	grève générale	اضراب عام
General survey mission	mission d'étude générale	بعثة استطلاعية عامة
Generalised tariff preferences	préférences tarifaires généralisées	المزايا التعرفية العامة–المزايا التعرفية المعممة
Generating capacity (*electricity*)	capacité de production (*électricité*)	طاقة التوليد – طاقة الانتاج (كهرباء)
Generation of income	génération de revenus	ادرار دخل – توليد دخل

Gentleman's agreement	accord de gentleman	اتفاق ضمني
Geographical distribution	répartition géographique	التوزيع الجغرافي – التوزيع الاقليمي
Geometric mean	moyenne géométrique	متوسط هندسي – وسط هندسي
Gestation lag	délai de maturation	اجل النضج
Gestation period	période de maturation	فترة النضج
	période de gestation	
Gift	don	هبة – منحة – عطية – نحلان
Gift tax	impôt sur les donations	ضريبة على الهبات
Gilt-edged securities	valeurs de premier ordre	أوراق مالية ممتازة – أوراق مالية مأمونة
	titres de père de famille	
Glass and glass products industry	industrie du verre et de la verrerie	صناعة الزجاج والمنتجات الزجاجية
Gliding parity system	système des parités mobiles	نظام التعادل المتحرك
Global plan	plan global	خطة شاملة
Global quota	contingent global	حصة كلية – حصة اجمالية
Glut	pléthore	فيض – وفرة – تكدس
	surabondance	
Glut of money	pléthore de monnaie	وفرة النقود
Goal variable	variable-but – variable-objectif	متغير هدفي
Going concern	affaire active	مشروع عامل – مشروع نشط
Going wages	salaires courants	الأجور الجارية – الأجور الدارجة
Gold backing	couverture-or	غطاء ذهبي
Gold bar	lingot d'or	سبيكة ذهبية
Gold bullion	or en barres – or en lingots	سبائك ذهبية
Gold bullion standard	étalon de lingots-or	قاعدة السبائك الذهبية
Gold clause	clause-or	شرط الذهب
Gold coins	pièces d'or	مسكوكات ذهبية – سكة ذهبية
Gold content	teneur en or – titre	عيار الذهب – المحتوى الذهبي
Gold cover	couverture-or	غطاء ذهبي – غطاء الذهب
Gold-exchange standard	étalon de change-or	قاعدة الصرف الذهبي – قاعدة الصرف بالذهب
Gold guarantee	garantie-or	ضمان ذهبي – ضمان ذهب
Gold holdings	avoirs en or	ارصدة ذهبية
	réserves-or	
Gold parity	parité-or	سعر التعادل الذهبي – سعر التعادل مع الذهب
Gold points	points d'or	حدود الذهب
	gold points	
Gold pool	pool de l'or	مجمع ذهب
Gold rush	ruée vers l'or	تهافت على الذهب
Gold specie standard	étalon de monnaie-or	قاعدة المسكوكات الذهبية
Gold standard	étalon-or	قاعدة الذهب
Gold tranche	tranche-or	شريحة ذهبية – شريحة الذهب
Gold-value clause	clause-or	شرط الذهب

Gold-value guarantee	garantie-or	ضمان الذهب – ضمان القيمة الذهبية
Goods	biens – marchandises	سلع
Goods and services	biens et services	سلع وخدمات
Goods and services account	compte de biens et services	حساب السلع والخدمات
Goods traffic	trafic des marchandises	حركة نقل السلع
Goodness of fit	qualité de l'ajustement	حسن التوفيق
Goodwill	clientèle	الشهرة التجارية – الاسم التجاري
	réputation	
Government accounts	comptes de l'Etat	حسابات الحكومة
	comptes publics	
Government agency	administration publique	جهاز حكومي – جهاز عام
	organisme public	
Government aid	aide gouvernementale	معونة حكومية – مساعدة حكومية – اعانة حكومية
Government bonds	obligations d'Etat	سندات حكومية
Government budget	budget de l'Etat	موازنة الدولة – ميزانية الدولة
Government consumption	consommation publique	استهلاك حكومي – استهلاك عام
Government corporation	entreprise publique	شركة عامة – مؤسسة عامة
	entreprise étatique	
Government debt	dette publique	الدين العام – الدين الحكومي
Government enterprise	entreprise publique	مشروع عام
Government expenditures	dépenses publiques	نفقات عامة
Government finance	finances publiques	المالية العامة
Government guarantee	garantie de l'Etat	ضمان حكومي – ضمان الدولة
Government interference	ingérence du gouvernement	تدخل حكومي – تدخل الحكومة
	ingérence de l'Etat	
Government loan	emprunt public	قرض عام – قرض حكومي
Government monopoly	monopole d'Etat	احتكار حكومي
Government obligations	obligations de l'Etat	سندات حكومية
	titres publics	
Government paper	effets publics	سندات حكومية
Government procurement	marchés publics	توريدات حكومية – مشتريات حكومية
Government receipts	recettes publiques	ايرادات عامة
Government revenue	revenus de l'Etat	الايرادات العامة – ايرادات الدولة
Government securities	titres publics	سندات عامة – صكوك حكومية
	fonds d'Etat	
Government services	services de l'administration	خدمات الحكومة – مرافق عامة
	services publics	
Government subsidy	subvention publique	اعانة حكومية
Government take	quote-part du gouvernement	حصة الدولة – نصيب الدولة
Governmental priorities	priorités gouvernementales	اولويات الحكومة – اولويات حكومية
Grace period	différé d'amortissement	فترة الامهال – فترة الانظار – فترة السماح
	délai de grâce	
	période de franchise	

Grading	gradation	تصنيف – ترتيب
	classement	
Graduated tariff	tarif progressif	تعرفة تصاعدية
Graduated tax	impôt progressif	ضريبة تصاعدية
Grain exchange	marché des grains	سوق الحبوب – بورصة الحبوب
Grain market		
Grant	don	منحة – هبة – عطية – نحلان
	subvention	
	donation	
Grant a credit, a loan, to	accorder un crédit, un prêt	منح ائتماناً أو قرضاً – قدم ائتماناً أو قرضاً
	octroyer un crédit, un prêt	
Grant a respite, to	accorder un délai	منح مهلة – امهل
Grant amount	montant-donation	مبلغ المنح – مبلغ العطاء – مبلغ النحلان
	valeur-don	
Grant basis, on a	à titre gracieux	على أساس الهبة
Grant element	élément de subvention	عنصر المنح – عنصر العطاء
	élément-don	عنصر الهبة – عنصر التيسير
	élément de libéralité	
Grant equivalent	équivalent-don	معادل المنح – معادل العطاء
Grant-in-aid	don	منحة – اعانة – مساعدة
	subvention	
Grant in kind	don en nature	منحة عينية – اعانة عينية – مساعدة عينية
Grant-like contribution	quasi-don	شبه هبة
Graph	graphe	رسم بياني
	graphique	
	diagramme	
Grazing lands	pâturages	مراعي – مراع
Green revolution	révolution verte	الثورة الخضراء
Grey market	marché parallèle	سوق موازي – سوق موازية
Gross	brut	اجمالي
Gross capital formation	formation brute de capital	اجمالي تكوين الرسمال
Gross disbursements	déboursements bruts	اجمالي السحوبات
Gross domestic product (GDP)	produit intérieur brut (PIB)	اجمالي الناتج المحلي
Gross fixed capital formation	formation brute de capital fixe	اجمالي تكوين الرسمال الثابت
Gross income	revenu brut	اجمالي الدخل – الدخل الاجمالي
Gross investment	investissement brut	اجمالي الاستثمار
Gross margin	marge de bénéfice brut	اجمالي هامش الربح – هامش الربح الإجمالي
Gross national expenditure	dépense nationale brute	اجمالي الانفاق القومي
Gross National Product (GNP)	produit national brut (PNB)	اجمالي الناتج القومي
Gross national turn-over	ressources disponibles brutes	اجمالي الموارد المتاحة
Gross payments	paiements bruts	اجمالي المدفوعات
Gross profit	bénéfices bruts	اجمالي الربح – اجمالي الأرباح
Gross revenue	recettes brutes	إجمالي الايرادات

Gross sales	chiffre d'affaires brut	اجمالي المبيعات
Gross savings	épargne brute	اجمالي الادخار
Gross value	valeur brute	اجمالي القيمة
Ground rent	rente foncière	ريع عقاري
Ground water	eau souterraine	مياه جوفية
Grouping	groupement	تجمع
Growth	croissance	نمو – نماء
Growth economics	économie de la croissance	اقتصاديات النمو
Growth factor	facteur de croissance	عامل نمو – عامل انمائي
Growth fund	fonds d'investissement à croissance	صندوق استثمار نمائي
Growth model	modèle de croissance	نموذج نمو
Growth paths	sentiers de croissance	مسالك النمو – مسارات النمو
Growth poles	pôles de croissance	اقطاب انمائية
Growth potential	potentiel de croissance	طاقة النمو – قدرة النمو
Growth rate	taux de croissance	معدل النمو
Growth shares	actions de croissance	اسهم نمائية
Guarantee	garantie	ضمان – كفالة
Guaranty	caution	
Guarantee agreement	contrat de garantie	اتفاقية ضمان
	accord de garantie	
Guarantee fund	fonds de garantie	صندوق ضمان
Guarantee mechanism	mécanisme de garantie	جهاز ضمان
Guaranteed loan	emprunt garanti	قرض مضمون – قرض مكفول
	emprunt avec garantie	
Guaranteed price	prix garanti	سعر مكفول
Guaranteed wage	salare garanti	اجر مكفول
Guarantor	garant	ضامن – كفيل
Guarantee	donneur de caution	
"Guesstimates"	estimations conjecturelles	تقديرات تخمينية
Guest worker	travailleur immigré	عامل وافد
Guidelines	directives	توجيهات عامة – ارشادات
	principes directeurs	
	principes d'orientation	
Guild	corporation	طائفة – نقابة حرفية
	corps de métier	
Guild economy	économie corporative	اقتصاد الطوائف
	économie de corps de métiers	
Guild socialism	socialisme corporatif	الاشتراكية الحرفية
Guinea	guinée	جنيه

H

Habitat	habitat	بيئة – نزل – موطن
Haggle, to	marchander	ماكس – ساوم
Haggling	marchandage	مماكسة – مساومة
Handicraft	artisanat	حرفة
Handicraft enterprise	entreprise artisanale atelier artisanal	مشروع حرفي
Handicraft industry	industrie artisanale	صناعة حرفية
Handling	manutention – maniement manoeuvre	مباشرة – تناول
Handling charges	droits de manutention frais de manutention	رسوم المباشرة
Harbour fees	droits portuaires	رسوم ميناء – رسوم مرفئية
Harbour installations	installations portuaires	منشآت الميناء – منشآت مرفئية
Harbour traffic	trafic portuaire	حركة الميناء – الحركة المرفئية
Hard cash	argent liquide liquide	نقد سائل – نقد فوري
Hard currency	monnaie forte devise forte	عملة قوية – عملة صعبة
Hard loan	prêt non-concessionnel	قرض غير ميسر
Hard terms	conditions commerciales	شروط تجارية – شروط غير ميسرة
Hardening of loan terms	durcissement des conditions de prêt	تشديد شروط الاقراض
Hardware	matériel	اجهزة – معدات
Harmonisation	harmonisation	تنسيق
Harmonic growth	croissance harmonisée	نمو متناسق
Harmonic mean	moyenne harmonique	وسط توافقي – متوسط توافقي
Harvest	moisson récolte	محصول
Harvesting	moissonnage	حصاد
Haulage	transport	نقل
Haves and havenots	nantis et déshérités	اثرياء وفقراء – اهل اليسر واهل العسر
Hawker	colporteur	بائع متجول
Head of the household	chef de ménage	رب الاسرة
Head office	siège principal	المركز الرئيسي
Head tax	capitation	ضريبة الاشخاص – الفردة
Health aid	aide sanitaire	معونة صحية – مساعدة صحية
Health assistance	assistance sanitaire	

Health insurance	assurance-maladie	تأمين صحي
Health services	services de la santé	مرافق صحية
Heavy equipment	gros équipement	اجهزة ثقيلة
Heavy industry	industrie lourde	صناعة ثقيلة – معدات ثقيلة
Heavy market	marché alourdi marché lourd	سوق متقاعس – سوق ناعسة
Hedging	couverture des opérations à terme	تغطية العمليات الآجلة
Hedging clause	clause de sauvegarde	شرط تحفظي – شرط احتياطي
Hedonism	hédonisme	مبدأ اللذة – مذهب اللذة
Hesitant market	marché indécis	سوق متردد – سوق عائم
Heterogeneity	hétérogénéité	عدم التجانس
Hidden dividends	dividendes occultes	ارباح خفية – ارباح مستترة
Hidden dumping	dumping occulte	اغراق مستتر
Hidden reserve	réserve occulte	احتياطي مستتر
Hidden tax	impôt occulte	ضريبة مستترة
High finance	haute finance	دوائر المال العليا
High income countries	pays à revenu élevé	دول ذات دخل مرتفع
High level technology	technologie avancée	فن انتاجي رفيع – تكنولجية رفيعة
High priority project	projet de haute priorité	مشروع مرتفع الأولوية
High productivity	haute productivité – productivité élevée	انتاجية مرتفعة
High-yielding seed varieties	variétés de semences à haut rendement	انواع بذور مرتفعة العائد–بذور مرتفعة الانتاجية
Higher income brackets	groupes à revenu élevé tranches de revenus élevés	فئات الدخل المرتفع
Highest bidder	plus offrant	اعلى مزايد
Highway budget	budget du réseau routier	موازنة شبكة الطرق الرئيسية – ميزانية المشاعب
Highway planning	planification des auto-routes	تخطيط الطرق الرئيسية – تخطيط المشاعب
Highway transportation	transport routier	النقل البري
Hinterland	arrière-pays	الريف – المناطق الداخلية
Hire, to	louer	اجّر
Hire-purchase	location-vente vente à tempérament	شراء بالتقسيط
Histogram	histogramme	مدرج تكراري
Historic cost	coût original – coût d'acquisition	تكلفة اصلية – كلفة اصلية
Historical materialism	matérialisme historique	المادية التاريخية
Historical school	école historique	المدرسة التاريخية
Historicism	historicisme	مذهب التاريخية
Historiogram	historiogramme	منحنى زمني – خط زمني
Hoard, to	thésauriser	اكتنز
Hoarding	thésaurisation	اكتناز
Holder	détenteur	حامل (اسهم، سندات)
Holder of shares	actionnaire - détenteur d'actions	مساهم – صاحب اسهم – حامل اسهم

Holding company	holding – société de contrôle	شركة قابضة
	société de portefeuille	
Home consumption	consommation intérieure	استهلاك محلي
Home economics	économie domestique	تدبير منزلي – اقتصاد منزلي
Home market	marché intérieur	سوق محلي – سوق داخلي
	marché national	
Home worker	ouvrier à domicile	عامل بمنزله
	travailleur à domicile	
Homo economicus	*homo economicus*	الانسان الاقتصادي
Homogeneity	homogénéité	تجانس
Homogeneous equations	équations homogènes	معادلات متجانسة
Homogeneous product	produit homogène	انتاج متجانس – سلعة متجانسة
Horizontal integration	intégration horizontale	تكامل افقي
Horticulture	horticulture	زراعة البساتين
Host country	pays-hôte	دولة مضيفة
	pays d'accueil	
	pays d'implantation	
Host government	Etat-hôte	حكومة مضيفة
	Etat d'accueil	
Hot money	capitaux errants – argent fugueur	اموال رحاحلة – اموال متنقلة – اموال رحل
	capitaux flottants – capitaux fébriles	
Hotel industry	industrie hôtelière	قطاع الفنادق
House property	biens-fonds – immeubles	عقارات
Household	ménage	اسرة
Household behaviour	comportement des ménages	سلوك الاسر
Household budget	budget familial	موازنة الاسرة – ميزانية الاسرة
Household goods	biens ménagers – mobilier	سلع منزلية – اثاثات
Household savings	épargne des ménages	ادخار الافراد
Household sector	secteur des ménages	قطاع الاسر – القطاع المنزلي
Housing	logement	اسكان
Housing construction	construction de logements	بناء المساكن
Housing economics	économie du logement	اقتصاديات الاسكان
Housing estates	immeubles résidentiels	مباني سكنية
Housing policy	politique du logement	سياسة الاسكان
Housing shortage	crise du logement	ازمة السكن
Human capital	capital humain	رسمال بشري
Human costs	coûts humains	كلفة بشرية
	coûts de l'homme	
Human economy	économie humaine	اقتصاد انساني
Human environment	environnement humain	البيئة الانسانية
Human factor	facteur humain	عامل بشري
Human investment	investissement humain	استثمار بشري
Human resources	ressources humaines	موارد بشرية
	potentiel humain	

Human resource planning	planification des ressources humaines	تخطيط الموارد البشرية
Human rights	droits de l'homme	حقوق الانسان
Human settlements	agglomérations humaines établissements humains – habitat humain	مستوطنات بشرية
Human skills	compétences humaines	مهارات بشرية
Humane economy	économie humaine – économie humanitaire	اقتصاد انساني
Humanism	humanisme	المذهب الانساني
Husband resources, to	ménager les ressources	دبر الموارد – اقتصد الموارد
Husbandry	agriculture industrie agricole	زراعة – فلاحة
Hybridisation	hybridation	تهجين
Hydroelectric power station	centrale hydroélectrique	محطة كهرمائية
Hydrology	hydrologie	دراسة الموارد المائية
Hydroponics	hydroponique	زراعة مائية – زراعة بلا تربة
Hyperinflation	hyperinflation	تضخم ضارم
Hypothecated account	compte nanti compte gagé	حساب مرتهن
Hypothesis	hypothèse	فرضية – فرض
Hypothesis testing	test d'hypothèse	اختبار الفرضية – اختبار الفرض

Identification (*econometrics*)	identification (*économétrie*)	تعيين – تحديد (اقتصاد قياسي)
Identification of projects	identification de projets	استقصاء مشاريع – استكشاف مشاريع
Identity	identité	مطابقة – متطابقة
Identity equation	équation d'identité	معادلة تطابق
Ideology	idéologie	مذهبية – عقيدة
Idle capacity	capacité inutilisée capacité excédentaire potentiel oisif	طاقة عاطلة – طاقة فائضة – طاقة معطلة
Idle capital	capital oisif	رسمال عاطل – رسمال معطل
Idle cash	encaisse oisive	ارصدة عاطلة
Idle liquidities	liquidités oisives	نقود عاطلة – ارصدة عاطلة
Idle resources	ressources inutilisées – ressources oisives	موارد عاطلة
Illicit profits	profits illicites	ارباح غير مشروعة

Illiquidity	manque de liquidité	لا سيولة – عجز السيولة
Illiteracy	analphabétisme	امية
Illiterate	analphabète	امي
Illusory correlation	corrélation illusoire	ارتباط وهمي
Illusory profits	profits illusoires	ارباح وهمية
Imbalance in international payments	déséquilibre des paiements internationaux	اختلال المدفوعات الدولية
Immigrant	immigrant	مهاجر – وافد – نقيل
Immigrant labour	travailleurs immigrés	عمال وافدون – عمال نقلاء
Immigration	immigration	هجرة-وفود-هجرة الى الداخل
Immigration quota	contingent d'immigration	حصة الهجرة
Immigration restrictions	restrictions à l'immigration	قيود الهجرة
Immiseration	paupérisation	افقار – املاق
Immiserising growth	croissance paupérisante	نمو املاقي-نمو مفقر
Immunity from taxation	immunité fiscale	حصانة ضريبية
Imperative planning	planification impérative	تخطيط اجباري – تخطيط آمر
Imperfect competition	concurrence imparfaite	منافسة غير كاملة
Imperialism	impérialisme	استعمار – امبريالية
Implementation	exécution réalisation	انجاز – تنفيذ
Implementation schedule (*projects*)	calendrier d'exécution (*projets*)	جدول التنفيذ – جدول الانجاز (مشاريع)
Implementation stage	stade d'exécution	مرحلة التنفيذ – مرحلة الانجاز
Implementing organisation	organisme exécutant	هيئة التنفيذ – هيئة الانجاز
Implicit costs	coûts implicites	تكاليف ضمنية
Implicit exchange rates	taux de change implicites	اسعار صرف ضمنية
Implicit deflator	déflateur implicite	آطر ضمني
Import Importation	importation	استيراد
Import, to	importer	استورد
Imports	importations	واردات
Import ban	prohibition d'importation	حظر استيراد
Import component (*projects*)	composante d'importation (*projets*)	عنصر الاستيراد (مشاريع)
Import content	contenu d'importation élément-importation	محتوى استيرادي – عنصر الاستيراد
Import controls	contrôle des importations	قيود الاستيراد
Import credit	crédit à l'importation	ائتمان واردات – ائتمان استيرادي
Import duty	droit d'importation	رسم استيراد
Import-export policy	politique des échanges	سياسة التصدير والاستيراد
Import goods	produits d'importation	سلع مستوردة – سلع استيراد
Import license Import permit	permis d'importation	اذن استيراد – ترخيص استيراد
Import price	prix à l'importation	ثمن الاستيراد – سعر الاستيراد
Import prohibition	prohibition d'importation	حظر استيراد

Import quotas	contingents d'importation	حصص استيراد
Import requirements	besoins d'importations	حاجات الاستيراد
Import restrictions	restrictions à l'importation	قيود الاستيراد
Import substitute	produit de substitution d'importations	بديل استيراد – بديل واردات
Import substituting industrialisation	industrialisation par remplacement d'importations	تصنيع باستبدال الواردات
Import substitution	remplacement des importations	استبدال الواردات
Import substitution policy	politique de substitution des importations	سياسة استبدال الواردات
Import tax	taxe à l'importation droits d'importation	رسم على الواردات – رسم استيراد
Import trade	commerce d'importation	تجارة الاستيراد
Import regulations	régime de l'importation	نظام الاستيراد – لائحة الاستيراد
Import restrictions	restrictions à l'importation	قيود الاستيراد
Imported inflation	inflation importée	تضخم مستورد
Imported technology	technologie importée	فن انتاجي مستورد – تكنولجية مستوردة تكنية مستوردة
Importer	importateur	مستورد
Importing country	pays importateur	دولة مستوردة
Imposition	imposition	فرض الضريبة – اخضاع للضريبة
Impoverism	appauvrissement	افتقار
Impulse buying	achat impulsif	شراء اندفاعي
Imputation	imputation	اسناد
Imputation theory	théorie de l'imputation	نظرية الاسناد
Imputed cost	coût imputé coût attribué	تكلفة مسندة – تكلفة اعتبارية
Imputed interest	intérêt imputé intérêt fictif	فائدة مسندة – فائدة اعتبارية
In-plant training	formation sur le tas	تدريب عملي
Inactive account	compte inactif	حساب عاطل
Inadequacy of monetary reserves	insuffisance des réserves monétaires	قصور الارصدة النقدية
Incentive	stimulant incitation	حافز – دافع
Incentive wage	salaire d'encouragement	اجر تشجيعي
Incentive fee	bonus d'encouragement	مكافأة تشجيعية
Incidence of taxation	incidence des impôts	مسقط الضرائب – رجعية الضرائب عبء الضريبة
Incidental expenses	faux frais	مصاريف نثرية
Income	revenu – recette	دخل – ايراد
Income account	compte des revenus	حساب الدخل
Income after taxes	revenu net d'impôts	صافي الدخل بعد الضرائب
Income and expenditure account	compte des recettes et dépenses	حساب الايرادات والمصروفات
Income and expenditure schedule	échéancier des recettes et dépenses	جدول الايرادات والمصروفات

Income bonds	obligations de revenu	سندات الدخل
Income bracket	classe de revenu	شريحة الدخل – فئة الدخل
	tranche de revenu	
Income differentials	différences de revenus	فروق الدخل
Income disparity	inégalité des revenus	تفاوت الدخول
Income inequality		
Income distribution	distribution des revenus	توزيع الدخل
Income effect	effet de revenu	اثر الدخل – عامل الدخل
Income elasticity	élasticité-revenu	مرونة دخلية
	élasticité au revenu	
Income formation	formation des revenus	تكوين الدخول
Income from capital	revenu du capital	دخل الرسمال – عائد الرسمال
Income from holdings	revenu de portefeuille	دخل حافظة الاستثمار – دخل الحافظة
Income fund	fonds d'investissement à revenu	صندوق استثمار دخلي
Income group	catégorie de revenu	فئة دخل
Income in kind	revenu en nature	دخل عيني
Income on investments	revenu des investissements	دخل الاستثمارات
Income policy	politique du revenu	سياسة الدخل
Incomes policy	politique des revenus	سياسة الدخول
Income property	immeuble de rapport	عقار مدر للدخل
Income redistribution	redistribution des revenus	اعادة توزيع الدخول
Income return	déclaration des revenus	اقرار الدخل
Income statement	compte des profits et pertes	حساب الدخل – حساب الارباح والخسائر
Income stream	flot des revenus	تيار الدخل
	flux des revenus	
Income tax	impôt sur le revenu	ضريبة الدخل
Income tax return	déclaration de revenu	اقرار الدخل
Income terms of trade	termes de l'échange-revenus	معدل التبادل الدخلي
Inconvertible currency	monnaie inconvertible	عملة غير قابلة للتحويل
Inconvertibility	inconvertibilité	عدم القابلية للتحويل
Increase in stocks	accroissement des stocks	زيادة المخزون – تزايد الكداس
Increasing returns	rendements croissants	غلة متزايدة – عائد متزايد
Increasing returns to scale	rendements croissants à l'échelle	انتاجية متزايدة لتغير الحجم – عائد متزايد لتغير الحجم
Incremental benefits	avantages différentiels	منافع اضافية
Incremental capital output ratio	coefficient marginal du capital	المعامل الحدّي لانتاجية الرسمال
Incremental cost	coût additionnel	تكلفة اضافية – كلفة فرقية
	coût différentiel	
Incremental rate of return	taux différentiel de rentabilité	معدل العائد الاضافي – معدل العائد الفرقي
Incur losses, to	subir des pertes	تحمّل خسائر
Indebtedness	endettement – dette	مديونية – دين
Indemnification	indemnisation	تعويض
Indemnify, to	indemniser	عوّض

Indemnity	indemnité cautionnement	تعويض – ضمان
Indemnity bond	cautionnement	كفالة – ضمان
Indent	commande ordre d'achat engagement	امر شراء – تعهد
Indenture	contrat accord	عقد – اتفاق
Independent variable	variable indépendante	متغير مستقل
Index	index – indicateur indice	مؤشر
Index clause	clause d'indexation	نص تأشير – شرط تأشير
Index fund	fonds-indice	صندوق مؤشر
Index numbers	indices – nombre-indices	مؤشرات – ارقام قياسية
Index of prices	indice des prix	رقم قياسي للاسعار – مؤشر الاثمان
Index-tied loan	prêt indexé emprunt indexé	قرض مؤشر
Indexation Indexing	indexation	تأشير
Indexation scheme	système d'indexation	نظام تأشير
Indexed bond	obligation indexée	سند مؤشر
Indexed debt	dette indexée	دين مؤشر
Indexed loan	emprunt indexé	قرض مؤشر
Indicative planning	planification indicative	تخطيط توجيهي – تخطيط ارشادي
Indifference curve	courbe d'indifférence	منحنى السواء
Indifference map	champ d'indifférence	خريطة السواء
Indirect benefits	avantages indirects	منافع غير مباشرة
Indirect economies	économies indirectes	وفورات غير مباشرة
Indirect expenses	frais généraux	نفقات عامة – نفقات غير مباشرة
Indirect taxes	impôts indirects contributions indirectes	ضرائب غير مباشرة
Individual income tax	impôt sur le revenu personnel	ضريبة على الدخل الفردي
Individual welfare	bien-être individuel	رفاهية فردية – رفاهة فردية
Individualism	individualisme	المذهب الفردي – الفردية
Indivisibilities	indivisibilités	عناصر غير قابلة للتقسيم
Indorsement	endossement	تظهير
Indorser	endosseur	مظهر
Induced capital movement	mouvement de capitaux induit	حركة رسمال تابعة
Induced demand	demande induite demande dérivée	طلب مشتق – طلب تابع
Induced investment	investissement induit investissement dérivé	استثمار مشتق – استثمار تابع
Industrial accidents	accidents du travail	حوادث العمل

Industrial age	époque industrielle – ère industrielle	العصر الصناعي – العهد الصناعي
Industrial bank	banque industrielle	مصرف صناعي – بنك صناعي
Industrial capital	capital industriel	رسمال صناعي
Industrial capitalism	capitalisme industriel	الرسمالية الصناعية
Industrial census	recensement industriel	احصاء صناعي
Industrial centre	centre industriel	مركز صناعي
Industrial complex	complexe industriel	مجمع صناعي
Industrial concentration	concentration industrielle	تركز صناعي
Industrial country	pays industriel	دولة صناعية
Industrial credit	crédit industriel	ائتمان صناعي
Industrial crops	cultures industrielles	حاصلات صناعية
Industrial democracies	démocraties industrielles	الديمقراطيات الصناعية
Industrial democracy	démocratie industrielle	الديمقراطية الصناعية
Industrial development	développement industriel	تنمية صناعية – انماء صناعي
Industrial dispute	conflit de travail	نزاع عمالي
Industrial economics	économie industrielle	اقتصاديات الصناعة
Industrial economy	économie industrielle	اقتصاد صناعي
Industrial engineering	construction mécanique organisation industrielle	هندسة صناعية
Industrial enterprise	entreprise industrielle	مؤسسة صناعية – مشروع صناعي
Industrial espionage	espionnage industriel	جاسوسية صناعية – تجسس صناعي
Industrial estate	zone industrielle	منطقة صناعية
Industrial expansion	expansion industrielle	توسع صناعي
Industrial exports	exportations industrielles	صادرات صناعية
Industrial extension	vulgarisation industrielle	خدمات ارشاد واعلام صناعي
Industrial fair	foire industrielle	معرض صناعي
Industrial finance company	société de financement industriel	شركة تمويل صناعي
Industrial geography	géographie industrielle	الجغرافية الصناعية
Industrial growth	croissance industrielle	نمو صناعي
Industrial information	information industrielle	اعلام صناعي
Industrial legislation	législation industrielle	تشريعات صناعية
Industrial location	localisation industrielle	توطن صناعي
Industrial machinery	machines industrielles	آلات صناعية – معدات صناعية
Industrial management	gestion industrielle	ادارة صناعية
Industrial organisation	organisation industrielle	تنظيم صناعي
Industrial planning	planification industrielle	تخطيط صناعي
Industrial plant	équipement industriel usine – installations industrielles	مصنع – معدات صناعية – منشآت صناعية
Industrial policy	politique industrielle	سياسة صناعية
Industrial potential	potentiel industriel	طاقة صناعية – قدرة انتاج صناعية
Industrial product	produit industriel	سلعة صناعية
Industrial production	production industrielle	إنتاج صناعي
Industrial profiles	fiches technico-économiques profils industriels	سمات صناعية

Industrial promotion	promotion industrielle	تشجيع الصناعة – حفز الصناعة
Industrial property	propriété industrielle	ملكية صناعية
Industrial property rights	droits de propriété industrielle	حقوق الملكية الصناعية
Industrial psychology	psychologie industrielle	علم النفس الصناعي
Industrial rationalisation	rationalisation industrielle	الترشيد الصناعي
Industrial redeployment	redéploiement industriel	اعادة توزيع الطاقات الصناعية
Industrial relations	relations patron-ouvriers	علاقات العمل
	relations industrielles	
Industrial research	recherches industrielles	الابحاث الصناعية
Industrial residential centre	cité ouvrière	مدينة عمالية
Industrial revolution	révolution industrielle	الثورة الصناعية
Industrial sabotage	sabotage industriel	تخريب صناعي
Industrial sector	secteur industriel	قطاع صناعي
Industrial society	société industrielle	مجتمع صناعي
Industrial sociology	sociologie industrielle	علم الاجتماع الصناعي
Industrial standards	normes industrielles	انماط صناعية
Industrial structure	structure industrielle	هيكل صناعي
Industrial tradition	tradition industrielle	تقاليد صناعية
Industrial union	syndicat industriel	نقابة صناعية
Industrial unit	unité industrielle	وحدة صناعية
Industrial workers	ouvriers industriels	عمال الصناعة
Industrialisation	industrialisation	التصنيع
Industrialised countries	pays industrialisés	دول صناعية
Industrialism	industrialisme	النظام الصناعي
Industrialisation plan	plan d'industrialisation	خطة تصنيع
Industry	industrie	صناعة – فرع انتاجي
	branche économique	
Inelastic demand	demande inélastique	طلب غير مرن
Inelastic supply	offre inélastique	عرض غير مرن – انتاج غير مرن
	production inélastique	
Inelasticity	inélasticité	لامرونة – عدم المرونة
Inequalities	inégalités	فروق
Inequality of incomes	inégalité des revenus	عدم تكافؤ الدخول – تفاوت الدخول
Infant industry	industrie naissante	صناعة ناشئة
Infant mortality rate	taux de mortalité infantile	معدل وفيات الأطفال – معدل وفيات الرضع
Inference	induction	استدلال – استخلاص
Inferior goods	biens inférieurs	سلع دنيا – سلع فقيرة
Inflation	inflation	تضخم
Inflation-accounting	comptabilité d'inflation	محاسبة تضخم
Inflation rate	taux d'inflation	معدل تضخم
Inflationary boom	boom inflationniste	رواج تضخمي
Inflationary gap	écart inflationniste	فجوة تضخمية
Inflationary pressures	tensions inflationnistes	ضغوط تضخمية
Inflationary tensions		

Inflationary spiral	spirale inflationniste	لولب تضخمي
Inflow of capital	entrée de capitaux	دخول رسمال – وفود الرسمال
Influx of capital		
Informal sector	secteur non-organisé	القطاع غير المنظم
Information system	système d'information	نظام اعلام
Information theory	informatique	نظرية الاعلام
Infrastructure	infrastructure	بنية أساسية – هياكل أساسية
Infrastructure facilities	équipement infrastructurel	تجهيزات أسية – تجهيزات أساسية
Ingot	lingot	سبيكة
Initial capital	capital initial	رسمال مبدئي – رسمال أولي
Initial capital cost	frais de premier établissement	مصاريف التأسيس
Initial outlays		
Initial contribution	contribution initiale	مساهمة مبدئية – مساهمة أولية
Initial cost	coût initial	تكلفة أولية
Initial investment	investissement initial	استثمار أولي
Initial payment	acompte	عربون – قسط أول
	premier versement	
Initial subscription	souscription initiale	اكتتاب أولي – اكتتاب مبدئي
Inland navigation	navigation fluviale	ملاحة نهرية
Inland transport	transports intérieurs	نقل داخلي – نقل بري
	transports routiers	
Innovation	innovation	ابتكار – ابتداع
Innovation policy	politique de l'innovation	سياسة الابتكار
Input	input – intrant	مستخدم
Input-output analysis	analyse des échanges intersectoriels	تحليل المستخدم – المنتج
	analyse input-output	
	analyse entrées-sorties	
Input-output coefficients	coefficients techniques	معاملات الانتاج – المعاملات الفنية
	coefficients de production	
Input-output matrix	matrice d'échanges industriels	مصفوفة المستخدم – المنتج
In-service training	formation sur le tas	تدريب بالممارسة – تدريب عملي
Insolvency	insolvabilité – faillite	افلاس
Installation period	période d'installation	فترة التشييد – فترة التركيب
Installations	installations	منشآت
Installed capacity	puissance installée	طاقة مركبة
Instalment	versement – échéance	قسط
Instalment buying	achat à crédit	شراء بالتقسيط
Instalment credit	crédit à tempérament	قرض تقسيط – تمويل شراء بالتقسيط
Instalment loan	crédit à la consommation	قرض استهلاك
Instalment plan	plan de versements échelonnés	برنامج اقساط
Institution	institution	نظام – تنظيم – هيئة – مؤسسة

Institution building	promotion d'institutions	تدعيم الهيئات – بناء الاطار النظامي
		بناء الاطار المؤسسي
Institutional constraints	contraintes institutionnelles	قيود نظامية – حدود نظامية – قيود مؤسسية
Institutional credit	crédit institutionnel	ائتمان منظم
Institutional economics	économie institutionnelle	اقتصاديات النظم
Institutional framework	cadre institutionnel	اطار نظامي – اطار مؤسسي
	structure institutionnelle	
Institutional investors	investisseurs collectifs	هيئات استثمار جماعي – هيئات استثمار
	organismes de placement collectif	
Institutional sectors	secteurs institutionnels	قطاعات نظامية – قطاعات نظمية
Institutional setting	cadre institutionnel	وضع نظمي – اطار مؤسسي
Institutionalism	institutionnalisme	المذهب النظمي – المذهب المؤسسي
Instrument variable	variable-instrument	متغير اداتي – متغير وسيلي
	variable instrumentale	
Insurable risk	risque assurable	خطر صالح للتأمين
Insurance	assurance	تأمين
Insurance benefits	prestations d'assurances	عوائد التأمين
Insurance charges	frais d'assurance	تكاليف التأمين
Insurance cover	étendue de l'assurance	نطاق التأمين – مدى التأمين
Insurance policy	police d'assurance	وثيقة تأمين
Insurance premium	prime d'assurance	قسط تأمين
Insurance value	valeur assurée	قيمة مؤمنة – قيمة التأمين
Insured value	valeur d'assurance	
Insure, to	assurer	أمّن – ضمن
	garantir	
Intangible assets	actif incorporel	اصول معنوية
Intangible property	biens incorporels – biens immatériels	
Intangible benefits	avantages intangibles	منافع غير ملموسة
	avantages impondérables	
Intangible factors	impondérables	عوامل غير ملموسة
Integrated development	développement intégré	انماء متكامل – تنمية متكاملة
Integrated industry	industrie intégrée	صناعة متكاملة
Integrated project	projet intégré	مشروع متكامل
Integrated rural development	développement rural intégré	تنمية ريفية متكاملة – انماء ريفي متكامل
Integrated transportation system	système de transport intégré	نظام نقل متكامل – شبكة نقل متكاملة
Integration methods	méthodes d'intégration	أساليب التكامل
Integration process	processus d'intégration	مجرى التكامل
Integration project	projet d'intégration	مشروع تكامل
Intended investment	investissement prévu	استثمار مستهدف
	investissement projeté	
Intended saving	épargne prévue	ادخار مستهدف
	épargne projetée	
Intensive agriculture	agriculture intensive	زراعة كثيفة

Intensive farming	culture intensive	فلاحة كثيفة
Inter-bank deposits	dépôts interbancaires	ودائع ما بين البنوك – ودائع بين مصرفية
Inter-bank loans	prêts interbancaires	قروض ما بين البنوك – قروض بين مصرفية
Inter-bank market	marché interbancaire	سوق مصرفي – سوق المصارف
Inter-bank rate	taux interbancaire	سعر بين مصرفي
Interdependence	interdépendance	ترابط – اعتماد متبادل
Interdisciplinary approach	approche interdisciplinaire	منهج التضافر
Interdisciplinary research	recherche interdisciplinaire	تضافر فروع المعرفة-بحث متضافر
Inter-enterprise market	marché inter-entreprises	سوق المشروعات – سوق المؤسسات
Inter-firm market		
Interest	intérêt	فائدة – مصلحة
Interest account	compte d'intérêts	حساب فوائد
Interest arbitrage	arbitrage d'intérêt	موازنة الفوائد – موازنة أسعار الفائدة
Interest-bearing securities	titres portant intérêts	سندات مدرة لفوائد – صكوك مدرة لفوائد
Interest-earning securities	titres productifs d'intérêts	
Interest calculation	calcul d'intérêts	حساب الفوائد
Interest costs	coût d'intérêts	تكلفة الفوائد – كلفة الفوائد
Interest coupon	coupon d'intérêts	قسيمة الفوائد – كعب الفوائد
Interest differential	écart entre les taux d'intérêt	فرق بين أسعار الفائدة
		فرق أسعار الفائدة
Interest due	intérêts dus	فوائد مستحقة
Interest during construction	intérêts inter-calaires	فوائد فترة التنفيذ
	intérêts courus durant la construction	فوائد مستحقة خلال التنفيذ
Interest equalisation tax	taxe de péréquation des intérêts	ضريبة معادلة الفوائد
Interest-free loan	prêt sans intérêts	قرض بلا فوائد – قرض مجاني
	prêt gratuit	
Interest on arrears	intérêts moratoires	فوائد تأخير
Interest spread	marge d'intérêts	هامش الفوائد – فرق الفوائد
Interest-subsidised loan	prêt à intérêt bonifié	قرض بفوائد معوضة
Interest subsidy	bonification d'intérêts	اعانة تعويض الفوائد
Interest subsidy fund	fonds de bonification d'intérêts	صندوق تعويض الفوائد
Inter-governmental loans	emprunts inter-étatiques	قروض ما بين الحكومات – قروض بين حكومية
	prêts inter-gouvernementaux	
Intergovernmental transfers	transferts inter-administrations	تحويلات بين الادارات الحكومية
Interim accounts	comptes provisoires	حسابات مؤقتة – حسابات انتقالية
Interim budget	budget intérimaire	موازنة مؤقتة – موازنة انتقالية
Interim due dates	échéances intercalaires	استحقاقات جزئية
Interim credit	crédit intérimaire	ائتمان انتقالي – ائتمان مؤقت
Interim dividend	dividende provisoire	قسط أرباح
Interim financial statement	bilan provisoire	ميزانية مؤقتة
Interim financing	financement provisoire	تمويل انتقالي – تمويل مؤقت
	financement intérimaire	
Interim payments	versements provisoires	أقساط – مدفوعات مؤقتة

Inter-industrial analysis	analyse des relations inter-industrielles	تحليل التداخل الصناعي
		تحليل التشابك الصناعي
Inter-industrial flows	flux inter-industriels	تيارات التداخل الصناعي
Inter-industrial relations	relations inter-industrielles	علاقات التداخل الصناعي
Interlocking directorates	conseils d'administration entrelacés	مجالس ادارة متداخلة
	directorats croisés	
Intermediaries	intermédiaires	وسطاء
Intermediate demand	demande intermédiaire	طلب وسيط
Intermediate consumption	consommation intermédiaire	استهلاك وسيط
Intermediate financing facility	facilité de financement intermédiaire	طاقة تمويل وسطى
Intermediate goods	biens intermédiaires	سلع وسيطة
Intermediate inputs	intrants intermédiaires	مستخدمات وسيطة
	inputs intermédiaires	
Intermediate regime	régime intermédiaire	نظام وسيط
Intermediate technology	technologie intermédiaire	فنون انتاجية وسيطة – تكنية متوسطة
		فنون انتاجية متوسطة
Intermediation	intermédiation	وساطة – توسيط – توسط
Internal cash generation	capacité d'autofinancement	قدرة التمويل الذاتي
Internal colonialism	colonialisme interne	الاستعمار الداخلي – الاستعمار المحلي
Internal economies	économies internes	وفورات داخلية
Internal migration	migration interne	هجرة داخلية – هجرة محلية
Internal rate of return	taux de rentabilité interne	معدل العائد الذاتي
	taux de rendement intrinsèque	
Internal revenue	recettes fiscales	ايرادات ضريبية
International aid	aide internationale	معونات دولية – مساعدات دولية
International assistance	assistance internationale	اعانات دولية
International capital market	marché international des capitaux	السوق المالية الدولية
International capital movements	mouvements internationaux des capitaux	حركات دولية للرسمال
		حركات رسمال دولية
International cartel	cartel international	كارتل دولي – احتكار دولي
International commerce	échanges internationaux	تجارة دولية
	commerce international	
International commodity agreements	accords internationaux sur les produits de base	اتفاقيات سلعية دولية
International competitive bidding	adjudication internationale	نظام العطاءات الدولية المفتوحة
	appel d'offres international	مناقصة دولية مفتوحة – مناقصة عامة دولية
International development tax	impôt pour le développement international	ضريبة تنمية دولية – ضريبة انماء دولية
International division of labour	division internationale du travail	تقسيم دولي للعمل – تقسيم دولي للانتاج
International economic cooperation	coopération économique internationale	تعاون اقتصادي دولي
International economic interdependence	interdépendance économique internationale	ترابط اقتصادي دولي
International economic interpenetration	interpénétration économique internationale	تداخل اقتصادي دولي

International economic order	ordre économique international	نظام اقتصادي دولي
International economic relations	relations économiques internationales	علاقات اقتصادية دولية
International economy	économie internationale	الاقتصاد الدولي
International finance	finances internationales	المالية الدولية
International financial markets	marchés financiers internationaux	أسواق مالية دولية
International financial organisation	organisation financière internationale	منظمة مالية دولية
International financing	financement international	تمويل دولي
International integration	intégration internationale	تكامل دولي
International lending agencies	institutions financières internationales	مؤسسات الاقراض الدولية
International liquidity	liquidités internationales	سيولة دولية – أرصدة سائلة دولية
International markets	marchés internationaux	أسواق دولية
International migration	migration internationale	هجرة دولية
International monetary system	système monétaire international	نظام النقد الدولي
International payments	paiements internationaux	مدفوعات دولية
International prices	prix internationaux	أسعار دولية
International public tendering	adjudication publique internationale	نظام العطاء الدولي العلني
		مناقصة عامة دولية
International reserves	réserves internationales	أرصدة دولية
International rivers and waterways	fleuves et canaux internationaux	الأنهر والممرات المائية الدولية
International securities issue	émission de titres internationaux	اصدار سندات دولية
		اصدار صكوك دولية
International trade	commerce international échanges internationaux	تجارة دولية – مبادلات دولية
International transports	transports internationaux	نقل دولي
International tourist trade	tourisme international	سياحة دولية
Internationalisation	internationalisation	تدويل
Internationalisation of aid	internationalisation de l'aide	تدويل المعونات – تدويل المساعدات
Internationalisation of capital	internationalisation du capital	تدويل الرأسمال
Internationalisation of production	internationalisation de la production	تدويل الانتاج
Interpolation	interpolation	استيفاء
Interquartile range	intervalle interquartile	المدى الربيعي
Inter-regional economic relations	relations économiques inter-régionales	علاقات اقتصادية بين اقليمية
		علاقات اقتصادية بين الأقاليم
Inter-regional trade	commerce inter-régional échanges inter-régionaux	تجارة بين اقليمية
Intersectoral allocation of investments	allocation inter-sectorielle des investissements	التوزيع القطاعي للاستثمار
Intersectoral model	modèle intersectoriel	نموذج متعدد القطاعات
Intertemporal choice	choix intertemporel	خيار زمني
Interval estimation	estimation d'intervalle	تقدير المدى
Intervention currency	monnaie d'intervention	عملة التدخل

Intervention point	niveau d'intervention	حد التدخل
	seuil d'intervention	
Interventionism	interventionnisme	مذهب التدخل
Intra-firm trade	commerce intra-firmes	تجارة بين فروع المشروع
Intra-regional exports (*imports*)	exportations (*importations*) intra-régionales	صادرات (واردات) اقليمية
Intra-regional trade	commerce intra-régional	تجارة اقليمية – مبادلات اقليمية
	échanges intra-régionaux	
Intrinsic value	valeur intrinsèque	قيمة ذاتية
Invention	invention	اختراع – ابتكار
Inventor	inventeur	مخترع – مبتكر
Inventorize, to	inventorier	جرد
Inventory, to	faire l'inventaire	
Inventory (*stocks*)	stocks	مخزون – كداس – ركام
	inventaire	
Inventory	inventaire	جرد
Inventory accumulation	accumulation de stocks	تراكم المخزون – زيادة المخزون
		تجمع الكداس
Inventory book	livre d'inventaire	دفتر الجرد
Inventory control	contrôle des stocks	رقابة المخزون – رقابة الكداس
	gestion des stocks	ادارة المخزون
Inventory cycle	cycle d'inventaire	دورة المخزون – دورة كداسية
Inventory evaluation	évaluation des stocks	تقدير المخزون – تقدير الكداس
Inventory investment	investissement en stocks	استثمار كداسي
Inventory profits	bénéfices d'inventaire	أرباح كداسية
Inventory-sales ratio	ratio de la rotation des stocks	نسبة تدوير المخزون – نسبة تدوير الكداس
Inverse matrix	matrice inverse	مصفوفة عكسية – مصفوفة معكوسة
Invest, to	investir – placer	استثمر – وظف
Invest capital, to	investir des capitaux	استثمر رسمالاً – وظف رسمالاً
	placer des capitaux	
Investable funds	fonds investibles	أموال قابلة للاستثمار – أموال تثمير
Investable surplus	surplus investible – plus-value investible	فائض قابل للاستثمار
Invested capital	capital investi	رسمال مستثمر – رسمال موظف
Invested funds	fonds investis	أموال مستثمرة – أموال موظفة
Investment	investissement	استثمار – توظيف أموال
	placement de fonds	
Investment advisory service	bureau de conseil financier	مكتب استشارة مالية
Investment agreement	contrat d'investissement	اتفاقية استثمار
Investment allocation	répartition des investissements	توزيع الاستثمارات
Investment appraisal	évaluation des investissements	تقييم الاستثمار – روز الاستثمار
Investment bank	banque d'affaires	بنك استثمار – مصرف استثمار
Investment budget	budget d'équipement	موازنة استثمارية – ميزانية استثمارية

Investment capital	capital d'investissement capital de placement	رسمال استثماري
Investment climate	climat de l'investissement ambiance d'accueil des investissements	مناخ الاستثمار
Investment consultant	conseiller financier	مستشار استثماري
Investment costs	coûts d'investissement	تكاليف الاستثمار – تكاليف استثمارية
Investment counseling	conseil en placements	استشارة استثمارية – استشارة مالية
Investment criteria	critères d'investissement	معايير الاستثمار
Investment currency	monnaie d'investissement	عملة الاستثمار
Investment decisions	décisions d'investissement	قرارات الاستثمار
Investment demand	demande d'investissement	طلب استثماري
Investment efficiency **Investment effectiveness**	efficacité de l'investissement	فاعلية الاستثمار – جدوى الاستثمار
Investment evaluation	évaluation des investissements	تقيم الاستثمار
Investment financing	financement des investissements	تمويل الاستثمار
Investment fund	fonds de placement	صندوق استثمار
Investment guarantee **Investment guaranty**	garantie des investissements	ضمان الاستثمار
Investment goods	biens d'équipement biens d'investissement	سلع استثمارية
Investment horizon	horizon de l'investissement	افق الاستثمار
Investment insurance	garantie des investissements	ضمان الاستثمار – تأمين الاستثمار
Investment management	gestion de portefeuille	ادارة الحافظة المالية
Investment media	instruments d'investissement	أدوات الاستثمار – وسائل الاستثمار
Investment opportunities	possibilités d'investissement	فرص الاستثمار
Investment plan	plan d'investissements	خطة استثمار – خطة استثمارية
Investment planning	planification de l'investissement	تخطيط الاستثمار
Investment policy	politique d'investissement	سياسة استثمارية – سياسة الاستثمار
Investment portfolio	portefeuille-titres	حافظة سندات – حافظة أوراق مالية
Investment priorities	priorités d'investissement	أولويات الاستثمار
Investment programme	programme d'investissements	برنامج استثماري – برنامج الاستثمارات
Investment programming	programmation des investissements élaboration des programmes d'investissement	برمجة الاستثمار – وضع برامج الاستثمار
Investment project	projet d'investissement	مشروع استثماري
Investment promotion	promotion des investissements	حفز الاستثمار – تشجيع الاستثمار ترويج الاستثمار
Investment protection measures	mesures de protection des investissements	تدابير حماية الاستثمار
Investment selection	choix des investissements sélection des investissements	انتقاء الاستثمارات – اختيار الاستثمارات
Investment shares **Investment stocks**	titres de placement	أسهم استثمار – أسهم توظيف

Investment strategy	stratégie de l'investissement	سياسة الاستثمار – استراتيجية الاستثمار
Investment transactions	opérations d'investissement	عمليات استثمارية – عمليات استثمار
Investment trust	société d'investissement	شركة استثمار
Investment variants	variantes d'investissement	بدائل الاستثمار
Investor	investisseur	مستثمر
Invisible exports and imports	exportations et importations invisibles	الصادرات والواردات غير المنظورة
Invisible hand	main invisible	اليد الخفية
Invisible trade	commerce invisible	تجارة غير منظورة
Invisible transactions	opérations invisibles	عمليات غير منظورة
Invitation to bid	avis d'adjudication	دعوة مناقصة – اعلان مناقصة – طلب عطاءات
Invitation to tender	appel d'offres	
Invoice	facture	فاتورة – حسبونة
Invoice, to	facturer	فوتر – حسبن
Invoicing	facturation	حسبنة – وضع فاتورة – فوترة
Involuntary unemployment	chômage involontaire	بطالة غير ارادية – بطالة جبرية
IOU	reconnaissance de dette	سند دين
Iron and steel industry	industrie du fer et de l'acier	صناعة الحديد والصلب
Iron law of wages	loi d'airain des salaires	قانون الأجر الحديدي
Irredeemable bonds	obligations non remboursables	سندات غير قابلة للسداد
Irrevocable agreement to reimburse	garantie irrévocable de remboursement	تعهد نهائي بتغطية الدفع
Irrevocable letter of credit	accréditif irrévocable	اعتماد نهائي – اعتماد غير قابل للالغاء
Irrigable area	surface irrigable	منطقة قابلة للري – مساحة قابلة للري
Irrigated area	périmètre irrigué	منطقة ري – منطقة مروية
Irrigation economics	économie de l'irrigation	اقتصاديات الري
Irrigation installations	installations d'irrigation	منشآت الرى
Irrigation projects	projets d'irrigation	مشاريع ري
Island countries	pays insulaires	دول جزيرية
Iso-cost curve	courbe d'iso-coûts	منحنى التكاليف المتكافئة
		منحنى التكاليف المتساوية
Iso-product curve	courbe d'iso-produits	منحنى الناتج المتكافئ
		منحنى الناتج المتساوي
Iso-profit curve	courbe d'iso-profits	منحنى الربح المتكافئ
		منحنى الربح المتساوي
Iso-quant curve	courbe iso-quante	منحنى الكميات المتكافئة
		منحنى الكميات المتساوية
Isolationism	isolationnisme	المذهب الانعزالي
Issue	émission	اصدار
Issue, to	émettre	اصدر
Issue market	marché des émissions	سوق الاصدار
Issue price	prix d'émission	سعر الاصدار
	taux d'émission	
Issued capital	capital émis	رسمال مصدر

Issuer	émetteur	مصدر (أوراق مالية)
Issuing	émission – délivrance distribution	اصدار – توزيع – صرف
Issuing house	maison d'émission maison émettrice	بيت اصدار – مؤسسة اصدار
Items of the budget	postes du budget	بنود الموازنة – بنود الميزانية
Iteration	itération	معاودة
Iterative method	méthode itérative	اسلوب المعاودة
Itinerant trade	colportage – commerce ambulant	تجارة متجولة

Job classification	classification des emplois	تصنيف الوظائف
Job creation	création d'emplois	خلق عمالة – ايجاد عمالة
Job description	description d'emploi	وصف الوظيفة
Job engineering	organisation du travail	تنظيم العمل
Job evaluation	évaluation des emplois	تقييم الوظائف
Job planning	organisation du travail	تنظيم العمل
Job security	sécurité de l'emploi	استقرار التوظف
Job seeker	chercheur d'emploi	باحث عن عمل
Job vacancies	postes vacants	وظائف خالية
Jobber	marchand de titres intermédiaire commercial	تاجر أوراق مالية – وسيط تجاري
Joint account	compte joint	حساب مشترك
Joint costs	coûts liés	تكاليف مشتركة – نفقات مشتركة
Joint debtor	co-débiteur	مدين متضامن – مدين مزامل
Joint demand	demande liée	طلب متلازم
Joint distribution	distribution conjointe	توزيع مشترك
Joint financing	financement conjoint	تمويل مشترك
Joint governmental activities	activités administratives conjointes	مرافق ادارية مشتركة
Joint loan	prêt conjoint	قرض مشترك
Joint marketing arrangements	mesures de commercialisation collective	تدابير تسويق جماعي
Joint ownership	co-propriété	ملكية مشتركة
Joint production	co-production	انتاج مشترك
Joint project	projet conjoint	مشروع مشترك
Joint stock	capital social	رسمال المؤسسة
Joint stock company	société par actions	شركة مساهمة
Joint supply	offre liée	عرض متلازم

Joint venture	entreprise conjointe	مشروع اقتصادي مشترك
Joint adventure	opération conjointe	
Journeyman	journalier	عامل مياوم – مياوم – عامل
	ouvrier	
Junior capital	capital ordinaire	رسمال عادي
Junior debt	dette de rang inférieur	دين تابع
Junior partner	associé en second	شريك ثنيان
	associé minoritaire	
Junk-market	marché aux puces	سوق الخردة – سوق الكنتو
Jurisdiction clause	clause de compétence judiciaire	نص الاختصاص القضائي-نص الولاية القضائية
Just price	juste prix	ثمن عادل

Kerb-stone market (*stock exchange*)	marché hors-cote (*bourse*)	سوق غير رسمي (سوق مالي)
Key currency	monnaie clé	عملة رئيسية
Key industry	industrie clé	صناعة اساسية
Key money	pas de porte	خلو – خلو رجل
Key project	projet clé	مشروع أساسي
Key resources	ressources de base	موارد أساسية
Key sector	secteur clé	قطاع أساسي
Key variable	variable décisive	متغير حاسم
Keynesian economics	économie keynésienne	الاقتصاد الكينزي
Keynesianism	keynésianisme	الكينزية
Khozratchet (USSR)	*khozratchot* (URSS)	محاسبة اقتصادية (الاتحاد السوفييتي)
Kibboutz	*Kibboutz*	مزرعة جماعية
Kinked demand courve	courbe brisée de la demande	منحنى طلب أكوع
Know-how	savoir-faire	خبرة – حيل – دراية
	know-how	
Kolkhoze (USSR)	*kolkhoze* (URSS)	مزرعة جماعية (الاتحاد السوفييتي)
Krach	*krach*	انهيار
Kulaks (USSR)	*koulaks* (URSS)	الكولاك (الاتحاد السوفييتي)
		كبار المزارعين

L

Labelling	étiquetage	نعت
Labour	main-d'œuvre – travail	قوة العمل – العمال – العمل
Labour absorption	absorption de la main-d'œuvre	استيعاب العمل – تشغيل
Labour aristocracy	aristocratie du travail	ارستقراطية العمل – ارستقراطية عمالية
	aristocratie ouvrière	
Labour conflict	conflit du travail	نزاع عمالي
Labour dispute		
Labour contract	contrat de travail	عقد عمل
Labour costs	coûts de main-d'œuvre	تكاليف العمل – تكاليف عمالية
	coûts du travail	
Labour division	division du travail	تقسيم العمل
Labour economics	économie du travail	اقتصاديات العمل
Labour exchange	bourse du travail	بورصة العمل – سوق العمل
Labour force	main-d'œuvre	قوى عاملة
	population active	
Labour intensity	intensité du travail	كثافة العمل
Labour-intensive industry	industrie à travail intensif	صناعة كثيفة العمل
Labour-intensive technology	technologie à travail intensif	فن انتاجي كثيف العمل – تكنية كثيفة العمل
		تكنولوجية عمالية
Labour legislation	législation du travail	تشريعات العمل
Labour management relations	relations patrons-ouvriers	علاقات العمل – علاقات عمالية – علاقات صناعية
Labour relations	relations industrielles	
Labour market	marché du travail	سوق العمل
Labour mobility	mobilité de la main-d'œuvre	سيولة العمل – حراكية العمل
Labour movement	mouvement ouvrier	الحركة العمالية
Labour-output ratio	rapport travail-production	نسبة انتاجية العمل – نسبة العمل للناتج
Labour power	force de travail	قوة العمل
Labour productivity	productivité du travail	انتاجية العمل
Labour-saving techniques	techniques épargnant du travail	تكنية موفرة للعمل – فن موفر للعمل
Labour shortage	pénurie de main-d'œuvre	ندرة العمل – قصور الايدي العاملة
Labour supply	offre de main-d'œuvre	عرض العمل – توفر العمل
Labour surplus economy	économie à main-d'œuvre excédentaire	اقتصاد وفير العمل
Labour theory of value	théorie de la valeur-travail	نظرية كمية العمل – نظرية العمل (في القيمة)

Labour turn-over	changement du personnel – rotation du personnel	تغير العاملين
Labour union	syndicat ouvrier	نقابة عمالية
Labour unionization	syndicalisation ouvrière	تكوين نقابات العمال
Labour unrest	agitation sociale	قلق عمالي
Labourer	ouvrier	عامل
Labourism	travaillisme	المذهب العمالي – العمالية
Lading	chargement	شحن
Lagged variable	variable décalée	متغير مستأخر
Laisser-faire capitalism	capitalisme libéral	نظام رسمالي حر
Laisser-faire economics	économie libérale	مذهب الاقتصاد الحر
Laisser-faire economist	économiste libéral	اقتصادي من المذهب الحر
Laisser-faire economy	économie libérale	اقتصاد حر
Land	terre – nature – terrain	أرض – طبيعة – قطعة أرض
Land adaptation	aménagement du sol	تهيئة الأراضي – تمهيد الأرض
Land appropriation	appropriation de la terre	تملك الأراضي
Land assets	capital foncier	رسمال عقاري
Land bank	crédit foncier – banque hypothécaire	بنك عقاري – مصرف عقاري
Land clearing	défrichage – défrichement	تجلية الأرض – تمهيد الأرض
Land conservation	conservation du sol	حفظ التربة
Land consolidation	remembrement des terres agricoles	تجميع الحيازات الزراعية
Land development	mise en valeur des terres aménagement foncier	استصلاح الأراضي – احياء الأراضي
Land economics	économie foncière	اقتصاديات الأراضي – الاقتصاد العقاري
Land-holding	propriété foncière	حيازة عقارية
Land improvement	amélioration des terres aménagement agricole	استصلاح الأراضي – تحسين الأراضي
Land labour	main-d'œuvre agricole	عمل زراعي – عمال الريف
Land laws	lois agraires	تشريعات عقارية
Land levelling	nivellement des terres	تسوية الأرض
Land-locked country	pays sans littoral – pays enclavé	دولة بلا سواحل – دولة حصراء
Land management	gestion foncière – gestion agraire	ادارة الأراضي – الادارة العقارية الادارة الزراعية
Land ownership **Land property**	propriété foncière	ملكية عقارية
Land parcel	lopin de terre – terrain	قطعة أرض
Land parcelling	morcellement des terres	تجزئة الأراضي
Land reclamation	mise en valeur des terres – défrichement	استصلاح الأراضي – احياء الأراضي
Land reform	réforme agraire	اصلاح زراعي
Land rent	rente foncière	ريع عقاري
Land settlement	colonisation rurale – mise en valeur des terres	تعمير الأراضي – استيطان الأراضي

Land speculation	spéculation foncière	مضاربة عقارية
Land surveyor	géomètre – arpenteur	مساح – مساح أراضي – خبير هندسي
Land system	système agraire	نظام عقاري
Land tax	impôt foncier	ضريبة عقارية
Land tenure system	régime foncier	نظام الملكية العقارية – نظام الحيازة العقارية
Land transportation	transports terrestres	نقل بري
Land use Land utilisation	utilisation des terres	استخدام الأراضي
Land values	prix des terres	ثمن الأراضي – قيمة الأراضي
Landlord	propriétaire	مالك أراض – صاحب أملاك
Large-scale industry	grosse industrie grande industrie	صناعة كبيرة
Large-sized firm	grosse entreprise grande entreprise	مشروع كبير – منشأة كبيرة
Late capitalism	capitalisme tardif	الرسمالية المتأخرة
Late development	développement attardé	النمو المتأخر
Latent inflation	inflation latente	تضخم كامن
Latifundia	*latifundia*	ضيع كبيرة – ضياع كبيرة
Law of comparative advantage	théorie des avantages comparés théorie des avantages comparatifs	نظرية المزايا النسبية
Law of comparative costs	théorie des coûts comparés théorie des coûts comparatifs	نظرية التكاليف النسبية – نظرية النفقات النسبية
Law of diminishing returns	loi des rendements décroissants	قانون الغلة المتناقصة
Law of diminishing marginal utility	loi de l'utilité marginale décroissante	قانون المنفعة الحدية المتناقصة
Law of large numbers	loi des grands nombres	قانون الاعداد الكبيرة
Laws of return	lois des rendements	قوانين العائد
Law of supply and demand	loi de l'offre et de la demande	قانون العرض والطلب
Law of uneven economic development	loi du développement économique inégal	قانون النمو الاقتصادي غير المتكافئ
Law of value	loi de la valeur	قانون القيمة – نظرية القيمة
Law of variable proportions	lois des proportions variables	قانون النسب المتغيرة
Lawful reserve	réserve légale	احتياطي قانوني
Laying off (*workers*)	licenciement (*ouvriers*) désembauche	تسريح (عمال)
Lay-out of a project	plan de masse d'un projet	تصميم عام للمشروع
Lead manager of an issue	chef de file d'une émission	عميد الاصدار – رائس الاصدار
Leading firm	entreprise dominante	مشروع مسيطر – مشروع رائد
Leading indicators	indicateurs de conjoncture	مؤشرات الدورة
Leading sector	secteur moteur	قطاع رائد – قطاع رئيسي
Leads and lags	termaillages décalages chronologiques avances et retards	الاخر والقدم
Leakage	fuite	تسرب

Leaks and injections	fuites et injections	التسرب والحقن
Learning effect	effet d'apprentissage	أثر التعلم – أثر الاستيعاب
Lease	bail	إيجار – كراء
Lease, to	louer	أجر
Lease-back	lease-back – relocation	إيجار البيع
Leasing	crédit-bail – prêt-bail	إيجار الشراء
Least-cost	coût minimum	التكلفة الدنيا – أقل تكلفة – أدنى تكلفة
Least-cost analysis	analyse du moindre coût	تحليل أدنى التكاليف
Least-cost equilibrium	équilibre du moindre coût	توازن التكلفة الدنيا – توازن أقل تكلفة
Least-developed countries	pays les moins développés	الدول الأقل تطوراً – الدول الأقل نمواً
Least-squares method	méthode des moindres carrés	منهج المربعات الدنيا – منهج تضييل المربعات منهج أقل المربعات
Leather industry	industrie du cuir	صناعة الجلود
Ledger	grand livre	دفتر الاستاذ
Legal monopoly	monopole légal	احتكار قانوني
Legal reserve	réserve légale couverture obligatoire	احتياطي قانوني
Legal reserve requirements	obligations légales de couverture	التزامات الغطاء القانوني التزامات الاحتياطي القانوني
Legal tender (currency)	monnaie à cours légal	نقود رسمية – نقود قانونية
Leisure activities	loisirs	نشاطات ترفيهية
Leisure class	classe oisive	السباندة-السبادرة
Lend, to	prêter	أقرض
Lend-lease	prêt-bail	إيجار الشراء
Lender	prêteur	مقرض
Lender of last resort	prêteur ultime prêteur en dernier ressort	المقرض الأخير
Lending	prêt	اقراض
Lending agency **Lending institution**	organisme de financement	مؤسسة اقراض – جهاز اقراض
Lending country	pays prêteur	دولة مقرضة
Less developed countries (LDCs)	pays moins développés	دول أقل نمواً – الدول المتأخرة – الدول المتخلفة
Letter of commitment	lettre d'engagement	كتاب تعهد – كتاب التزام
Letter of credit	lettre de crédit	خطاب اعتماد
Letter of intent	lettre d'intention	اعلان النية
Level of aid	volume de l'aide	حجم المعونة – مستوى المعونة
Level of development	niveau de développement	مستوى التطور
Level of growth	niveau de croissance	مستوى النمو
Level of prices	niveau des prix	مستوى الأسعار – مستوى الاثمان
Level of production	niveau de la production	مستوى الانتاج
Level of significance	seuil de signifiance	حد الدلالة – مستوى الدلالة
Leverage **Leveraging**	leviérage greffage	مرابعة- إرباع

Levy	prélèvement	فرض – مكس – ضريبة
	taxe	
	impôt	
Levy taxes, to	lever des impôts	فرض ضرائب – حصّل ضرائب
	taxer – imposer	
Liability	obligation	التزام – خصم
Liability management	gestion du passif	ادارة الخصوم – تدبير الخصوم
Liabilities	passif	خصوم – التزامات
	engagements	
Liable to tax	assujetti à l'impôt	خاضع للضريبة
Liberalisation	libéralisation	تحرير – اطلاق
Liberalisation of capital transfers	libéralisation des transferts de capitaux	تحرير التحويلات الرسمالية
Liberalisation of trade	libéralisation des échanges	تحرير المبادلات
Liberalism	libéralisme	المذهب الحر
License	licence	رخصة – ترخيص
	permis	
Licensee	concessionnaire	مرخص له
Licenser	concesseur	مرخص
Licensing	octroi d'une licence	منح ترخيص – ترخيص
Licensing agreement	accord de licence	اتفاق ترخيص
Lien	privilège – droit de gage	حق امتياز – حق حبس
Life annuity	rente viagère	دخل مدى الحياة – ريع العمرى – ريع مدى الحياة
Life expectancy	espérance de vie	احتمال الحياة – الحياة المحتملة
Life index of depletable resources	indice de longévité des ressources non-renouvelables	مؤشر فترة استنفاد الموارد غير المتجددة
Life insurance	assurance-vie	تأمين على الحياة
Life of a loan	durée d'un prêt	فترة القرض – مدة القرض
Life of the project	durée du projet	أجل المشروع – مدة المشروع
Life-span of a plant Life-span of equipment	durée de l'équipement	أجل المعدات – فترة استخدام المعدات
Life tables	tables de longévité	جداول الحياة
Life style	mode de vie	نمط حياتي
Light industry	industrie légère	صناعة خفيفة
Lightning strike	grève-surprise	اضراب مفاجيء – اضراب فجائي
Limit order	ordre à prix fixe	أمر محدد الثمن
Limit price	prix limite – prix limitatif	حد الثمن – الحد الثمني
Limitation of the market	étroitesse du marché	ضيق السوق
Limited convertibility	convertibilité partielle	قابلية محدودة للتحويل
Limited liability company	société à responsabilité limitée	شركة ذات مسئولية محدودة
Limited partnership	société en commandite	شركة توصية
Line of credit	ligne de crédit	اعتماد

Linear correlation	corrélation linéaire	ارتباط خطي
Linear depreciation	amortissement linéaire	استهلاك متساوى الأقساط
Linear equation	équation linéaire	معادلة خطية
Linear model	modèle linéaire	نموذج خطي
Linear programme	programme linéaire	برنامج خطي
Linear programming	programmation linéaire	برمجة خطية
Linear regression	régression linéaire	ارتداد خطي
Linear trend	tendance linéaire	اتجاه خطي
Liner conference	conférence maritime	مؤتمر بحري
Linkages	liens – liaisons – jonctions	روابط
Linkage effects	effets de liaison – effets de jonction	آثار الترابط
Liquid assets	avoirs liquides liquidités disponibilités	أصول سائلة – اصول حاضرة
Liquid capital	capital liquide	رسمال سائل
Liquid funds	fonds liquides liquidités	أموال سائلة
Liquid money	argent liquide	نقد سائل
Liquid natural gas	gaz naturel liquide	غاز طبيعي سائل
Liquid reserves	réserves liquides réserves de trésorerie	أرصدة سائلة
Liquidation	liquidation	تصفية – حل
Liquidation of a debt	amortissement d'une dette remboursement d'une dette	سداد دين – استهلاك دين
Liquidation of holdings	réalisation d'avoirs	تصرف في أصول
Liquidation prices	prix de liquidation	أثمان تصفية – أسعار تصفوية
Liquidity creation	création de liquidités	خلق سيولة
Liquidity preference	préférence pour la liquidité	تفضيل السيولة – الميل للسيولة
Liquidity premium	prime de liquidité	علاوة سيولة
Liquidity ratio	coefficient de liquidité ratio de trésorerie	نسبة السيولة – معامل السيولة
Liquidity requirements	besoins de trésorerie	احتياجات السيولة
Liquidity reserve	réserve de liquidité	احتياطي السيولة
Liquidity shortage	déficit de liquidité	قصور السيولة – عجز السيولة
Liquidity squeeze	crise de liquidité	ازمة سيولة
Liquidity trap	trappe de la liquidité piège de la liquidité	فخ السيولة
List of goods	nomenclature des marchandises liste des biens	قائمة السلع – قائمة البضائع
List of quotations	bulletin des cours	قائمة أسعار الصرف – قائمة الأسعار
Listed securities	valeurs cotées (en bourse)	أوراق مالية مقيدة – أوراق مالية مسجلة
Listing	cotation	ادراج – تسجيل

Listing a security	coter un titre	سجل سندا في البورصة- أدرج سنداً
Livelihood	gagne-pain	الرزق – وسائل العيش
Livestock	bétail	الماشية
Livestock breeding	élevage du bétail	تربية المواشي
Livestock industry	industrie de l'élevage	قطاع تربية المواشي
Livestock products	produits de l'élevage	منتجات الثروة الحيوانية
Living conditions	conditions de vie	ظروف المعيشة – الأحوال المعيشية
Living labour	travail vivant	عمل حي
Living space	espace vital	مجال حيوي
"Lebensraum"		
Living wage	salaire de subsistance	أجر الكفاف
Loading port	port de chargement	ميناء الشحن
Loan	prêt	قرض – سلفة –سلفية
Loan account	compte de prêt	حساب قرض
Loan administration	administration des prêts	ادارة القروض
Loan agreement	accord de prêt	اتفاقية قرض
Loan application	demande de prêt	طلب قرض
	requête de prêt	
Loan applicant	demandeur d'emprunt	طالب القرض – مستقرض
Loan capital	capital emprunté	رسمال مقترض
	capital d'emprunt	
Loan charges	frais de crédit	رسوم القرض
Loan commission	commission de prêt	عمولة القرض
Loan commitment	engagement de prêt	تعهد اقراض
Loan contract	contrat de prêt	عقد قرض
Loan department	service des prêts	دائرة القروض
Loan effectiveness	entrée en vigueur de l'accord de prêt	نفاذ اتفاقية القرض – نفاذ القرض
	entrée en vigueur du prêt	
Loan officer	chargé des prêts	مسئول القروض
Loan on collateral	prêt sur titres – prêt sur nantissement	قرض على أوراق مالية – قرض برهن
Loan regulations	règlement des prêts	لائحة القروض – لائحة الاقراض
Loan resources	fonds prêtables	موارد اقراضية – موارد مقترضة
	fonds empruntés	
Loan shark	usurier	مرابي – مراب
Loan terms	conditions de prêt – modalités de	شروط القرض
	l'emprunt	
Loan turndowns	cas de refus de prêt	حالات رفض الاقراض
Loanable funds	fonds prêtables	أموال اقراضية – أموال قابلة للاقراض
Loans make deposits	les crédits font les dépôts	القروض تخلق الودائع
Loans outstanding	encours des prêts	القروض القائمة
Local administration	administration locale	ادارة محلية
Local contribution	contribution locale	إسهام محلي-نصيب محلي- مساهمة محلية
	quote-part locale	

Local costs	dépenses locales	تكاليف محلية – نفقات محلية
Local currency	monnaie locale	عملة محلية – نقد محلي
	monnaie nationale	
Local economy	économie locale	اقتصاد محلي
Local finance	finances locales	مالية محلية
Local government	collectivité locale	الحكومة المحلية – الادارة المحلية
	administration publique locale	
Local industry	industrie locale	صناعة محلية
Local interests	intérêts locaux	مصالح محلية
Local manufacture	manufactures locales	صناعات محلية – صناعة محلية
	fabrication locale	
Local market	marché locale	سوق محلي
Local partner	associé local – partenaire local	شريك محلي
Local personnel	personnel local	جهاز العاملين المحليين
Local preferences	préférences locales – préférences domestiques	تمييزات محلية – تفضيلات محلية
Local production	production locale	انتاج محلي
Local rates	impôts locaux	ضرائب محلية
Local resources	ressources locales	موارد محلية
Local tax	impôt local	ضريبة محلية
	impôt municipal	
Local traffic	trafic local	حركة النقل المحلي
Localization	localisation	توطن – توطين
	implantation	
Location theory	théorie de l'implantation	نظرية التوطن
Lock-out	lock-out – grève patronale	غلق – غلق المصنع
Logarithmic chart	graphe logarithmique	لوحة لوغاريتمية – رسم لوغاريتمي
Logistics	logistique	الامداد والنقل
Lognormal distribution	distribution lognormale	توزيع لوغسوي
Lombard loan	prêt sur gage	قرض رهني – قرض على رهونات
Long term	long terme	طويل الأجل
Long-term capital	capitaux à long terme	رسمال طويل الاجل
Long-term credit	crédit à long terme	ائتمان طويل الأجل
Long-term planning	planification à long terme	تخطيط طويل الأجل
Long waves	cycles longs	دورات طويلة الأجل
Loop	boucle	قويس
Loose-foot industries	industries mobiles	صناعات متحركة
Loss	perte	خسارة
Loss assessment	estimation des pertes – estimation des dégâts	تقدير الاضرار – تقدير الخسائر
Lot (of shares)	paquet (d'actions)	مجموعة أسهم
Lot (of ground)	lotissement – parcelle (de terrain)	قسيمة – قطعة أرض
Lottery bonds	obligations à lots	سندات يانصيب – سندات سحب
		سندات بجوائز

Low-income country	pays à faible revenu	دولة ذات دخل منخفض – دولة فقيرة
Low-level equilibrium trap	piège de l'équilibre à bas niveau	فخ التوازن الوطيء – فخ التوازن المنخفض
Low-level technology	technologie simple	فن انتاجي بسيط – تكنية بسيطة
Low-price stores	magasins populaires	متاجر شعبية
Low-priority project	projet à faible priorité	مشروع منخفض ألأولوية
Low productivity	basse productivité	انتاجية منخفضة
Lower quartile	premier quartile	الربيع الأدنى – الربيع الأول
Lowest bid	offre la plus avantageuse	أحسن العروض – العرض الأقل تكلفة
Lowest bidder	moins-disant	صاحب أحسن عرض – أقل عطاء
Lucrative capital	capital lucratif capital rentable	رسمال مربح – رسمال مجز – رسمال كاسب
Lump of labour theory	théorie de la motte de travail	نظرية كومة العمل
Lump price	prix forfaitaire	ثمن جزافي
Lump sum	somme forfaitaire	مبلغ جزافي–مبلغ مجمل
Lump-sum appropriation	crédit forfaitaire	اعتماد جزافي – اعتماد مجمل
Lump-sum price	prix forfaitaire	سعر جزافي – ثمن جزافي
Lump-sum tax	impôt forfaitaire	ضريبة جزافية
Lumpen-bourgeoisie	*lumpen-bourgeoisie*	بورجوازية حطبة – ذنانة البورجوازية
Lumpen-proletariat	sous-prolétariat	الرعاع
Lumpiness of an investment	indivisibilité d'un investissement	عدم قابلية الاستثمار للتجزئة
Luxury commodities Luxury goods	articles de luxe	سلع ترفية – سلع كمالية
Luxury goods industry	industrie de luxe	صناعة ترفية
Luxury tax	impôt sur les articles de luxe taxe de luxe	ضريبة ترفية – ضريبة السلع الكمالية
Luxury tourism	tourisme de luxe	سياحة ترفية
Luxury trade	commerce de luxe	تجارة الكماليات – تجارة ترفية

Machinery	matériel	أجهزة – آلات
Machinism	machinisme	نظام الآلة – الآلية
Macro-dynamic model	modèle macro-dynamique	نموذج كلي حركي
Macro-economic aggregates	agrégats macro-économiques	كليات اقتصادية
Macro-economic model	modèle macro-économique	نموذج اقتصادي كلي
Macro-economics	macro-économique macro-économie	التحليل الاقتصادي الكلي – الاقتصاد الكلي
Macro-function	macro-fonction	دالة كلية
Macro-variable	macro-variable	متغير كلي

Mail-order business	vente par correspondance	تجارة بريدية – بيع بالمراسلة
Mail transfer	transfert par courrier	تحويل بريدي
	virement postal	
Maintaining capital intact	maintien du capital intact	حفظ الرسمال – حفظ سلامة الرسمال
	préservation du capital	
Maintenance	maintien – maintenance	صيانة
	entretien	
Maintenance allowance	allocation d'entretien	مخصص صيانة
Maintenance costs	frais d'entretien	تكاليف صيانة
Maintenance of value clause	clause de maintien de la valeur	شرط حفظ القيمة – نص ثبات القيمة
Maintenance services	services d'entretien	خدمات صيانة
Major equipment	gros équipement	أجهزة ثقيلة
Majority holding	participation majoritaire	تملك غالبية الرسمال – مساهمة غالبة
Majority interest	participation majoritaire	مساهمة غالبة
mala fide **holder**	porteur de maùvaise foi	حامل سيء النية
Malinvestment	mésinvestissement	استثمار سيء – سوء الاستثمار
Malnutrition	sous-alimentation	سوء التغذية – تعييل
	déficience alimentaire	
Malthusianism	malthusianisme	المالتسية
Man-day	journée de travail	يوم عمل
	journée de main-d'œuvre	
Man-hour	heure de travail	ساعة عمل
	heure de main d'œuvre	
Man-land ratio	densité de la population	كثافة السكان
Man-month	mois de travail	شهر عمل
	mois de main-d'œuvre	
Man-power	main-d'œuvre	قوة عمل – عمل
Man-power planning	planification de la main-d'œuvre	تخطيط القوى العاملة
Man-power requirements	besoins en main-d'œuvre	احتياجات العمل
Man-power resources	ressources de main-d'œuvre	موارد عمالية
Man-power survey	enquête sur la main d'œuvre	مسح عمالي
Managed currency	monnaie dirigée	نقد موجه
Managed floating (*of a currency*)	flottement contrôlé (*d'une monnaie*)	تعويم موجه (لعملة)
	flottaison contrôlée	
Management	gestion – administration	ادارة – تسيير – تدبير
	direction – gérance	
Management agreement	contrat de gestion	عقد ادارة – عقد تسيير – عقد تدبير
Management contract		
Management consultant	conseiller de gestion	مستشار اداري – مستشار تدبير – مستشار تسيير
	organisateur-conseil	
Management engineering	organisation de la gestion	تنظيم ادارة المشروعات
Management fee	rétribution de gestion	رسم ادارة – رسم تسيير – رسم تدبير
	commission de service	عمولة اصدار
	commission de direction	

Management needs	besoins en cadres	احتياجات ادارية
Management requirements		
Management plan	plan de gestion	خطة ادارية – خطة تسيير
Management team	équipe de direction	جهاز الادارة
Management techniques	techniques de gestion	أساليب الادارة – أساليب التسيير
Manager	directeur – gérant – administrateur manageur dirigeant	مدير – مدبر
Managerial control	contrôle de la direction	سيطرة على الادارة – سيطرة على ادارة المؤسسات
Managerial personnel	cadres	جهاز اداري – كوادر
Managerial revolution	révolution managérielle révolution des technocrates révolution des manageurs	ثورة المديرين – ثورة المدبرين ثورة المدراء
Managerial skill	compétence managérielle compétence administrative	مهارة ادارية – مهارة تدبيرية
Managerial society	société des manageurs – société managérielle	المجتمع الاداري – مجتمع المدراء
Managing agent	agent de gérance	وكيل ادارة – وكيل تدبير
Managing syndicate (*issues*)	syndicat de direction (*émissions*)	حلقة تنظيم-دارة تدبير (اصدارات)
Mandatory redemption	remboursement obligatoire	سداد جبري – وفاء جبري استهلاك جبري
Manipulation of accounts	tripotage des comptes	تلاعب بالحسابات
Manipulation of prices	manipulation des prix	تلاعب بالأسعار
Manipulation of the market	manipulation du marché	تلاعب بالسوق
Manual labour	travail manuel	عمل يدوي
Manufactory	manufacture fabrique	مصنع – ورشة
Manufacture	fabrication	تصنيع – صناعة
Manufactured goods	produits manufacturés	سلع مصنعة – سلع صناعية
Manufacturer's price	prix de fabrique	ثمن المصنع
Manufacturing costs	coûts de fabrication	تكاليف الانتاج
Manufacturing industry	industrie manufacturière	صناعة تحويلية
Manufacturing licence	licence de fabrication	رخصة انتاج – ترخيص انتاج
Manure	engrais – fumier	سماد (طبيعي)
Mapping	cartographie	وضع الخرائط – رسم الخرائط
Margin	marge limite	هامش – حد
Margin call	appel de provision	طلب تغطية
Margin of error	marge d'erreur	هامش خطأ
Margin of preference	marge de préférence	هامش تفضيل – هامش تمييز
Margin of profit	marge de bénéfice marge bénéficiaire	هامش ربح
Margin requirements	couverture requise couverture légale	مقتضيات الغطاء – الغطاء القانوني

Marginal	marginal	حدي
Marginal analysis	analyse marginale	تحليل حدي
Marginal cost	coût marginal	تكلفة حدية – نفقة حدية
Marginal cost pricing	fixation du prix au coût marginal	تسعير بالتكلفة الحدية
	tarification au coût marginal	
Marginal efficiency of capital	efficacité marginale du capital	الفاعلية الحدية للرسمال
		الانتاجية الحدية للرسمال
Marginal efficiency of investment	efficacité marginale de l'investissement	الفاعلية الحدية للاستثمار
		الانتاجية الحدية للاستثمار
Marginal export revenue	revenu marginal d'exportation	الايراد الحدي للتصدير
Marginal firm	entreprise marginale	مشروع حدي
Marginal growth contribution	contribution marginale à la croissance	الاسهام الحدي في النمو
Marginal import cost	coût marginal d'importation	النفقة الحدية للاستيراد
Marginal producer	producteur marginal	منتج حدي
Marginal product	produit marginal	ناتج حدي – منتج حدي
Marginal productivity	productivité marginale	انتاجية حدية
Marginal project	projet marginal	مشروع حدي
Marginal propensity to consume	propension marginale à consommer	الميل الحدي للاستهلاك
Marginal propensity to import	propension marginale à importer	الميل الحدي للاستيراد
Marginal propensity to save	propension marginale à épargner	الميل الحدي للادخار
Marginal rate of substitution	taux marginal de substitution	المعدل الحدي للاستبدال
Marginal revenue	recette marginale	ايراد حدي
Marginal social benefit	rendement social marginal	منفعة اجتماعية حدية
		عائد اجتماعي حدي
Marginal social cost	coût social marginal	الكلفة الاجتماعية الحدية
Marginal social productivity	productivité sociale marginale	الانتاجية الاجتماعية الحدية
Marginal utility	utilité marginale	منفعة حدية
Marginalism	marginalisme	تحليل حدي
Marginalist school	école marginaliste	المدرسة الحدية
Marine insurance	assurance maritime	تأمين بحري
Marine resources	ressources maritimes	موارد بحرية
Maritime freight rates	taux de fret maritime	أسعار الشحن البحري
Maritime transportation	transports maritimes	نقل بحري
Marker crude (oil)	brut de référence (pétrole)	نفط القياس
Market	marché	سوق
Market area	marché	منطقة السوق
Market arrangements	arrangements commerciaux	تدابير سوقية – تدابير تجارية
	arrangements en matière de marchés	
Market behaviour	comportement du marché	اتجاه السوق
Market conditions	conditions du marché	أوضاع السوق – أحوال السوق
Market dominance	domination du marché	سيطرة على السوق
Market distortions	imperfections du marché	شوائب السوق
Market imperfections		

118

Market economy	économie de marché	اقتصاد أسواق – اقتصاد سوقي
Market efficiency	efficacité du marché	فاعلية السوق
Market exploitation	exploitation marchande – utilisation commerciale	استغلال سوقي
Market forces	forces du marché	عوامل السوق – قوى السوق
Market forecast	prévision du marché	توقعات السوق – استنباء السوق
Market forms Market types	types de marché formes de marché	أنواع السوق – أشكال السوق
Market fragmentation	fragmentation du marché	تجزؤ السوق – تشتت السوق –تقسم السوق
Market glut	saturation du marché pléthore du marché	طفاح السوق – اكتظاظ السوق فيضة السوق – تكدس السوق
Market information	information sur les marchés	بيانات سوقية
Market integration	intégration du marché – intégration par le marché	تكامل السوق – تكامل عن طريق السوق
Market maker	contrepartiste	مسوق – سويق
Market mechanism	mécanisme du marché	جهاز السوق
Market organization	organisation des marchés	تنظيم الأسواق
Market outlook	perspectives du marché	طالع السوق
Market penetration	pénétration du marché	ولوج السوق – دخول السوق – فتح السوق
Market performance	performance commerciale état du marché	أداء تجاري – أداء سوقي – أداء السوق
Market perturbations	troubles du marché perturbations du marché	تقلبات السوق – اضطرابات السوق
Market place	marché	سوق
Market potential	possibilités de vente – potentiel du marché	طاقة السوق
Market price	prix du marché prix courant	سعر السوق – ثمن السوق – السعر الجاري
Market prospection	prospection du marché	دراسة السوق–سبر الأسواق
Market rally	reprise des cours	انتعاش السوق (المالية)
Market research	étude de marché	دراسة تسويقية
Market segmentation	segmentation du marché	تجزؤ السوق–تشتت السوق–تقسم السوق
Market share	part du marché	نصيب في السوق – نصيب من الأسواق
Market sharing	partage du marché	اقتسام السوق – توزيع السوق
Market size	dimension du marché étendue du marché	حجم السوق – نطاق السوق
Market socialism	socialisme de marché	اشتراكية سوقية
Market sounding	sondage du marché	سبر السوق
Market structure	structure du marché	هيكل السوق
Market support	soutien du marché	مساندة السوق
Market survey	enquête sur les marchés	مسح سوقي – دراسة سوقية
Market transparency	transparence du marché	شفافية السوق
Market trends	tendances des marchés	اتجاهات السوق

Market value	valeur sur le marché	قيمة سوقية
	valeur marchande	
Marketability	négociabilité	القابلية للتسويق – القابلية للبيع
Marketable	négociable – commercialisable	قابل للتسويق – قابل للبيع
	vendable	
Marketable securities	titres négociables	أوراق مالية قابلة للتداول
		سندات قابلة للتداول
Marketing	commercialisation	تسويق
	marchéage	
	mercatique	
	placement – distribution	
Marketing board	office de vente	جهاز تسويق – هيئة تسويق
	organisme de commercialisation	
Marketing campaign	campagne de vente	حملة تسويقية
Marketing cartel	cartel de vente	كارتل تسويق
Marketing channels	circuits de commercialisation	مسالك التسويق
Marketing cooperative	coopérative de vente	تعاونية تسويق
Marketing expert	expert en commercialisation	اخصائي تسويق
	expert en mercatique	
Marketing management	gestion commerciale	ادارة التسويق
Marketing policy	politique de vente	سياسة التسويق
	politique de commercialisation	
Marketing research	étude de mercatique	بحث تسويقي – دراسة تسويقية
Marking	marquage	وسم
Mark-up	marge (commerciale)	هامش (تجاري)
Mark-up pricing	fixation du prix par marge de bénéfice	تسعير هامشي
Marriage rate	taux de nuptialité	معدل الزواج
Marxian economics	économie marxiste	الاقتصاد الماركسي
Marxian socialism	socialisme marxiste	الاشتراكية الماركسية
Marxism	marxisme	الماركسية – المذهب الماركسي
Marxist dogmas	dogmes marxistes	فرض ماركسية
Marxist ideology	ideologie marxiste	المذهبية الماركسية
Mass consumption	grande consommation	الاستهلاك الكبير
Mass consumption goods	biens de grande consommation	منتجات الاستهلاك الكبير
	produits de grande consommation	سلع الاستهلاك الكبير
Mass media	moyens d'information publique	وسائل الاعلام
Mass-produced goods	produits de grande série	سلع الانتاج الكبير
Mass production	production de masse	انتاج كبير
	production à la chaîne	
Mass tourism	tourisme populaire	سياحة شعبية
Mass transports	transports collectifs	نقل جماعي
Mass unemployment	chômage massif	بطالة متفشية – بطالة واسعة
Masses	masses	جماهير
Master-plan	maître-plan – plan d'ensemble	خطة رئيسية

Matching of maturities	équilibrage des échéances – harmonisation des échéances	تنسيق الآجال – تنسيق الاستحقاقات
Material balances	balances-matières	موازين مادية
Material costs	coûts de matériaux	تكلفة المواد – كلفة المواد
Material incentives system	système d'incitations matérielles	نظام حوافز مادية
Material intensity	intensité matérielle	كثافة مادية
Material-financial balances	balances matério-financières	موازين مادية ،مالية
Mathematical economics	économie mathématique	الاقتصاد الرياضي
Mathematical expectation	espérance mathématique	احتمال رياضي
Mathematical model	modèle mathématique	نموذج رياضي
Matrix	matrice	مصفوفة
Matrix of input-output coefficients	matrice des coefficients inter-industriels	مصفوفة معاملات المستخدم المنتج
Mature economy	économie développée	اقتصاد ناضج – اقتصاد متقدم
Matured debt	dette échue	دين حال – دين حل اجله
Maturity	échéance	أجل الاستحقاق – أجل الدفع
Maturity acceleration	accélération de l'échéance déchéance du terme	تعجيل الاستحقاق – اسقاط الأجل
Maturity mismatch	discordance des échéances	تخالف الآجال
Maximax criterion	critère du maximax	معيار اقصاء القصى – معيار اذراء الذرو
Maximin criterion	critère du maximin	معيار اذراء النزير معيار اقصاء المضيل
Maximisation	maximisation maximation	اقصاء – اذراء – تعظيم
Maximise, to	maximiser	قصّى – اذرى – عظّم
Maximum	maximum	القصى – الحد الأقصى – الذرو – النهاية الكبرى النهاية العظمى
Maximum likelihood	maximum de vraisemblance	الاحتمال الأقصى – أقصى احتمال
Maximum-likelihood estimate	estimation d'après le maximum de vraisemblance	تقدير الاحتمال الأقصى – تقدير الجوازية الكبرى
Maximum price	prix maximum	السعر الأقصى – أقصى سعر – أقصى الأسعار
Maximum satisfaction	satisfaction maximum satisfaction maximale	أقصى الاشباع
Mean	moyenne	وسط – متوسط
Mean deviation	écart moyen écart à la moyenne	الانحراف الوسط
Mean value	valeur moyenne	قيمة وسط – قيمة متوسطة
Means of communication	voies de communication	وسائل المواصلات
Means of financing	moyens de financement	وسائل تمويل ٢ موارد تمويل
Means of payment	moyens de paiement	وسائل دفع
Means of production	moyens de production	وسائل انتاج
Means of subsistence	moyens d'existence	موارد الحياة-موارد المعيشة-موارد معيشية

Mechanised agriculture **Mechanised farming**	agriculture mécanisée motoculture	زراعة آلية – فلاحة آلية
Median	médiane	وسيط
Medical care	soins médicaux	خدمات طبية – عناية طبية
Medium of exchange	instrument d'échange	اداة تبادل
Medium term	moyen terme	الأجل المتوسط
Meet a deficit, to	couvrir un déficit	واجه عجزاً – غطى عجزاً
Meet cash requirements, to	faire face à des besoins de liquidités	واجه حاجة للسيولة
Mercantile marine	marine marchande	البحرية التجارية
Mercantile system	système mercantiliste	النظام التجاري – نظام التجاريين
Mercantilism	mercantilisme	المذهب التجاري
Merchandise	marchandises	بضاعة – بضائع – بياعات – سلع
Merchandise trade	commerce des marchandises	تجارة البضائع – تجارة السلع
Merchandise traffic	trafic des marchandises trafic commercial	حركة نقل البضائع – حركة نقل السلع
Merchandising	marchandisage	تسويق
Merchant	négociant commerçant	تاجر
Merchant banks	"merchant banks" banques d'affaires	بنوك أعمال – مصارف أعمال
Merchant fleet	flotte marchande flotte commerciale flotte de commerce	اسطول تجاري
Merger	fusion	دمج – اندماج
Merit wants	besoins privilégiés	حاجات متميزة
Metal industry **Metallurgy**	métallurgie industrie métallurgique	صناعة معدنية – صناعة التعدين
Metallic money	monnaie métallique	نقود معدنية – عملة معدنية
Methodology	méthodologie	دراسة مناهج البحث – المنهجية منهج البحث
Micro-economics	micro-économie micro-économique	التحليل الاقتصادي الجزئي – الاقتصاد الجزئي
Middle class	classe moyenne bourgeoisie	الطبقة الوسطى
Middle-income developing countries	pays en développement à revenu intermédiaire	دولة نامية وسيطة الدخل دول نامية متوسطة الدخل
Middleman	intermédiaire	وسيط
Migration	migration	هجرة – رحيل
Migrant workers **Migrating labour**	travailleurs migrants	عمال مهاجرون – عمال رحل
Mileage statistics	statistiques kilométriques	احصاءات كيلومترية – احصاءات المسافات
Military aid **Military assistance**	aide militaire assistance militaire	معونة عسكرية – مساعدة عسكرية

Military budget	budget militaire	موازنة عسكرية – ميزانية عسكرية
Military expenditures	dépenses militaires	نفقات عسكرية – مصروفات عسكرية
Military-industrial complex	complexe militaro-industriel	الكتلة العسكرية الصناعية
Milling industry	meunerie	صناعة الطحن
Mine economics	économie minière	اقتصاديات المناجم
Mineral concession	concession minière	امتياز منجمي
Mineral exploration	exploration minière	تنقيب منجمي
Minerals fuels and lubricants	combustibles minéraux et lubrifiants	وقود معدني وزيوت تشحيم
Mineral resources	richesses du sous-sol	موارد منجمية – موارد جوفية
Mineral wealth	richesses minières	ثروة منجمية – ثروة جوفية
Mineral resources development	mise en valeur des ressources minérales	استغلال الموارد المنجمية استغلال الموارد الجوفية
Minimal nutritional level	niveau nutritif minimum	الحد الأدنى للمستوى الغذائي
Minimax criterion	critère du minimax	معيار تنزير الذرو معيار تضييل القصى
Minimisation	minimisation minimation	تضييل – تنزير – ادناء
Minimise, to	minimiser	دنّى – نزّر – ضيّل
Minimum	minimum	الحد الأدنى – التنزير – المضيل – النهاية الصغرى
Minimum cash requirements	encaisse minimum obligatoire	رصيد نقدي اجباري
Minimum cost	coût minimum – coût minimal	التكلفة الدنيا – أدنى تكلفة
Minimum lending rate	taux de prêt minimum	الحد الأدنى لسعر الاقراض
Minimum of subsistence	minimum vital	حد الكفاف
Minimum price	prix minimum	السعر الأدنى – الثمن الأدنى
Minimum reserves	réserves obligatoires – réserves minimums	احتياطي جبري – أرصدة اجبارية
Minimum wage	salaire minimum	الحد الأدنى للأجور
Mining and quarrying	industrie d'extraction	الصناعة الاستخراجية – المناجم والمحاجر
Mining company	société minière	شركة منجمية
Mining concession	concession minière	امتياز منجمي
Mining economy	économie minière	اقتصاد منجمي
Mining industry	industrie minière	الصناعة المنجمية
Mining production	production minière	انتاج منجمي .
Mining rights	concessions minières	امتيازات منجمية
Minority holding	participation minoritaire	مساهمة نقيصة – تملك اقلية الرسمال
Minority interest		
Mint, the	hôtel des monnaies	دار السك – دار السكة
Mintage	frappe de la monnaie	سك النقود
Misallocation of resources	mauvaise distribution des ressources mésallocation des ressources	سوء توزيع الموارد – سوء تخصيص الموارد
Miscellaneous income	revenus divers	دخول متنوعة
Misdevelopment	développement mal orienté	نمو منحرف – سوء النمو

Misevaluation of a project	mésévaluation d'un projet	سوء تقييم المشروع
	malévaluation d'un projet	
Mismanagement	mauvaise gestion	سوء ادارة – سوء تدبير
	malgestion	
Mixed economy	économie mixte	اقتصاد مختلط
Mixed enterprise	entreprise d'économie mixte	مشروع مختلط – مشروع اقتصاد مختلط
Mixed farming	polyculture	فلاحة مختلطة – زراعة متنوعة
	agriculture et élevage	زراعة وتربية
Mobilisation of resources	mobilisation des ressources	تعبئة الموارد
Mobilise capital, to	mobiliser du capital	تعبئة الرسمال
Mobility of capital	mobilité du capital	سيولة الرسمال – حراكة الرسمال
Mobility of labour	mobilité de la main-d'œuvre	سيولة العمل – حراكة العمل
Mobility of the factors of production	mobilité des facteurs de production	سيولة عوامل الانتاج – حراكة عوامل الانتاج
Modal consumer	consommateur modal	المستهلك المنوالي
Mode (*statistics*)	mode (*statistique*)	منوال (احصاء)
Mode of life	mode de vie	نمط الحياة – نمط حياتي – نمط حضاري
Mode of payment	mode de paiement	وسيلة الدفع – كيفية الدفع
Mode of production	mode de production	نظام الانتاج
Modes of transportation	moyens de transports	وسائل النقل
Model farm	ferme modèle	مزرعة نموذجية
Model installation	installation pilote	منشأة نموذجية
Model specification	spécification du modèle	توصيف النموذج – تحديد النموذج – تعيين النموذج
Model testing	testage de modèles	اختبار النموذج – اختبار النماذج
Modelling	modélisation	نمذجة – صياغة نموذج
Modern sector	secteur moderne	قطاع حديث
Modernisation	modernisation	تطوير – تحديث
Modus operandi	*modus operandi*	كيفية العمل
Modus vivendi	*modus vivendi*	نهج التعايش – كيفية التعايش
Moment(s)	moment(s)	عزم (عزوم)
Monetarism	monétarisme	المذهب النقدي
Monetarists	monétaristes	أنصار المذهب النقدي
Monetary agreement	accord monétaire	اتفاق نقدي
Monetary area	zone monétaire	منطقة نقدية
Monetary authorities	autorités monétaires	سلطات نقدية
Monetary aggregates	agrégats monétaires	كليات نقدية
Monetary circulation	masse monétaire	حجم النقود المتداولة – تداول نقدي
Monetary cooperation	coopération monétaire	تعاون نقدي
Monetary economics	économie monétaire	اقتصاديات النقود
Monetary equilibrium	équilibre monétaire	توازن نقدي
Monetary erosion	érosion de la monnaie – érosion	تفتت نقدي – تفتت قيمة النقود
	monétaire	
Monetary expansion	expansion monétaire	توسع نقدي
Monetary flows	flux monétaires	تدفقات نقدية – تيارات نقدية
	flots monétaires	

Monetary gold	or monétaire	ذهب نقدي
Monetary income	revenu monétaire	دخل نقدي
Monetary instability	instabilité monétaire	تقلبات نقدية – لا استقرار نقدي
Monetary integration	intégration monétaire	تكامل نقدي
Monetary law	loi monétaire	قانون نقدي – قانون النقد
Monetary management	gestion monétaire	ادارة الشئون النقدية – سياسة نقدية
Monetary operations	opérations monétaires	عمليات نقدية
Monetary policy	politique monétaire	سياسة نقدية
Monetary reform	réforme monétaire	اصلاح نقدي
Monetary reserves	réserves monétaires	أرصدة نقدية
Monetary situation	situation monétaire	حالة نقدية – وضع نقدي
Monetary stability	stabilité monétaire	استقرار نقدي
Monetary stabilization	stabilisation monétaire	تثبيت نقدي – تثبيت الأوضاع النقدية
Monetary standard	étalon monétaire	قاعدة نقدية
Monetary stock	masse monétaire	كمية النقود
Monetary stringency	austérité monétaire	تقشف نقدي
Monetary survey	relevé monétaire enquête monétaire	بيانات نقدية – مسح نقدي
Monetary system	système monétaire	نظام نقدي
Monetary theory	théorie monétaire	نظرية نقدية
Monetary union	union monétaire	اتحاد نقدي
Monetary unit	unité monétaire	وحدة نقدية
Monetisation	monétisation	اسباغ الصفة النقدية
Monetisation of a debt	monétisation d'une dette	تسييل دين
Money	monnaie	نقد – نقود – عملة
Money at call	argent au jour le jour	سلفية معجلة–سلفة تحت الطلب–ائتمان معجل
Money changer	changeur	صراف
Money circulation	circulation monétaire	نقد متداول
Money economy	économie monétaire	اقتصاد نقدي
Money illusion	illusion monétaire	وهم نقدي – أخذة نقدية
Money income	revenu monétaire	دخل نقدي
Money lender	bailleur de fonds prêteur	مقرض
Money lending	prêt d'argent	تسليف – اقراض
Money market	marché monétaire marché de l'argent	سوق نقدي – سوق النقود
Money order	mandat-poste	حوالة بريدية
Money squeeze	disette de fonds pénurie de fonds	شح النقود – ندرة نقدية
Money stock	masse monétaire – stock monétaire	كمية النقود – حجم النقود
Money substitutes	succédanés monétaires	بدائل نقدية
Money supply	massé monétaire stock monétaire – offre monétaire disponibilités monétaires	حجم النقود – كمية النقود – عرض النقود

Money transfer	transfert de monnaie	تحويل نقدي
	transfert monétaire	
Money veil	voile monétaire	قناع نقدي – ستار نقدي
Money wage rate	taux du salaire nominal	معدل الأجر الاسمي
Moneyed classes	classes aisées	الطبقات الثرية
Monitoring of aid	supervision de l'aide	متابعة المعونات – رقابة المساعدات
Monitoring system	système de surveillance	نظام رقابة – نظام مراقبة
Monoculture	monoculture	زراعة المحصول الواحد
Monometallism	monométallisme	نظام المعدن النقدي الواحد
		نظام المعدن الواحد
Monopolisation	monopolisation	احتكار
Monopolise, to	monopoliser – accaparer	احتكر
Monopolist	monopoliste – monopoleur	محتكر
Monopolistic competition	concurrence monopolistique	منافسة احتكارية
Monopoly	monopole	احتكار
Monopoly power	pouvoir de monopole	سلطة احتكارية – قوة احتكارية
Monopoly price	prix de monopole	ثمن احتكاري
Monopoly profits	profits de monopole	أرباح احتكارية
Monopoly rent	rente de monopole	ريع احتكاري
Monopsony	monopsone	احتكار الشراء
Monotonic trend	tendance monotonique	اتجاه رتيب
Monthly averages	moyennes mensuelles	متوسطات شهرية
Monthly payments	mensualités	أقساط شهرية
Moonlighting	cumul d'emplois	ازدواج العمل – تعدد العمل
Moral restraint	contrainte morale	مانع أدبي – امتناع أدبي
Moral suasion	persuasion morale	اقناع أدبي
Moratorium	moratorium	مكابلة
Mortality rate	taux de mortalité	معدل الوفيات
Mortality tables	tables de mortalité	جداول الوفيات
Mortgage bank	banque hypothécaire	بنك رهون عقارية – بنك ائتمان عقاري
Mortgage bond	obligation hypothécaire	سند عقاري – سند رهن عقاري
Mortgage debenture		
Mortgage credit	crédit hypothécaire	ائتمان عقاري
Mortgage debt	dette hypothécaire	دين عقاري
Mortgage financing	financement hypothécaire	تمويل عقاري
Mortgage loan	prêt hypothécaire	قرض عقاري
Mortgage market	marché hypothécaire	سوق الرهون العقارية
Most-favoured nation clause	clause de la nation la plus favorisée	نص الدولة الأولى بالرعاية
Most seriously affected countries	pays les plus gravement atteints	الدول الأكثر تأثراً
Movable assets	biens meubles	منقولات – أموال منقولة
Movables		

Moving average	moyenne mobile	متوسط متحرك – وسط متحرك
Moving averages method	méthode des moyennes mobiles	منهج المتوسطات المتحركة
Multicollinearity	multicollinéarité	ترابط متسامت متعدد
Multidimensional project	projet polyvalent	مشروع متعدد الأبعاد
Multi-end company	société polyvalente	شركة متعددة الأغراض
Multi-purpose company		
Multilateral aid	aide multilatérale	معونة دولية – مساعدة دولية
Multilateral assistance	assistance multilatérale	اعانة متعددة الأطراف
Multilateral compensation	compensation multilatérale	مقاصة متعددة الأطراف
Multilateral guarantee mechanism	mécanisme de garantie multilatérale	جهاز للضمان المتعدد الأطراف
		جهاز للضمان الدولي
Multilateral investment insurance	garantie multilatérale des investissements	ضمان دولي للاستثمار
Multilateral lending agency	organisme multilatéral de prêt	مؤسسة اقراض دولية
		مؤسسة اقراض متعددة الأطراف
Multilateral payments	paiements multilatéraux	مدفوعات متعددة الأطراف
Multilateral payments agreement	accord de paiements multilatéral	اتفاق دفع متعدد الأطراف
Multilateral trade	commerce multilatéral	تجارة متعددة الأطراف
Multilateralism	multilatéralisme	تعدد الأطراف – نظام تعدد الأطراف
Multi-level planning	planification multi-polaire	تخطيط متعدد المستويات
		تخطيط متعدد الأقطاب
Multinational company	société multinationale	شركة متعددة الجنسية – شركة دولية
Multinational corporation	entreprise multinationale	شركة متعددة الجنسيات
Multinational firm	firme multinationale	
Multinational project	projet multinational	مشروع متعدد الأطراف
Multinationalisation	multinationalisation	تدويل
Multiple correlation	corrélation multiple	ارتباط متعدد
Multiple currency option	option de change multiple	خيار صرف متعدد
Multiple exchange rate system	système de taux de change multiples	نظام تعدد سعر الصرف
Multiple lines of production	fabrications multiples	انتاج متعدد الفروع – انتاج متعدد
Multiple objective decision model	modèle de décision à objectifs multiples	نموذج بت متعدد الهدف
	modèle décisionnel à objectifs multiples	
Multiple objective planning	planification multi-objectifs	تخطيط متعدد الأهداف
Multiplier	multiplicateur	مضاعف
Multiplier-accelerator model	modèle de l'interaction multiplicateur-accélérateur	نموذج تفاعل المضاعف والمعجل
Multiplier effect	effet multiplicateur	أثر مضاعف – أثر المضاعف
Multiplier process	mécanisme du multiplicateur	مجرى المضاعف
Multi-product firm	entreprise à production multiple	مؤسسة متعددة المنتجات
		مؤسسة متعددة الانتاج

Multi-purpose project	projet polyvalent	مشروع متعدد الأغراض
Multi-regional analysis	analyse multi-régionale	تحليل متعدد الأقاليم
Multi-sectoral model	modèle multi-sectoriel	نموذج متعدد القطاعات
Multi-sectoral project	projet multi-sectoriel	مشروع متعدد القطاعات
Multivariate analysis	analyse multivariable	تحليل متعدد المتغيرات
Multi-year budget	budget pluri-annuel	موازنة متعددة السنوات – ميزانية متعددة السنوات
Multi-year programme	programme pluri-annuel	برنامج متعدد السنوات
Municipal bonds	obligations municipales	سندات بلدية
Municipal finance	finances locales	المالية المحلية
Municipal taxes	impôts locaux	ضرائب محلية – ضرائب بلدية
mutatis mutandis	*mutatis mutandis*	مع اجراء التغييرات المناسبة
Mutual aid	aide mutuelle	معونة متبادلة – مساعدة متبادلة
Mutual assistance	assistance mutuelle	
Mutual benefit society	mutuelle	تعاونية – جمعية تعاونية
Mutual cooperation	coopération mutuelle	تعاون متبادل
Mutual fund	société d'investissement à capital variable	صندوق استثمار مشترك
	fonds commun de placement	صندوق استثمار جماعي
Mutual insurance	assurance mutuelle	تأمين متبادل

N

Naïve-model test	test du modèle naïf	اختبار النموذج الساذج
Narrow market	marché étroit	سوق ضيق
Nascent industry	industrie naissante	صناعة ناشئة
National accounting	comptabilité nationale	محاسبة قومية
National accounts	comptes nationaux	حسابات قومية
National bourgeoisie	bourgeoisie nationale	البورجوازية الوطنية
National currency	monnaie nationale	عملة وطنية – نقد وطني
National debt	dette nationale	الدين القومي – دين الدولة
National dividend	dividende national	العائد القومي – الدخل القومي
National economic budget	budget économique national	موازنة اقتصادية قومية – ميزانية اقتصادية قومية
National economic independence	indépendance économique nationale	الاستقلال الاقتصادي القومي
National economic priorities	priorités économiques nationales	أولويات اقتصادية قومية
National economic profitability criterion	critère de rentabilité macro-économique	معيار الأرحية الاقتصادية القومية
National economy	économie nationale	الاقتصاد القومي
National income	revenu national	الدخل القومي
National income accounts	comptes du revenu national	حسابات الدخل القومي

National income aggregates	agrégats du revenu national	كليات الدخل القومي
National investment bank	banque nationale d'investissement	بنك وطني للاستثمار
National liberation	libération nationale	التحرر الوطني
National loan	emprunt national	قرض وطني
National plan	plan national	خطة قومية
National planning	planification nationale	التخطيط القومي
National priorities	objectifs prioritaires nationaux	أولويات قومية
National product	produit national	الناتج القومي
National self-reliance	efforts propres nationaux – autonomie nationale	الاعتماد القومي على النفس
National-socialism	national-socialisme	الاشتراكية الوطنية
National wealth	richesse nationale	الثروة القومية
Nationalisation	nationalisation	تأميم
Nationalise, to	nationaliser	أمّم
Nationalised industry	industrie nationalisée	صناعة مؤممة
Nationalism	nationalisme	القومية
Natural calamities Natural disasters	désastres naturels	الجوائح
Natural endowments Natural wealth	richesse naturelles	ثروات طبيعية
Natural monopoly	monopole naturel	احتكار طبيعي
Natural order	ordre naturel	النظام الطبيعي
Natural resources	ressources naturelles	موارد طبيعية
Nazism	nazisme	النازية
Near-money	quasi-monnaie	شبه نقود
Needs	besoins	حاجات
Need for assistance	besoins d'assistance	الحاجة إلى معونات – الحاجة إلى مساعدات
Negative capital formation	formation négative de capital	تكوين سالب للرسمال
Negative correlation	corrélation négative	ارتباط سالب
Negative investment	investissement négatif désinvestissement	استثمار سالب
Negative rate of interest	taux d'intérêt négatif	سعر فائدة سالب
Negative pledge clause	clause d'engagement négatif clause de maintien du rang	نص التعهد السالب نص حفظ الرتبة
Negative saving	épargne négative – désépargne	ادخار سالب
Negotiable bills Negotiable paper	effets négociables papier négociable	سندات قابلة للتداول – أوراق قابلة للتداول
Negotiate a loan, to	négocier un emprunt	عقد قرضاً – تفاوض على قرض
Negotiated price	prix négocié	سعر تفاوضي – سعر اتفاقي
Negotiated procurement	marché de gré à gré	توريد بالممارسة – شراء بالممارسة
Negotiation techniques	techniques de la négociation	أساليب التفاوض
Neo-classical economics	économie néo-classique	النظرية الاقتصادية التقليدية الجديدة الاقتصاد التقليدي الجديد

Neo-colonialism	néo-colonialisme	الاستعمار الجديد
Neo-keynesianism	néo-keynésianisme	الكينزية الجديدة
Neo-marginalism	néo-marginalisme	المدرسة الحدية الجديدة
Neo-marxism	néo-marxisme	الماركسية الجديدة
Neo-mercantilism	néo-mercantilisme	المذهب التجاري الجديد
Neo-protectionism	néo-protectionnisme	مذهب الحماية الجديد
Net	net	صافي
Net assets	actif net	صافي الاصول
Net assets value	valeur d'aprés l'actif net	القيمة على أساس صافي الاصول
Net borrowing	montant net des emprunts	صافي المبالغ المقترضة
Net current assets	actif net réalisable	صافي الاصول الجارية
Net disbursements	déboursements nets	صافي المسحوبات
Net domestic product	produit domestique net	صافي الناتج المحلي
Net earnings	gain net	صافي المكسب – صافي الكسب صافي الربح
Net economic welfare	bien-être économique net	صافي الرفاهة الاقتصادية
Net fixed assets	actif net immobilisé	صافي الأصول الثابتة
Net income	revenu net	صافي الدخل
Net investment	investissement net	صافي الاستثمار
Net lending	montant net des prêts	صافي الاقراض
Net national product	produit national net	صافي الناتج القومي
Net official holdings	avoirs officiels nets	صافي الأرصدة الرسمية
Net present worth	valeur nette actualisée	صافي القيمة الحالية – صافي القيمة المستحطة
Net profit	bénéfice net	صافي الربح
Net realisable value	valeur réalisable nette	صافي القيمة السوقية – صافي القيمة السائلة
Net production rate	taux net de reproduction	صافي معدل التناسل – صافي معدل التكاثر
Net return	rendement net	صافي العائد
Net sales	chiffre d'affaires net	صافي المبيعات
Net saving	épargne nette	صافي الادخار
Net transfer of resources	transfert net de ressources	صافي الموارد المحولة صافي تحويل الموارد
Net value	valeur nette	صافي القيمة – القيمة الصافية
Network analysis	analyse de réseaux	التحليل الشبكي
Net worth	actif net	صافي الاصول – صافي الذمة المالية
Net yield	rendement net	صافي العائد
Neutral money	monnaie neutre	نقد محايد
New class	nouvelle classe	طبقة جديدة
New combinations	combinaisons nouvelles	أساليب انتاجية جديدة – توليفات جديدة
New deal (U.S.A.)	New deal – "Nouvelle donne" (E.U.)	السياسة الجديدة (الولايات المتحدة)
New economic policy (USSR)	Nouvelle politique économique (URSS)	السياسة الاقتصادية الجديدة (الاتحاد السوفيتي)
New lines of production	productions nouvelles	فروع انتاج جديدة
No-growth economy	économie sans croissance	اقتصاد بلا نمو
No-load fund	fonds d'investissement sans frais d'acquisition	صندوق استثمار بلا مقدم
No-par value shares	actions sans valeur nominale	أسهم بلا قيمة إسمية

Nomadism	nomadisme	الرحل
Nomadic pastoralists	pasteurs nomades	رعاة رحل
Nomads	nomades	رحل – رحاحلة
Nominal charges	charges symboliques	اعباء رمزية – رسوم رمزية
Nominal exchange rate	taux de change nominal	سعر صرف اسمي
Nominal interest	intérêt nominal	فائدة اسمية
Nominal value	valeur nominale	قيمة اسمية
Nominal wage rate	taux du salaire nominal	معدل الأجر الاسمي
Non-cash debt issues	émissions sans contrepartie monétaire	اصدارات غير نقدية
Non-cash transactions	opérations non-monétaires	عمليات غير نقدية
Non-commercial risks	risques non-commerciaux	مخاطر غير تجارية
Non-competing groups	groupes non-concurrentiels	جماعات غير متنافسة
Non-competitive markets	marchés non-compétitifs	أسواق غير متنافسة
Non-concessional loan	prêt non-concessionel	قرض غير ميسر
Non-delivery	non-livraison	عدم التسليم
Non-development	non-développement	لا نمو
Non-discrimination	non-discrimination	لا تمييز – معاملة متكافئة
Non-discriminatory tariff preferences	préférences tarifaires non-discriminatoires	مزايا جمركية لا تمييزية
Non-discriminatory treatment	traitement non-discriminatoire	معاملة لا تمييزية – معاملة متكافئة
Non-durable goods	biens non-durables biens périssables	سلع غير معمرة
Non-equivalent exchange	échange inégal	تبادل غير متكافئ
Non-essential goods	articles non-essentiels	سلع غير أساسية
Non-factor services	services non-factoriels	خدمات غير العوامل
Non-farm rural sector	secteur rural non-agricole	القطاع الريفي غير الفلاحي القطاع الريفي غير الزراعي
Non-financial sector	secteur non-financier	قطاع غير مالي
Non-ferrous metal industry	industrie des métaux non-ferreux	صناعة المعادن غير الحديدية
Non-interest bearing securities	titres non-productifs d'intérêts	سندات بلا فوائد
Non-linear correlation	corrélation non-linéaire	ارتباط غير خطي
Non-linear regression	régression non-linéaire	ارتداد غير خطي
Non-manual worker	travailleur non-manuel	عامل غير يدوي
Non-marketable securities	valeurs non-négociables	سندات غير قابلة للتداول
Non-monetary income	revenu non-monétaire	دخل غير نقدي
Non-price competition	concurrence non-monétaire	منافسة غير سعرية
Non-profit organisation	organisme sans but lucratif	مؤسسة لا تجارية – مؤسسة غير هادفة للربح
Non-project aid	aide hors-projet	معونة غير مرتبطة بمشروع – مساعدة غير مرتبطة بمشروع
Non-proprietary technology	technologie non-privative	تكنولجية حرة –
Non-reciprocal tariff preferences	préférences tarifaires non-réciproques	مزايا جمركية غير متبادلة
Non-reciprocal treatment	traitement non-réciproque	معاملة غير متبادلة
Non-renewable resources	ressources non-renouvelables	موارد غير متجددة

Non-reproducible tangible wealth	richesse matérielle non reproductible	الثروة المادية غير المتجددة
Non-tariff barriers	barrières non-tarifaires	عوائق غير تعرفية
Non-traded goods	bien non-échangeables	سلع غير متبادلة – سلع لا تبادلة
Non-traditional exports	exportations non-conventionnelles	صادرات غير تقليدية
Non-user benefits	avantages aux non-usagers	منافع غير المستفيدين – منافع غير المتفعين
Non-user costs	coûts des non-usagers	تكاليف غير المتفعين
Normal curve	courbe normale	المنحنى السوى
Normal distribution	distribution normale	توزيع سوى
Normal price	prix normal	سعر عادي
Normal profit	profit normal	ربح عادي
Normative economics	économie normative	الاقتصاد الوصائي
Nostro account	compte *nostro*	حسابنا
Note	bon	اذن – سند
Note issue	émission de billets	اصدار اذون – اصدار اذونات – اصدار نقدي
Note issue (*central banking*)	émission fiduciaire (*banque centrale*)	الاصدار النقدي (بنك مركزي)
Notice	préavis – avis	انذار – اخطار – اعلان
Nuclear energy	énergie nucléaire	طاقة ذرية
Null hypothesis	hypothèse nulle	فرض العدم
Numbered accounts	comptes numérotés	حسابات مرقمة
Numeraire	numéraire	وحدة قياس – وحدة عد
Numismatics	numismatique	علم المسكوكات القديمة
Nuptiality rate	taux de nuptialité	معدل الزواج
Nutrients	éléments nutritifs	عناصر غذائية
Nutrition	nutrition	تغذية

Objective	objectif	هدف
Objective function	fonction-objectif fonction économique	دالة الهدف – دالة هدفية
Objective income	revenu objectif	دخل موضوعي – دخل فعلي
Obligations	obligations	التزامات
Obligations (*securities*)	obligations (*titres*)	سندات (أوراق مالية)
Observation period	période d'observation	فترة الملاحظة
Observed behaviour	comportement observé	سلوك ملاحظ – سلوك فعلي
Obsolescence	obsolescence désuétude	قدم – بلى – بلاء
Obsolescent technology	technologie surannée	فن انتاجي بال – تكنولجية بالية

Obsolete technology	technologie obsolète technologie désuète	تكنية بالية
Occupation	profession emploi	مهنة – عمل
Occupational disease	maladie professionnelle	مرض مهني
Occupational hazards	risques professionnels	مخاطر العمل
Occupational mobility	mobilité professionnelle	سيولة مهنية
Occupational structure	structure des professions – structure de l'emploi	هيكل التوظف – هيكل العمالة
Ocean floor	fonds sous-marins	قاع المحيطات – قاع البحار
Ocean freight	fret maritime	شحن بحري
Ocean resources	ressources maritimes	موارد البحار
Odd lot (securities)	petit paquet (de titres)	رزمة صغيرة (من الأوراق المالية)
Odd lot (trade)	solde (commerce)	بواقي (تجارة)
Off-balance-sheet financing	financement hors bilan	تمويل خارج الميزانية
Offer	offre	عرض
Offering of bonds	mise en vente d'obligations	عرض سندات
Offering price	prix offert	ثمن معروض – ثمن العرض
Official development assistance	aide publique au développement aide officielle au développement	معونات انمائية رسمية – مساعدات انمائية رسمية
Official holdings	avoirs officiels	أرصدة رسمية
Official rate of exchange	cours de change officiel	السعر الرسمي للصرف – سعر العملة الرسمي
Offset credit	crédit compensatoire	ائتمان موازن
Offset the losses, to	compenser les pertes	عوّض الخسائر
Offsetting book entries	entrées compensatrices	قيود مقابلة
Off-shore bank	banque extra-territoriale	بنك لا اقليمي – مصرف لا اقليمي
Off-shore financial centre	centre financier extra-territorial	مركز مالي لا أقليمي
Off-shore funds	fonds d'investissement extra- territoriaux	صناديق استثمار لا اقليمية
Off-shore production	production en zone maritime production off-shore	انتاج المنطقة البحرية
Oil and by-products	pétrole et dérivés	نفط ومشتقاته
Oil concession	concession pétrolière	امتياز نفطي
Oil conservation measures	mesures de conservation pétrolière	تدابير حفظ الموارد النفطية
Oil country	pays pétrolier	دولة نفطية
Oil crisis	crise du pétrole	ازمة النفط
Oil deposits	gisements de pétrole	رواسب نفطية
Oil embargo	embargo pétrolier	حظر تصدير النفط
Oil era	ère du pétrole	عهد النفط – عهد البترول
Oil exporting country	pays exportateur de pétrole	دولة مصدرة للنفط
Oil facility (IMF)	facilité pétrolière (FMI)	تسهيلات نفطية (صندوق النقد الدولي)
Oil fields	champs pétrolifères	حقول نفط – نفاطات
Oil pipeline	oléoduc – pipeline	بيب نفطي – خط أنابيب نفط

Oil producing country	pays producteur de pétrole	دولة منتجة للنفط
Oil production	production pétrolière	انتاج نفطي
Oil refinery	raffinerie de pétrole	معمل تكرير نفط
Oil revenues	revenus pétroliers	ايرادات نفطية
Oil-rich country	pays pétrolifère	دولة نفطية
Oil shortage	pénurie de pétrole	شح النفط – قصور النفط
Oil tanker	pétrolier	ناقلة نفط
Oil weapon	arme du pétrole	سلاح النفط
Oil wells	puits de pétrole	آبار نفط – آبار نفطية
Old-age allowances	prestations-vieillesse	اعانات الشيخوخة
Oligopologistic market	marché d'oligopole marché oligopolistique	سوق احتكار القلة (بيع)
Oligopoly	oligopole	احتكار القلة (بيع)
Oligopsony	oligopsone	احتكار القلة (شراء)
On-farm development	aménagement des exploitations- agricoles	تنمية المزارع – تنمية الاستغلالات الزراعية
On-lending	sous-prêt – sous-financement	اقراض مشتق – اقراض فرعي
On-the-job-training	formation sur le tas	تدريب عملي
One-crop economy	économie de monoculture	اقتصاد المحصول الواحد
Open account	compte courant compte ouvert	حساب جاري
Open cheque	chèque non barré	شيك غير مسطر
Open-door policy	politique de la porte ouverte	سياسة الباب المفتوح – سياسة الانفتاح
Open economy	économie ouverte	اقتصاد مفتوح
Open-end investment company	société d'investissement à capital variable (sicav)	شركة استثمار مفتوحة شركة استثمار ذات رسمال متغير
Open-end investment trust	fonds de placement à capital variable	مؤسسة استثمار مفتوحة مؤسسة استثمار ذات رسمال متغير
Open-market operations	opérations d'open market opérations de marché libre	عمليات السوق المفتوح
Open-market rate	taux du marché libre	سعر السوق الحر
Open order	ordre au mieux	أمر غير مقيد – أمر مفتوح
Open unemployment	chômage déclaré chômage manifeste	بطالة ظاهرة
Opening of bids	ouverture des plis	فتح العطاءات – فرز العروض
Opening prices	cours d'ouverture	أسعار الفتح
Operating account	compte d'exploitation	حساب استغلال – حساب تشغيل
Operating budget	budget d'exploitation budget de fonctionnement	موازنة الاستغلال – ميزانية التشغيل
Operating capital	capital d'exploitation	رسمال تشغيل -- رسمال متداول
Operating costs	coûts d'exploitation	تكاليف الاستغلال – تكاليف التشغيل
Operating deficit	déficit d'exploitation	عجز استغلال
Operating expenditures	dépenses d'exploitation	نفقات الاستغلال – نفقات التشغيل

Operating expenses	frais d'exploitation	
	dépenses de fonctionnement	
Operating period	période d'exploitation	فترة الاستغلال – فترة التشغيل
Operating principles	principes de gestion	مبادىء التسيير – مبادىء العمل
Operating profit	bénéfice d'exploitation	ربح الاستغلال – ربح التشغيل
Operating revenues	recettes d'exploitation	ايرادات الاستغلال – ايرادات التشغيل
Operational earnings		
Operating surplus	surplus d'exploitation	فائض الاستغلال – فائض التشغيل
Operation of a project	exploitation d'un projet	استغلال مشروع – تسيير مشروع
Operations evaluation	évaluation des opérations	تقييم العمليات
Operations research	recherche opérationnelle	دراسة العمليات
Opportunism	opportunisme	الانتهازية
Opportunity cost	coût de substitution	نفقة الخيار – كلفة بديلة
Opportunity investments	investissements d'opportunité	استثمارات الملاءمة
Optimal capital accumulation	accumulation optimale du capital	التراكم الأمثل للرسمال
Optimal choice	choix optimum	الخيار الأمثل
Optimal decision	décision optimale	القرار الأمثل
Optimal depletion rate	taux d'épuisement optimal	المعدل الأمثل للاستنفاد
Optimal location	implantation optimale	الموقع الأمثل – التوطين الأمثل
Optimal programme	programme optimal	البرنامج الأمثل
Optimal resource allocation	répartition optimale des ressources	التخصيص الأمثل للموارد
Optimal solution	solution optimale	الحل الأمثل
Optimal tariff	tarif optimal	التعرفة المثلى
Optimum tariff		
Optimal taxation	imposition optimale	ضريبة مثلى – فرض الضريبة المثلى
Optimality	optimalité	أمثلية
Optimisation	optimisation	إمثال
Optimisation model	modèle d'optimisation	نموذج – إمثال
Optimising model		
Optimise, to	optimiser	أمثل
Optimum	optimum	الحد الأمثل – الأمثل
Optimum growth	croissance optimale	النمو الأمثل
Optimal growth		
Optimum population level	niveau optimum de la population	المستوى الأمثل للسكان
Optimum price	prix optimal	السعر الأمثل – الثمن الأمثل
Optimum production programme	programme de production optimal	البرنامج الأمثل للانتاج
		برنامج الانتاج الأمثل
Optimum rate of population growth	taux optimum d'accroissement de la population	المعدل الأمثل لزيادة السكان
Optimum scale	dimension optimale	الحجم الأمثل
Optimum size	dimension optimale – taille optimale	الحجم الأمثل
Optimum use	utilisation optimale	الاستخدام الأمثل
Option	option – prime	حق خيار – خيار – علاوة

Option money	acompte – prime	عربون – علاوة
Option value	valeur d'option	قيمة الخيار
Optional currency loan	prêt à option de change	قرض بخيار الصرف
Optional redemption clause	clause de remboursement anticipé	نص خيار السداد
Ordinal utility	utilité ordinale	منفعة صفية – منفعة رتبية
Ordinary budget	budget général – budget ordinaire	موازنة عادية – ميزانية عادية
Ordinary shares	actions ordinaires	أسهم عادية
Organic composition of capital	composition organique du capital	التركيب العضوي للرسمال
Organic fertilizers	engrais organiques	سماد عضوي – أسمدة عضوية
Organization chart	organigramme	هيكل تنظيمي – مخطط تنظيمي
Organization of industrial zones	organisation des zones industrielles	تنظيم المناطق الصناعية
Organization of production	organisation de la production	تنظيم الانتاج
Organizational framework of planning	organisation de la planification	الاطار التنظيمي للتخطيط
Organized labour	syndicats ouvriers	المنظمات العمالية
Original cost	coût original	تكلفة أصلية – نفقة أصلية
Original securities	titres originaux	صكوك أصلية – سندات أصلية
Orthodox economics	pensée économique orthodoxe	الفكر الاقتصادي السائد
Oscillation	fluctuation	تقلب – تذبذب – رقص
	oscillation	
Oscillator	oscillateur	رقيص
Oscillatory model	modèle oscillatoire	نموذج رقصي – نموذج تذبذبي
Outbid, to	surenchérir	زايد – زاد
Outbidding	surenchère	مزايدة
Outflow of capital	sortie de capitaux	تصدير الرسمال – خروج الرسمال
Outlays	dépenses	انفاق – نفقات
	mises de fonds	
	débours	
Outlets	débouchés	أسواق تصريف
Out-migration	émigration	هجرة – هجرة الى الخارج
Out-of-pocket expenses	menus frais	نفقات نثرية – مصاريف نثرية
Output	production	انتاج
Output capacity	capacité de production	طاقة الانتاج
Output per man-hour	production par heure de travail	الانتاج لساعة العمل
		الانتاج للساعة من العمل
Outright gift	don pur et simple	منحة خالصة – نحلان – هبة خالصة
Outstanding amount	encours	المبلغ القائم
Outstanding bonds	obligations en circulation	سندات متداولة – سندات قائمة
Outstanding claim	créance à recouvrer	حق قائم
Outstanding debt	encours de la dette	دين قائم – رصيد المديونية
Outstanding external debt	encours de la dette extérieure	الدين الخارجي القائم
		رصيد الدين الخارجي
Outstanding interest	intérêts échus	فوائد مستحقة
Outstanding taxes	arriérés d'impôts – impôts dus	متأخر ضرائب – ضرائب غير مسددة

Overall aid	aide globale	اجمالي المعونات – اجمالي المساعدات
Overall deficit	déficit global	عجز اجمالي – اجمالي العجز
Overall demand	demande globale	طلب اجمالي – اجمالي الطلب
Overall development	développement global	نمو شامل – انماء شامل
Overall economy	économie globale	اجمالي الاقتصاد القومي
Overall growth	croissance globale	نمو شامل
	croissance générale	
Overall planning	planification globale	تخطيط شامل – تخطيط كلي
Over-allotment	sur-attribution	تخصيص مفرط – زيادة التخصيص
Over-commitment risk	risque de surengagement	خطر الافراط في الالتزام
Overbid, to	surenchérir	زايد
Overbidding	surenchère	مزايدة
Over-development	surdéveloppement	نمو مفرط – افراط النمو
Overdraft	découvert – avance	سلفية – سلفة
Overdraft facility	avance – facilité de caisse	سلفية – تسهيلات ائتمانية
Overdrawn account	compte découvert	حساب منكشف – حساب مكشوف
Overdue	échu – en souffrance	مستحق
Overdue payment	paiement échu	دفع مستحق – دين حال
Overemployment	suremploi	افراط العمالة – عمالة مفرطة
Over-estimate, to	surestimer	غالى في
Over-estimation	surestimation	تقدير مغالى
Over-exploitation of resources	surexploitation des ressources	انجاع الموارد – افراط استغلال الموارد
Overhead capital	investissement d'infrastructure	رسمال ثابت
Overhead costs	frais généraux	نفقات ثابتة – تكاليف عامة
Overhead expenses		
Overhead price	prix forfaitaire	ثمن اجمالي – ثمن جزافي
Overheating of the economy	surchauffe de l'économie	فورة النشاط الاقتصادي
Overindebtedness	surendettement	افراط المديونية
Overinvestment	surinvestissement	افراط الاستثمار
Overinvoicing	surfacturation	مغالاة في الفوترة – مغالاة في الحسبنة
		افراط الفيترة – افراط الحسبنة
Overissue	surémission	افراط الاصدار
Overpopulation	surpeuplement	ازدحام سكاني – ضغط سكاني
	surpopulation	
Overproduction	surproduction	افراط الانتاج
Oversaving	excès d'épargne – surépargne	افراط الادخار
Overseas countries	pays d'outre-mer	دول ما وراء البحار
Overseas sector	secteur extérieur	القطاع الخارجي
Overseas trade	commerce d'outre-mer	تجارة ما وراء البحار – تجارة خارجية
Overseer	contremaître	وهين
Over-selling	survente	بيع مفرط – افراط البيع
Overspecification of a model	surspécification d'un modèle	الافراط في تحديد النموذج
Over-the-counter market	marché hors-cote	السوق غير الرسمي – سوق خارج البورصة
	marché hors-bourse	

Overtime	heures supplémentaires	ساعات اضافية
Overevaluation	surestimation	افراط في التقدير – مغالاة في التقييم
Overvalued currency	monnaie surévaluée	عملة مغالى في سعرها عملة غالية
Own capital	capital propre	رسمال ذاتي
Own resources	fonds propres	موارد ذاتية
Ownership	droit de propriété	حق ملكية – ملكية
	propriété	

Package deal	transaction globale	اتفاق اجمالي – صفقة اجمالية
	accord d'ensemble	
Packaging	emballage	تعبئة – ادراج
Packaging industry	industrie d'emballage	صناعة التعبئة – صناعة الادراج
Packaging costs	frais d'emballage	تكاليف التعبئة – تكاليف الادراج
Packing costs		
Paid-in capital	capital versé	رسمال مدفوع
Paid-up capital	capital libéré	
Paid-up shares	actions libérées	أسهم مسددة
Paired observations	observations couplées	مشاهدات متزاوجة
Paper and paper board industry	industrie du papier et du carton	صناعة الورق والورق المقوى
Paper currency	papier-monnaie	عملة ورقية – نقد ورقي
Paper money	monnaie de papier	
Paper gold	papier-or	ذهب ورقي
Paper profits	profits fictifs	أرباح وهمية – أرباح على الورق
Paper standard (money)	étalon-papier (monnaie)	قاعدة النقد الورقية
par, at	au pair	عند سعر التعادل – بالقيمة الاسمية
		بسعر التعادل
par value (currency)	parité – paire (monnaie)	سعر التبادل (عملة)
Par value (securities)	pair (titres) – valeur nominale	قيمة اسمية (أوراق مالية)
Par-value system	système des parités	نظام أسعار التعادل
Paradox of thrift	paradoxe de l'épargne	تناقض الادخار
Paradox of value	paradoxe de la valeur	تناقض القيمة
Parallel finance	financement parallèle	تمويل موازي
Parallel market	marché parallèle	سوق موازية
Parameter	paramètre	ضابط – معامل
Parameter programming	programmation paramétrique	برمجة ضوابطية
Para-public institution	organisation para-publique	هيئة شبه حكومية

Para-statal body	organisme para-public	جهاز شبه حكومي
Para-tariff barriers	barrières para-tarifaires	عوائق شبه تعرفية – حواجز شبه جمركية
Parent company	société-mère	شركة أم – شركة أصلية
Parity	parité – pair	تعادل
Parity price	prix paritaire	سعر التعادل – ثمن التعادل
Partial correlation	corrélation partielle	ارتباط جزئي
Part-time employment	emploi à temps partiel	عمل جزئي – عمل غير متفرغ
Partial equilibrium	équilibre partiel	توازن جزئي
Partial guarantee	garantie partielle	ضمان جزئي – كفالة جزئية
Participating bonds	obligations participantes	سندات مشاركة
Participating countries	pays participants	دول مشاركة
Participating preference shares	actions privilégiées à participation	أسهم امتياز مشاركة
Participation	participation	مشاركة – مساهمة
Participation agreement	accord de participation	اتفاق مشاركة – اتفاقية مشاركة
Participation loan	prêt syndiqué	قرض حلقي
Partner	associé	شريك
Partnership	association	شراكة – مشاركة
Passenger-kilometer	kilomètre-passagers kilomètre-voyageur	كيلومتر/مسافر
Passenger traffic	trafic des passagers	نقل المسافرين
Passive debt	dette passive – dette dormante	دين عقيم – دين عاطل
Pastoral economy	économie pastorale	اقتصاد رعي
Pastoral stage	étape pastorale	مرحلة الرعي
Pasture-lands	pâturages	مراعي
Patent	brevet – patente	براءة اختراع
Patent holder	titulaire du brevet	صاحب براءة الاختراع
Patent office	bureau de brevets	مكتب براءات الاختراع
Patentability	brevetabilité	صلاحية التسجيل (براءات الاختراع)
Patented invention	invention brevetée	اختراع مسجل
Pater familias investments	investissements de père de famille	استثمارات رب اسرة – استثمارات آمنة
Paternalism	paternalisme	اباوة
Path of development	voie de développement	سبيل التنمية – مسار التنمية
Pattern of consumption	structure de la consommation	نمط الاستهلاك
Pattern of industrial output	composition de la production industrielle	نمط الانتاج الصناعي
Pattern of investment	structure de l'investissement	نمط الاستثمار – هيكل الاستثمار
Pattern of migration	structure de la migration	نمط الهجرة
Pattern of production	structure de la production	نمط الانتاج
Pattern of spending	structure des dépenses	نمط الانفاق
Pattern of taxation	structure de la fiscalité	النمط الضريبي
Pattern of trade	structure des échanges	نمط التجارة – هيكل التجارة
Pauperisation	paupérisation	افقار – املاق
Pauperism	paupérisme	فقر – عوز – ملق

Pawnbroker	prêteur sur gage	مقرض برهونات – مرابي رهونات
Pawned bills	effets en pension	اذون مرهونة – سندات مرتهنة
Pawnshop	établissement de prêts sur gage	محل رهونات – دار رهن
	mont-de-piété	
Pay	salaire	اجر
Pay, to	payer	دفع
Pay-as-you-earn (*taxes*)	retenu à la source (*impôts*)	حجز عند المنبع (ضرائب)
Pay-back period	période d'amortissement	فترة الاسترداد – فترة الاستهلاك
	période de récupération	
Pay cash, to	régler en espèces	دفع نقداً
Pay-day	jour de paie	يوم القبض
Pay off a debt, to	s'acquitter d'une dette	سدد دينا – قضى دينا
	rembourser une dette	
Pay-off period	période d'amortissement	فترة السداد – فترة الوفاء
Pay scale	barème des salaires	جدول الاجور – سلم الاجور
Payables	sommes dues	مبالغ مستحقة الدفع
Payable at sight	payable à vue	قابل للدفع عند الطلب – معجل
Payable on demand		
Payable-receivable basis	base des sommes dues	أساس مستحقات الدفع والتحصيل
	et perçues	
Payee	bénéficiaire	مستفيد
Payer	payeur	دافع
Paying agent	agent payeur	وكيل دفع – وكيل مالي
	agent financier	
	agent assurant le service financier	
Paying capacity	capacité de paiement	قدرة على الدفع
Payment	paiement	دفع
Payments agreement	accord de paiements	اتفاق دفع – اتفاق مدفوعات
Payment arrears	arriérés de paiement	متأخرات الدفع
Payments basis, on	sur base-paiements	على أساس المدفوعات
Payment in kind	paiement en nature	دفع عيني – الدفع عينا
Payment media	moyens de paiement	وسائل الدفع
Payment on account	acompte	دفع تحت الحساب – عربون
Payment order	ordre de paiment	أمر دفع
	ordonnancement	
Payment terms	conditions de paiement	شروط الدفع
Payment union	union de paiement	اتحاد مدفوعات – اتحاد دفع
Payoff	rendement	عائد – أربحية
	rentabilité	
Payroll	feuille de paye	قائمة الاجور – مجموع الاجور
	masse des salaires	
Payroll tax	impôt sur les salaires	ضريبة الاجور
Peaceful co-existence	co-existence pacifique	تعايش سلمي

Peak	point maximal	ذروة – حد أقصى – قمة
	pointe	
	pic	
	sommet	
Peaks and troughs	sommets et creux	القمم والحضض
Peak hours	heures de pointe	ساعات الذروة
Peak load	charge maximale	الحمل الأقصى – حمل الذروة
	charge de pointe	
Peasant	paysan	فلاح – مزارع
Peasant-proprietor	paysan-propriétaire	فلاح مالك – مزارع مالك
Peasantry	paysannerie	طبقة الفلاحين – الفلاحون
Pecuniary difficulties	embarras financiers	عقبات مالية – صعوبات مالية
Pecuniary economies	épargnes monétaires	مدخرات نقدية
Pecuniary gain	gain lucratif	ربح مجزي – ربح مادي
	gain pécuniaire	
Peddler	colporteur	بائع متجول
	marchand ambulant	
Pedology	pédologie	علم التربة
Peg the currency, to	rattacher la monnaie à ...	ربط العملة بـ – ثبّت العملة
	stabiliser le change	
Pegged price	prix de soutien	سعر مثبت – سعر مؤشر – ثمن مثبت
	prix indexé	
Pegged rate	taux bloqué	سعر محدد – سعر مثبت
	taux stabilisé	
Pegging of the exchange rate	stabilisation du cours du change	تثبيت سعر الصرف
Penalty clause	clause pénale	شرط جزائي
	clause de pénalité	
Penalty interest	intérêts de retard	فوائد تأخير
	intérêts moratoires	
Penalty money	dédit – indemnité	مبلغ جزائي – تعويض الفسخ
Pension fund	caisse de retraite	صندوق معاشات – صندوق تقاعد
	fonds de retraite	
Pension scheme	régime des retraites	نظام معاشات – نظام تقاعد
Pent-up demand	demande refoulée	طلب مكبوت – طلب كامن
	demande latente	
Pent-up inflation	inflation refoulée	تضخم مكبوت – تضخم كامن
	inflation latente	
Penury	disette – pénurie	شح – نقصان – عوز
Per capita	per capita	للفرد الواحد – للفرد
	par tête	
	par habitant	
Per capita consumption	consommation par habitant	متوسط الاستهلاك – استهلاك الفرد
	consommation moyenne	إستهلاك فردي

Per capita income	revenu per capita	متوسط الدخل – دخل الفرد
	revenu par habitant	دخل فردي
	revenu moyen	
Percentage distribution	ventilation en pourcentages	توزيع مئوي
Perennial irrigation	irrigation permanente	ري دائم
Perfect competition	concurrence parfaite	منافسة كاملة
Perfect market	marché parfait	سوق كامل
Perfect substitute	substitut parfait	بديل كامل
Performance	performance – rendement – exécution	اداء – انجاز
Performance assessment	évaluation de performance	تقدير الاداء – تقييم الاداء
Performance auditing	vérification de la conduite du projet	تدقيق اداء المشروع – تدقيق انجاز المشروع
Performance bond	caution de bonne fin	ضمان الاداء – ضمان الاتمام
	garantie de bonne fin	
Performance budget	budget fonctionnel	موازنة اداء – ميزانية اداء
	budget de performance	
Performance criteria	critères de performance	معايير اداء – مقاييس اداء
Performance fee	bonus de rendement – bonus de performance	مكافأة اداء
Performance guarantee	garantie de bonne fin	ضمان الانجاز
Performance indicator	indice de performance	مؤشر اداء
Performance standards	normes d'exécution – normes de performance	انماط الاداء – انماط الانجاز
Period analysis	analyse séquentielle	تحليل زمني – تحليل حقبي
	analyse par périodes	
Period of non-negotiability	délai de blocage	فترة عدم التداول
Period of production	période de production	فترة الانتاج
Period of stagnation	période de stagnation	فترة ركود
Periodical	périodique	دوري
Periodogram	périodographe	رسم زمني – رسم محقب
	périodogramme	
Peripheric capitalism	capitalisme périphérique	رسمالية ديرية – رسمالية هامشية
Peripheric technology	technologie marginale – technologie complémentaire	تكنولجية هامشية
Periphery	périphérie	هامش – محيط – دائرة
Perishable goods	denrées périssables	سلع هالكة – سلع قابلة للهلاك سلع غير معمرة
Permanent emergency	état d'urgence permanente	حالة طوارىء دائمة
Permanent income hypothesis	hypothèse du revenu permanent	فرض الدخل الدائم
Permanent irrigation	irrigation permanente	ري دائم
Permanent revolution	révolution permanente	الثورة الدائمة – الثورة المتواصلة
Perpetual bond	obligation perpétuelle	سند دائم – سند بلا أجل
Personal accounts	comptes personnels	حسابات شخصية – حسابات فردية
	comptes privés	

Personal consumption	consommation privée	استهلاك خاص
Personal credit	crédit personnel	ائتمان شخصي
Personal finance	finances privées	مالية خاصة – مالية الافراد
Personal income	revenu privé	دخل شخصي – دخل خاص
	revenu personnel	دخل فردي
Personal loan	prêt individuel – prêt personnel	قرض شخصي – قرض فردي
Personal property	propriété mobilière	ملكية المنقولات
Personnel	personnel	جهاز العاملين
Personnel management	gestion du personnel	ادارة شئون العاملين
Perspectives of growth	perspectives de la croissance	طالع النمو – احتمالات النمو
		توقعات النمو
"pert" system	système "pert"	اسلوب تقييم ومتابعة البرامج
	système d'évaluation des programmes	اسلوب «برت»
Perverse growth	croissance perverse	نمو محبط – نمو احباطي
Pest control	lutte contre les parasites	مكافحة الحشرات – مكافحة الآفات
Pesticides industry	industrie des produits pesticides	صناعة منتجات مكافحة الآفات
		صناعة منتجات مكافحة الحشرات
Petro-chemical industry	industrie pétro-chimique	صناعة بتروكيماوية
Petro-dollars	pétro-dollars	دولارات نفطية – دولارات النفط
Petro-funds	fonds pétroliers	أموال نفطية – أموال النفط
Petty expenses	menus frais	نفقات نثرية
Pharmaceutical industry	industrie pharmaceutique	صناعة الأدوية
Phase over time, to	échelonner	قسّط
Phasing	échelonnement	تقسيط – تعقيب – توزيع زمني
Physical capital	capital matériel	رسمال مادي
Physical infrastructure	infrastructure matérielle	البنية الأساسية المادية
Physical planning	planification matérielle	تخطيط مادي
Physiocracy	physiocratie	مدرسة الطبيعيين
Physiocrats	physiocrates	الطبيعيون
Picket (*strike*)	piquet de grève	حارس الاضراب
Piece-cost	coût unitaire	تكلفة الوحدة
Piece-wage	salaire à la pièce	أجر بالقطعة – أجر قطعي
Piece-work	travail à la pièce	عمل بالقطعة – عمل قطعي
Pier dues	droits de quai	رسوم رصيفية – رسوم رصيف
Pilot experience	expérience pilote	تجربة نموذجية – تجربة رائدة
Pilot farm	ferme pilote	مزرعة نموذجية
Pilot plant	usine pilote	مصنع نموذجي – مصنع تجريبي
Pilot project	projet pilote	مشروع تجريبي – مشروع نموذجي
Pioneer	pionnier	رائد
Pipeline	pipe-line	بيب – خط أنابيب
Pipeline of projects	portefeuille de projets	حافظة مشاريع
Placement service	service de placement	مكتب تخديم – مكتب تشغيل
Placing **Placement**	placement	توظيف (أموال)

Placing of an issue	placement d'une émission	تصريف اصدار – توزيع اصدار
Placing power	capacité de placement – capacité de vente	طاقة التوظيف – طاقة التوزيع – طاقة التصريف
Plan	plan	خطة
Plan, to	planifier	خطّط
Plan control	contrôle du plan	رقابة الخطة – متابعة الخطة
Plan coordination	coordination du plan	تنسيق الخطة
Plan directives	directives du plan	ارشادات الخطة – توجيهات الخطة
Plan formulation	élaboration du plan	صياغة الخطة – وضع الخطة
Plan frame	cadre du plan	اطار الخطة
Plan fulfillment	achèvement du plan	انجاز الخطة
Plan implementation	exécution du plan	تنفيذ الخطة
Plan of action	plan d'action	خطة عمل
Plan of operations	plan d'action programme des opérations	خطة عمل – برنامج العمل
Plan projects	projets du plan	مشاريع الخطة
Plan targets	objectifs du plan	أهداف الخطة – مستهدفات الخطة
Planned economy	économie planifiée	اقتصاد مخطط
Planned production	production planifiée	انتاج مخطط
Planned production targets	objectifs du plan de production	أهداف خطة الانتاج – أهداف انتاجية مخططة
Planner	planificateur	مخطط
Planning activity	activité planificative	نشاط تخطيطي
Planning agency	organisme de la planification	جهاز تخطيط
Planning authority Planning board	conseil du plan	مجلس تخطيط – هيئة تخطيط
Planning commission	commission de planification	لجنة تخطيط
Planning committee	comité de planification	لجنة تخطيط
Planning department	service du plan	دائرة التخطيط
Planning experiences	expériences de planification	تجارب التخطيط
Planning from the top	planification en partant du sommet	تخطيط من القمة – تخطيط من أعلى
Planning horizon	horizon de planification	افق التخطيط
Planning institute	institut de planification	معهد تخطيط
Planning methods	méthodes de planification	أساليب التخطيط – مناهج التخطيط
Planning models	modèles de planification	نماذج تخطيط
Planning objectives	objectifs du plan – objectifs de la planification	أهداف التخطيط
Planning of development aid	planification de l'aide au développement	تخطيط المعونات الانمائية تخطيط المساعدات الانمائية
Planning organization	organisme de planification	جهاز تخطيط
Planning process	processus de la planification	مجرى التخطيط
Planning, programming and budgeting system (PPBS)	système de rationalisation des choix budgétaires	منهج ترشيد الانفاق العام

Planning research	recherches de planification	أبحاث تخطيطية – دراسات تخطيطية
	recherches sur la planification	
Planning system	système de planification	نظام تخطيط
Planning targets	objectifs du plan	أهداف الخطة
Planning techniques	techniques de planification	أساليب التخطيط
Planning unit	unité de planification	وحدة تخطيط
Plant	usine	مصنع – أجهزة – منشآت – معدات
	gros équipement	
	installations	
Plant location	emplacement de l'usine	موقع المنشأة – موقع المصنع
Plantation	plantation	ضيعة – مزرعة
Plastics industry	industrie des matières plastiques	صناعة اللدائن
Pledge	gage	رهن – التزام – تعهد
	engagement	
Pledge value	valeur de gage	قيمة رهنية
Pledging	engagement – nantissement	تعهد – رهن
Pledging of securities	nantissement de titres	رهن أوراق مالية
Plethora of money	pléthore d'argent	وفرة النقد – فيضة النقود
Plot consolidation	remembrement des parcelles	دمج الحيازات – تجميع الحيازات
Plough back profits, to	réinvestir les bénéfices	اعاد استثمار الأرباح
Plow back profits, to		
Ploughed-back profits	bénéfices réinvestis	أرباح معاد استثمارها
Plowed-back profits		
Plural society	société multi-raciale	مجتمع متعدد الأجناس
Plutocracy	ploutocratie	حكم الأثرياء
Point elasticity	élasticité ponctuelle	مرونة نقطية
Point estimation	estimation ponctuelle	تقدير نقطي
Point prediction	prévision ponctuelle	تنبؤ نقطي – توقع نقطي
Pole of development	pôle de croissance	قطب انمائي – قطب تنمية
Policy makers	décisionnaires	واضعو السياسة – أصحاب البت
Policy package	ensemble de principes d'action	مجموعة تدابير – مجموعة اجراءات – سياسة اجمالية
Policy statement	déclaration de principes	اعلان مبادىء
Political economy	économie politique	الاقتصاد السياسي
Political risks	risques politiques	مخاطر سياسية
Political strike	grève politique	اضراب سياسي
Poll tax	impôt personnel	فردة – ضريبة الأشخاص
	impôt de capitation	
Pollutant	polluant	ملوث
Pollution	pollution	تلوث – تلويث
Pollution control	lutte anti-pollution	مكافحة التلوث
	lutte contre la pollution	
Pool of money	pool monétaire	مجمع نقود
Pooled samples	échantillons groupés	عينات مجمعة

Pooling of reserves	mise en commun des réserves	تجميع الأرصدة
Poor man's goods	biens inférieurs – biens pauvres	سلع فقيرة–سلع الفقراء
Popular consumption criterion	critère de la consommation populaire	معيار الاستهلاك الشعبي
Population	population	سكان – أهالي
Population ageing	vieillissement de la population	تكهل السكان
Population census	recensement démographique	تعداد سكاني – احصاء سكاني
Population explosion	explosion démographique	انفجار سكاني
Population growth	croissance démographique	نمو سكاني
Population planning	planification démographique	تخطيط سكاني
Population policy	politique démographique	سياسة سكانية
Population pressure	pression démographique	ضغط سكاني
Population statistics	statistiques démographiques	احصاءات سكانية – بيانات سكانية
Population trap	piège démographique	الفخ السكاني
Population trends	tendances démographiques	اتجاهات سكانية
Populism	populisme	الشعبية
Port dues	droits portuaires	رسوم الميناء–رسوم مرفئية
Port infrastructure	infrastructure portuaire	بنية مرفئية
Port installations	installations portuaires	منشآت الميناء – منشآت مرفئية
Port management	exploitation des ports	ادارة المواني
Portfolio	portefeuille-titres	حافظة أوراق مالية – حافظة مالية
Portfolio analysis	analyse de portefeuille	تحليل الحوافظ المالية
Portfolio diversification	diversification de portefeuille	تنويع الحافظة
Portfolio efficiency	efficacité du portefeuille rentabilité du portefeuille	فاعلية الحافظة–أربحية الحافظة
Portfolio investment	placements de portefeuille investissements de portefeuille	استثمارات الحافظة
Portfolio management	gestion de portefeuille	ادارة الحافظة المالية ادارة الحوافظ المالية
Portfolio securities	valeurs de portefeuille	سندات الحافظة – صكوك الحافظة
Portfolio selection	choix du portefeuille	اختيار عناصر الحافظة – اختيار الحافظة
Positive correlation	corrélation positive	ارتباط موجب
Positive economics	économie positive	الاقتصاد الوضعي
Possession	possession	حيازة – امتلاك
Possibilities of substitution	possibilités de substitution	امكانيات الاستبدال
Post-auditing	post-vérification vérification à *posteriori*	تدقيق لاحق
Post-dated check	chèque postdaté	شيك بتاريخ لاحق
Post-evaluation	évaluation à *posteriori*	تقييم لاحق
Post-industrial society	société post-industrielle	مجتمع ما بعد الصناعة – مجتمع بعد الصناعة مجتمع بعد صناعي
Post-keynesian economics	économie post-keynésienne	علم الاقتصاد بعد كينز
Post-oil era	ère de l'après-pétrole	عهد بعد البترول

Postqualification of bidders	vérification ultérieure des offres	التوصيف اللاحق للعطاءات
	post-vérification des offres	
Postal cheque	mandat-virement – chèque postal	حوالة بريدية – شيك بريدي
Postal savings bank	caisse d'épargne postale	صندوق ادخار البريد
Postal service	service postal	البريد
Posted price	prix affiché	سعر معلن – سعر اسناد
	prix posté	
	prix de référence	
Postulated behaviour	attitude supposée	سلوك مفترض – سلوك ظني
	attitude postulée	
Potential customers	clientèle potentielle	عملاء محتملون
	clients potentiels	
Potential demand	demande potentielle	طلب محتمل
Potential growth	croissance potentielle	نمو متاح – نمو ممكن
Poultry farming	élevage de volaille	تربية الدواجن
	aviculture	
Poverty	pauvreté	فقر
Poverty amidst plenty	misère au sein de l'abondance	فقر وسط الثراء
Poverty criteria	critères de la pauvreté	معايير الفقر
Poverty line	seuil de pauvreté	حد الفقر – عتبة الفقر
Power development	développement de l'énergie	تنمية الطاقة
Power generation	production d'énergie	انتاج الطاقة – توليد الطاقة
Power production		
Power plant	station électrique	محطة كهربائية
Power resources	ressources énergétiques	موارد الطاقة
Power supply	disponibilités énergétiques	الطاقة المتوفرة – الطاقة المتاحة
Pre-capitalist economy	économie pré-capitaliste	اقتصاد سابق على الرسمالية
		اقتصاد قبل الرسمالية
Precautionary motive	motif de sécurité	دافع الحيطة
Precious metals	métaux précieux	معادن نفيسة
Precision instruments	instruments de précision	آلات دقيقة
Predetermined variables	variables prédéterminées	متغيرات سابقة التحديد
Prediction	prévision	ابشار – تنبؤ – توقع
Prediction period	période de prévision	فترة الابشار – فترة التنبؤ – فترة التوقع
Predictive test	test de prévision	اختبار الابشار – اختبار التنبؤ
Pre-fabricated buildings	bâtiments préfabriqués	مباني جاهزة
Prefeasibility study	étude de préfaisabilité	دراسة تمهيدية – دراسة استطلاعية
	étude de préfactibilité	
Preference bonds	obligations privilégiées	سندات امتياز
Preference margin	marge de préférence	هامش تفضيل – هامش تمييز
Preferential margin	marge préférentielle	
Preference scheme	système de préférence	نظام تفضيل – نظام تمييز
Preference system		

Preference shares	actions privilégiées	أسهم امتياز
Preferred shares		
Preferential advantage	avantage préférentiel	ميزة تفضيلية
Preferential duties	droits préférentiels	رسوم تمييزية – رسوم تفضيلية
Preferential rate	taux préférentiel	معدل تمييزي – سعر تمييزي
		معدل تفضيلي
Preferential tariff	tarif préférentiel	تعرفة تفضيلية – تعرفة تمييزية
Preferential treatment	traitement privilégié – traitement de	معاملة تفضيلية – معاملة تمييزية
	faveur	
	traitement préférentiel	
Preferred bonds	obligations privilégiées	سندات امتياز
Preferred operating rate	taux d'exploitation préféré	معدل الاستغلال المفضل
		معدل التشغيل المفضل
Prefinancing	préfinancement	تمويل مسبق
Pre-industrial society	société pré-industrielle	مجتمع ما قبل الصناعة – مجتمع قبل الصناعة
		مجتمع قبل صناعي
Preinvestment aid	aide au préinvestissement	معونة لمشاريع استطلاعية
Preinvestment study	étude de préinvestissement	دراسة استطلاعية – دراسة سابقة على الاستثمار
Preliminary design	avant-projet	تصميم أولي – تصميم مبدئي
Preliminary prospectus	prospectus provisoire	نشرة مبدئية – نشرة اصدار مبدئية
	prospectus préliminaire	
Preliminary survey	enquête préliminaire	مسح مبدئي
Premium	prime	علاوة – جائزة
Premium on an issue	prime d'émission	علاوة اصدار
Premium saving bond	bon d'épargne à prime	سند ادخار بجائزة
Pre-oil era	ère de l'avant-pétrole	عهد قبل النفط
Prepaid expenses	frais payés d'avance	نفقات مسبقة الدفع
Preparation of projects	préparation des projets	اعداد المشاريع
Preparation of the budget	préparation du budget	اعداد الموازنة – اعداد الميزانية
Prepayment	paiement anticipé	دفع مسبق
Pre-project	avant-projet	مشروع أولي – مشروع مبدئي
Prequalification of bidders	présélection des soumissionnaires	التوصيف المسبق للمناقصين
Present value	valeur actuelle	قيمة راهنة – قيمة مستحطة
Present worth	valeur actualisée	
Preservation-of-source criterion	critère du maintien de la source	معيار بقاء المصدر
Pressure group	groupe de pression	مركز قوة – فئة ضغط
Pressure of demand	pression de la demande	ضغط الطلب
Prestige project	projet de prestige	مشروع ارائي – مشروع دعائي
Prevailing market rate	cours du marché – taux courant	السعر الجاري – سعر السوق
Prevailing price	prix courant – prix du marché	الثمن الجاري – السعر السائد
Prevision	prévision	توقع – ابشار – تنبؤ
Price	prix	سعر – ثمن
Price adjustment	ajustement du prix	تعديل السعر – تغيير الثمن
	changement du prix	

Price asked	prix demandé	السعر المطلوب – الثمن المطلوب
Price behaviour	comportement des prix	اتجاه الأسعار – اتجاه الأثمان
Price bid	cours acheteur	سعر الشراء
Price boom	boom des prix – hausse des prix	ارتفاع الأسعار – غلاء الأثمان
Price cartel	cartel de prix	كارتل أسعار –كارتل أثمان
Price consistency	cohérence des prix	توافق الأسعار – تناسق الأثمان
Price control	contrôle des prix	رقابة الأسعار
Price cutting	réduction des prix	خفض الأسعار – خفض الأثمان
	baisse des prix	تخفيض الأثمان
Price decontrol	libération des prix	تحرير الأسعار – تحرير الأثمان
	déblocage des prix	
Price determination	formation des prix	تكوين الأسعار – تكوين الأثمان
Price formation		
Price differentials	écarts de prix	فروق الأسعار – فروق الأثمان
Price discrimination	discrimination dans les prix	تمييز في الأسعار – تمييز في الأثمان
Price dispersion	dispersion des prix	تشتت الأسعار – تشتت الأثمان
Price distortions	distortions dans la structure des prix	ضلع هيكل الأسعار
		أعوجاج هيكل الأثمان
Price-earnings ratio	coefficient de capitalisation	معامل رسملة الأرباح
	rapport cours-bénéfices	نسبة السعر إلى الأرباح
Price effect	effet de prix	أثر الثمن
Price elasticity	élasticité-prix	مرونة سعرية
Price escalation clause	clause de révision des prix	شرط تعديل الأثمان
Price ex-factory	prix-départ usine	السعر عند المصنع – الثمن عند المصنع
Price fixing	taxation des prix	تحديد الأسعار – تحديد الأثمان
Price followers	suiveurs de prix	تبع الثمن –تبع التسعير
Price forecasts	prévisions des prix	توقعات الأسعار – توقعات الأثمان
Price formula	formule de prix	صيغة التسعير – صيغة التثمين
Price freeze	blocage des prix	تجميد الأسعار – تجميد الأثمان
Price index	indice des prix	رقم قياسي للأسعار – مؤشر الأسعار
Price inflation	inflation des prix	تضخم الأسعار
Price leadership	maîtrise de prix	قيادة الثمن
Price level	niveau des prix	مستوى الأسعار – مستوى الأثمان
Price list	liste des prix	قائمة الأسعار–قائمة الأثمان
	barème des prix	
Price-maker	faiseur de prix	صانع الثمن – واضع الثمن
	formulateur de prix	
Price mechanism	mécanisme des prix	جهاز الثمن – جهاز الأثمان
Price pattern	structure des prix	نمط الأسعار – نمط الأثمان
Price policy	politique des prix	سياسة الأسعار
Price range	gamme des prix	مدى الأسعار – نطاق الثمن
	écart des prix	
Price ratios	ratios de prix	نسب الأسعار -- نسب الأثمان
Price relatives	indices proportionnels de prix	أرقام نسبية للأسعار – أرقام نسبية للأثمان

Price rigging	tripotage des prix	تلاعب بالأسعار
Price rigidity	rigidité des prix	جمود الأسعار – جمود الأثمان
Price ring	cartel de prix	كارتل أسعار – كارتل أثمان
Price signals	signaux des prix	اشارات الأسعار – اشارات الأثمان
Price-specie-flow mechanism	mécanisme des flux métalliques et des prix	حركة النقود المعدنية والأسعار
Price stabilisation	stabilisation des prix	تثبيت الأسعار – تثبيت الأثمان
Price stability	stabilité des prix	استقرار الأسعار – ثبات الأثمان
Price statistics	statistiques des prix	احصاءات الأسعار – احصاءات الأثمان
Price stop	blocage des prix	تجميد الأسعار – تجميد الأثمان
Price structure	structure des prix	هيكل الأسعار – هيكل الأثمان
Price subsidy	subvention-prix	اعانة سعرية
Price support	soutien des prix	مساندة الأسعار – مساندة الأثمان سند الأسعار
Price support policy	politique de soutien des prix	سياسة مساندة الأسعار–سياسة سند الأثمان
Price system	système des prix	نظام الأسعار – نظام الأثمان
Price swing	fluctuation des prix	تقلب الأسعار – رقص الأثمان
Price tag	étiquette de prix	بطاقة السعر – بطاقة الثمن
Price-taker	accepteur de prix	آخذ السعر – آخذ الثمن
Pricing	fixation des prix tarification	تسعير–تثمين–تحديد السعر
Pricing policy	politique de prix – politique de fixation des prix politique de tarification	سياسة التسعير
Pricing system	régime des prix système de fixation des prix système de la détermination des prix	نظام التسعير – نظام تحديد الأثمان
Primal programme	programme primal	برنامج أصلي – برنامج رئيسي
Primary commodities	produits de base	منتجات أولية
Primary products	produits primaires	
Primary goods		
Primary industries	industries primaires	صناعات أولية
Primary inputs	inputs primaires – intrants primaires	مستخدمات أولية
Primary liquidity	liquidités primaires	سيولة أولية
Primary market	marché primaire marché des émissions	سوق الاصدار
Primary producers	producteurs de matières premières	منتجو المواد الأولية
Primary producing countries	pays de production primaire	دول منتجة للمواد الأولية
Primary sector	secteur primaire	القطاع الأولي
Prime bills	effets de premier ordre	سندات الدرجة الأولى
Prime costs	coûts primaires	تكاليف أساسية – تكاليف العوامل الأساسية
Prime rate (of interest)	taux d'intérêt de base taux d'intérêt préférentiel	سعر الفائدة الأساسي سعر الفائدة التفضيلي

Primitive accumulation of capital	accumulation primitive du capital	التراكم البدائي للرسمال
Primitive community	communauté primitive	جماعة بدائية – مجمعة بدائية
Primitive techniques	techniques primitives	فنون انتاج بدائية – تكنيات بدائية
Principal	capital – principal	أصل – رسمال
Principal exports	principales exportations	صادرات رئيسية
Principal place of business	établissement principal	مركز أعمال أساسي – مركز أعمال رئيسي
Priority	priorité	أولوية – أفضلية
Priority shares	actions privilégiées	أسهم امتياز – أسهم أولوية
Priority undertaking	entreprise prioritaire	مشروع أولوي
Private bank	banque privée	بنك خاص
Private capital	capital privé	رسمال خاص
Private consumption	consommation privée	استهلاك الافراد – الاستهلاك الخاص
Private credit	crédit privé	ائتمان خاص
Private enterprise	entreprise privée initiative privée	مشروع خاص – مبادرة خاصة
Private enterprise system	système de l'entreprise privée	نظام المشاريع الخاصة
Private foreign investment	investissement privé étranger	استثمار أجنبي خاص
Private income	revenu personnel	دخل شخصي
Private investments	investissements privés	استثمارات خاصة
Private ownership	propriété privée	ملكية خاصة
Private placement	placement privé	اصدار خاص – توظيف خاص
Private property	propriété privée	ملكية خاصة
Private sector	secteur privé	القطاع الخاص
Privileged debt	dette privilégiée	دين ممتاز
Prize bonds	obligations à lots	سندات بانصيب – سندات ذات جوائز
Probability calculus	calcul des probabilités	حساب الاحتمالات
Probability density	densité probabiliste densité aléatoire	كثافة احتمالية
Probability distribution	distribution des probabilités	توزيع الاحتمالات – توزيع احتمالي
Probability level	niveau de probabilité seuil de probabilité	مستوى الاحتمال
Probability sample	échantillon probabiliste échantillon aléatoire	عينة احتمالية – عينة عشوائية
Probable reserves	réserves probables	احتياطي محتمل
Probation period	période d'essai	فترة اختبار
Proceeds	produit recettes	حصيلة – ايرادات
Proceeds of a loan	fonds empruntés	حصيلة القرض
Process	processus procès	مجرى – مسير
Processed goods	biens transformés produits manufacturés	سلع مصنعة

Processing (*an application*)	instruction (*d'une demande*)	خدمة (طلب)
Processing (*a product*)	transformation (*d'un produit*)	تصنيع – تحويل (سلعة)
Processing factory	usine de traitement	مصنع تحويل
Processing industry	industrie de transformation	صناعة تحويلية
Procurement	fourniture – passation de marchés	توريد – شراء
	achat	
	marché	
Procurement policy	politique des achats	سياسة التوريد – سياسة الشراء
Procurement procedure	procédure de passation des marchés	اجراءات التوريد – اجراءات الشراء
Produce, to	produire	انتج
Producer	producteur	منتج
Producers' association	association de producteurs	اتحاد منتجين
Producer behaviour	comportement du producteur	سلوك المنتج – اتجاه المنتج
Producers' cooperative	coopérative de producteurs	تعاونية انتاج
Producers' goods	biens de production	سلع انتاج – سلع انتاجية
Producer price	prix à la production	سعر المنتج – ثمن المنتج
Producers' values	valeurs-producteurs	قيم المنتجين
Product	produit	ناتج – منتج
Product cycle	cycle du produit	دورة السلعة – دورة المنتجات
Product-life cycle		
Product differentiation	différentiation du produit	تغاير المنتجات – تمييز المنتجات
Product diversification	diversification du produit	تنوع المنتجات
Product groups	groupes de produits	مجموعات سلعية – فئات سلعية
Product-in-hand project	projet produits-en-main	مشروع جاهز الانتاج
Product-mix	gamme de produits	مزيج الانتاج – تشكيلة المنتجات
Production	production	انتاج
Production capacity	capacité de production	طاقة الانتاج – طاقة انتاجية
Productive capacity	potentiel productif	
Production commitments	engagements de production	تعهدات الانتاج
Production control	contrôle de la production	تدقيق الانتاج – رقابة الانتاج
Production costs	coûts de production	تكاليف الانتاج – نفقات الانتاج
Production cutbacks	baisse de production	خفض الانتاج
Production cycle	cycle de la production	دورة الانتاج
Production engineering	technique de la production	هندسة الانتاج
Production forecasts	prévisions de production	توقعات الانتاج
Production function	fonction de production	دالة الانتاج
Production incentives	stimulants de la production	حوافز الانتاج
Production index	indice de production	مؤشر الانتاج
Production instruments	instruments de production	أدوات الانتاج
Production-inventory process	cycle production-stocks	دورة الانتاج والمخزون
		دورة الانتاج والكداس
Production path	sentier de production	مسار انتاج

Production possibility curve	courbe de transformation	منحنى الانتاج المتاح
Production process	processus de production	مجرى الانتاج
Production-sharing agreement	accord de co-production	اتفاقية مشاركة الانتاج
		اتفاقية انتاج مشترك
Production target	objectif de production	هدف انتاجي – مستهدف انتاجي
Production techniques	méthodes de production	أساليب الانتاج
Production unit	unité de production	وحدة انتاج – وحدة انتاجية
Productire activities	activités productives	نشاطات انتاجية
Productive efficiency	efficience de la production	فاعلية الانتاج
Productive equipment	appareil de production	جهاز انتاجي – منشآت انتاجية
	installations productives	
Productive factor	facteur productif	عامل انتاجي
Productive forces	forces productives	قوى انتاجية
Productive investments	investissements productifs	استثمارات انتاجية – استثمارات منتجة
Productive labour	travail productif	عمل منتج
Productive resources	ressources productives	موارد انتاجية – موارد منتجة
Productive sector	secteur productif	قطاع انتاجي
Productive structure	structure économique	هيكل انتاجي – هيكل الانتاج
Productivity	productivité	انتاجية
Productivity criterion	critère de la productivité	معيار الانتاجية
Productivity factor	facteur de productivité	عامل الانتاجية
Productivity gap	écart de productivité	فجوة الانتاجية – ثغرة الانتاجية
Productivity index	indice de productivité	مؤشر الانتاجية
Produit net	produit net	الناتج الصافي
Professional staff	cadres	الجهاز الفني
Profit	bénéfice	الربح – المكسب
	profit	
Profit and loss account	compte profits et pertes	حساب الأرباح والخسائر
Profit-earning capacity	rentabilité	الأرحية
Profit expectations	bénéfices prévus	الأرباح المتوقعة
	prévision de bénéfices	
Profit margin	marge bénéficiaire	هامش الربح
Profit maximisation	maximisation des profits	تعظيم الأرباح – اقصاء الأرباح
		اذراء الأرباح
Profit motive	motif du profit	دافع الربح – دافع الكسب
Profit ratio	ratio de rentabilité	نسبة الأرحية
Profit-seeking association	association à but lucratif	جمعية هادفة للربح – شركة هادفة للربح
Profit-sharing scheme	système de participation aux bénéfices	نظام المشاركة في الأرباح
Profit squeeze	compression des bénéfices	تقلص الأرباح – ضغط الأرباح
Profit taking	prise de bénéfices	جني الأرباح
Profit tax	impôt sur les bénéfices	ضريبة الأرباح
Profit-to-turnover ratio	ratio profits-chiffre d'affaires – taux de	نسبة هامش الربح
	marque	نسبة الربح لرقم الأعمال

Profitability	rentabilité	أربحية – رابحية
Profitability ratio	ratio de rentabilité	نسبة الأربحية – مؤشر الأربحية
Profitable price	prix rentable	سعر مجزي – ثمن مجزي
Profiteering	réalisation de bénéfices excessifs	تحقيق أرباح استغلالية
	mercantilisme	تهافت على الربح
Pro-forma **balance sheet**	bilan *pro-forma*	ميزانية مؤقتة
Pro-forma **invoice**	facture *pro-forma*	فاتورة مؤقتة – حسبونة مؤقتة
Prognostic	pronostic	تنبؤ – نبؤة – توقع
	prédiction	
Prognostication	pronostication – prédiction –	استنباء – تنبؤ – ابشار – توقع
	prévision	
Programme	programme	برنامج
Programme, to	programmer	برمج
Programme aid	aide-programme	معونة برامج – اعانة برامج
Program evaluation and review technique	technique d'évaluation et de contrôle des programmes	اسلوب تقييم ومتابعة البرامج
Programme lending	financement de programme	اقراض برامج
Programme loan	prêt-programme	قرض لبرنامج
Programmed obsolescence	obsolescence programmée	قدم مخطط – بلى مدبر
	désuétude préméditée	
Programming	programmation	برمجة
Progress	progrès	تطور – تقدم
Progress chart	diagramme d'exécution	خريطة التنفيذ – خريطة الانجاز
Progress report	rapport sur l'état des travaux	تقرير المتابعة – تقرير سير العمل
Progressive tax	impôt progressif	ضريبة تصاعدية
Prohibitive cost	coût prohibitif	تكلفة مانعة – تكلفة حاظرة
Prohibitive duty	droit prohibitif	رسم مانع (جمارك)
Project(s)	projet(s)	مشروع (مشاريع)
Project-acceptance criteria	critères d'acceptation des projets	معايير قبول المشاريع
Project analysis	analyse de projets	تحليل المشروع – تحليل المشاريع
Project appraisal	évaluation (ex ante) de projets	تقييم المشروع – تقييم المشاريع
	évaluation du projet	التقييم المسبق للمشاريع
	appréciation de projets	
Project auditing	post-vérification du projet	التدقيق اللاحق للمشروع – تدقيق المشروع
Project-by-project approach	approche projet par projet	منهج المشاريع – منهج توالي المشاريع
Project completion	achèvement du projet	انجاز المشروع – اتمام المشروع
Project control	contrôle du projet	رقابة المشروع
Project cooperation	coopération sur la base de projets	تعاون على أساس مشاريع
Project coordination	coordination du projet	تنسيق المشروع
Project cost	coût du projet	تكلفة المشروع – كلفة المشروع
Project data	données du projet	بيانات المشروع – وصف المشروع
	coordonnées du projet	

Project description	description du projet	وصف المشروع
Project design	conception du projet	تصميم المشروع
Project development	développement du projet	بلورة المشروع – بلورة مشاريع
	élaboration de projet	
Project documentation	dossier du projet	ملف المشروع – وثائق المشروع
Project evaluation	évaluation (ex-post) de projets	تقييم المشاريع – تقييم المشروع
	évaluation du projet	التقييم (اللاحق) للمشاريع
	évaluation rétrospective des projets	
Projects evaluation and planning department	département de l'évaluation et de la planification des projets	دائرة تقييم وتخطيط المشاريع
Project evaluator	évaluateur de projets	مقيم المشروع – مقيم مشاريع
Project execution	exécution du projet	تنفيذ المشروع – انجاز المشروع
Project finance	financement de projet	تمويل المشاريع
Project follow-up	suivi d'exécution – suivi du projet	متابعة المشروع – متابعة مشاريع
Project formulation	élaboration du projet	صياغة المشروع
Project generation	génération de projets	ايجاد المشاريع – خلق المشاريع
	production de projets	
Project goals	buts du projet	أهداف المشروع – غايات المشروع
Project implementation	réalisation du projet	تنفيذ المشروع
Project inputs	intrants du projet	مستخدمات المشروع
	inputs du projet	
Project lending	financement de projet	اقراض المشاريع
Project longevity	durée du projet	مدة المشروع – أجل المشروع
Project management	gestion du projet	ادارة المشروع – تسيير المشروع
	direction du projet	
Project manager	directeur du projet	مدير المشروع
Project monitoring	contrôle du projet	رقابة المشروع – متابعة المشروع
	supervision du projet	
Project officer	responsable du projet	ضابط المشروع – مسئول المشاريع
	chargé de projets	
Project output	produit du projet	ناتج المشروع
Project performance	comportement du projet	اداء المشروع
	performance du projet	
Project performance audit	post-vérification du projet	التدقيق اللاحق لأداء المشروع
		تدقيق أداء المشروع
Project personnel	personnel du projet	جهاز العاملين بالمشروع
Project planning	planification du projet	تخطيط المشروع – تخطيط المشاريع
	planification des projets	
Project preparation	préparation du projet	اعداد المشروع
Project presentation	présentation du projet	تقديم المشروع – عرض المشروع
Project profile	caractéristiques générales du projet	سمات المشروع
	profil du projet	
Project purpose	objectif du projet	هدف المشروع – غرض المشروع

Project report	rapport sur le projet	تقرير المشروع
	rapport du projet	
Project selection	choix de projets	اختيار المشاريع
Project selection crtieria	critères du choix des projets	معايير اختيار المشاريع
Project site	location du projet	موقع المشروع
Project scale	dimension du projet	حجم المشروع
Project specifications	devis descriptif du projet	أوصاف المشروع
Project sponsor	parrain du projet	مروج المشروع
Project status	état du projet	وضع المشروع
Project study	étude du projet	دراسة المشروع
Project-tied aid	aide liée à des projets	معونة مشاريع – معونة مرتبطة بمشاريع
Project timing	date d'exécution du projet	توقيت المشروع
Projected balance-sheet	bilan prévisionnel	ميزانية مرتقبة
Projected cash-flow statement	compte prévisionnel des recettes nettes	البيان المتوقع للتدفقات النقدية
	compte d'exploitation prévisionnel	البيان المتوقع لصافي الايرادات النقدية
Project demand	demande projetée	طلب متوقع
	demande prévue	
Projected growth path	sentier de croissance projeté	المسار المرتقب للنمو – مسار النمو المستهدف
		المسار المستهدف للنمو
Projected rate of growth	taux de croissance projeté	المعدل المرتقب للنمو – معدل النمو المستهدف
		المعدل المستهدف للنمو
Projection	projection	اسقاط – توقع
Projection methods	méthodes de projection	أساليب الاسقاط
Projectist	projectiste	اخصائي مشاريع
Proletariat (e)	prolétariat	البروليترية – الأوفاض
Proletarian	prolétaire	وفيض
Promissory note	billet à ordre	سند اذني
Promoter	promoteur	مروج – مؤسس
Promotion of economic development	promotion du développement économique	تشجيع التنمية الاقتصادية حفز التنمية الاقتصادية
Promotion of trade	promotion des échanges	تشجيع المبادلات – تشجيع التجارة
Promotional period	période de lancement	فترة الترويج
Promotional pricing	tarification promotionnelle	تسعير دعائي – تسعير تشجيعي
	prix de promotion	
Promotional techniques	techniques de promotion	أساليب الترويج – أساليب التشجيع
Prompt date	date de livraison	تاريخ التسليم
Propensity	propension	ميل
Propensity to consume	propension à consommer	الميل للاستهلاك
Propensity to hoard	propension à thésauriser	الميل للاكتناز
Propensity to save	propension à épargner	الميل للادخار
Propensity to spend	propension à dépenser	الميل للانفاق
Propertied classes	classes possédantes	الطبقات المالكة – طبقة أصحاب الاملاك
Property developer	promoteur immobilier	مروج عقاري
Property development	promotion immobilière	تنمية عقارية – ترويج عقاري

Property income	revenus de la propriété	دخل الملكية
Property market	marché immobilier	سوق العقارات – سوق عقاري
Property rights	droits de propriété	حقوق الملكية
Property transfer taxes	droits de mutation	رسوم نقل الملكية
Property tax	impôt sur la fortune	ضريبة على الملكية – ضريبة على الثروة
		ضريبة الثروة
Proportional tax	impôt proportionnel	ضريبة نسبية
Proprietary technology	technologie privative	تكنولوجيا مملوكة
Pro-rationing	contingentement	تحديد حصص – احصاص
Prospecting	prospection	تنقيب
	fouilles	
Prospective buyer	acheteur éventuel	مشترى محتمل
Prospective investor	investisseur éventuel	مستثمر محتمل
Prospective plan	plan perspectif	خطة منظورية – خطة استطلاعية
Prospective value	valeur prospective	قيمة مقدرة – قيمة مرتقبة
Prospective yield	rendement prévisionnel	عائد مرتقب
Prospects	perspectives	طالع – توقعات
Prospects of development	perspectives de développement	توقعات التنمية – طالع النمو
Prospectus (of an issue)	prospectus (d'une émission)	نشرة (اصدار)
Prosperity	prospérité	رخاء
Protected market	marché protégé	سوق محمية
Protection of foreign investment	protection des investissements extérieurs	حماية الاستثمارات الخارجية
Protection of the consumer	protection du consommateur	حماية المستهلك
Protection of the domestic market	protection du marché national	حماية السوق المحلي – حماية السوق الوطني
Protectionism	protectionnisme	مذهب الحماية
Protectionist	protectionniste	حمائي
Protectionist measures	mesures protectionnistes	اجراءات حمائية – تدابير حمائية
Protective duty	droit protecteur	رسم حمائي
Protective tariff	tarif de protection	تعرفة حمائية
	tarif protecteur	
Protracted default	défaillance prolongée	اعسار ممتد – عجز ممتد عن الدفع
Proved reserves	réserves prouvées	احتياطي ثابت – احتياطي مؤكد
Proven reserves	réserves confirmées	
Provident fund	caisse de prévoyance	صندوق ادخار
Provision for doubtful debts	provision pour créances douteuses	مخصص الديون المشبوهة
Provision for contingencies	réserve de prévoyance	مخصص الطوارىء
	réserve d'imprévus	
Provisional budget	budget provisoire	موازنة مؤقتة – ميزانية مؤقتة
Proxy	fondé de pouvoir – mandat	وكيل – وكالة
	mandataire	
Proxy fight	lutte pour les droits de vote	معركة الأصوات
Psychic income	revenu pyschique	دخل نفسي

Public accounting	comptabilité publique	حسابات الحكومة
Public administration	administration publique	الادارة العامة
Public aid	assistance publique	معونة حكومية – اغاثة حكومية – مساعدة حكومية
Public assistance	aide publique	
Public auction	adjudication publique – enchères publiques	مزاد علني
Public authority	pouvoirs publics	السلطات العامة
Public "bads"	nuisances publiques	اضرار عامة – منتجات سالبة
Public body	organisme public	هيئة عامة
Public consumption	consommation de l'Etat	استهلاك الدولة – استهلاك الادارة الاستهلاك العام
Public corporation	établissement public	مؤسسة عامة
Public debt	dette publique	الدين العام
Public enterprise	entreprise publique	مؤسسة عامة – مشروع عام
Public finance	finances publiques	المالية العامة
Public funds	fonds publics	أموال عامة
Public goods	biens publics	أملاك عامة – أموال عامة
Public interest	intérêt public	المصلحة العامة
Public investments	investissements publics	استثمارات عامة
Public issue	émission publique	اصدار عام
Public land	terre domaniale	أرض حكومية
Public order	ordre public	النظام العام
Public ownership	propriété publique	ملكية عامة
Public property	domaine public	املاك عامة
Public sale	vente aux enchères publiques	بيع بالمزاد العلني
Public sector	secteur public	قطاع عام
Public stock market	marché des titres publics	سوق السندات العامة
Public subscription	souscription publique	اكتتاب عام
Public tender	adjudication publique	مناقصة عامة
Public transport	transports en commun	النقل العام – وسائل النقل العام
Public utility	service public	مرفق عام
Public utility corporation	entreprise de service public service public	مرفق عام – مؤسسة مرفق عام
Public works	travaux publics	أشغال عامة
Public-works programme	programme de travaux publics	برنامج أشغال عامة
Publicity campaign	campagne de publicité	حملة دعاية -- حملة دعائية
Pump priming	reflation	انفاق انعاشي
Purchase	achat	شراء
Purchasing	acquisition	
Purchase, to	acheter	اشترى
Purchase commitments	engagements d'achat	تعهدات شراء
Purchase contract	marché de fourniture	عقد شراء – عقد توريد
Purchase price	prix d'achat	سعر الشراء – ثمن الشراء

Purchase tax	impôt de consommation	ضريبة المشتريات
Purchaser	acheteur	مشترى
	acquéreur	
Purchasers' values	valeurs-acheteurs	قيم المشترين
Purchasing power	pouvoir d'achat	قوة شرائية
Purchasing power guarantee	garantie de pouvoir d'achat	ضمان القوة الشرائية – كفالة القوة الشرائية
Purchasing power index	indice du pouvoir d'achat	مؤشر القوة الشرائية
Purchasing power parity	parité des pouvoirs d'achat	تعادل القوة الشرائية
Pure competition	concurrence parfaite	منافسة كاملة
	concurrence pure	
Pure rent	rente pure	ريع خالص
Put option	option de vente	خيار بيع – علاوة بيع
	prime vendeur	

Quadratic programming	programmation quadratique	برمجة تربيعية
Qualified agreement to reimburse	garantie conditionnelle de remboursement	تعهد شرطي بتغطية الدفع
Qualitative targets (*of planning*)	objectifs qualitatifs (*de la planification*)	أهداف كيفية – أهداف غير كمية (للتخطيط)
Quality competition	concurrence qualitative	منافسة نوعية – منافسة كيفية
Quality control	contrôle de qualité	تدقيق النوعية – رقابة النوعية
Quality mark-up	prime de qualité	علاوة نوعية
Quality of life	qualité de la vie	نوعية الحياة
Quality of life index	indice de la qualité de la vie	مؤشر نوعية الحياة
Quantify, to	quantifier	حدّد الكم – عيّن الكم
Quantitative economics	économie quantitative	الاقتصاد الكمّي
Quantitative targets	objectifs quantitatifs	أهداف كمية
Quantity equation	équation quantitative	معادلة كمية النقود – معادلة الكمية
Quantity index	indice de quantité	مؤشر كمّي – مؤشر الكم
Quantum index		
Quantity theory of money	théorie quantitative de la monnaie	نظرية كمية النقود
Quarrying	exploitation des carrières	استغلال المحاجر
Quarterly payments	paiements trimestriels	مدفوعات ربع سنوية
Quartile	quartile	ربيع
Quartile deviation	déviation inter-quartile	انحراف ربيعي – مدى ربيعي
Quasi-corporate enterprise	quasi-société	شبه شركة
Quasi-equity	quasi-capital	شبه رسمال

Quasi-money	quasi-monnaie	شبه نقد
Quasi-monopoly	quasi-monopole	شبه احتكار
Quasi-rent	quasi-rente	شبه ريع
Quaternary sector	secteur quaternaire	القطاع الرباعي
Quayage	quayage	رسوم رصيف
Questionnaire	questionnaire	استبيان
Queueing theory	théorie de la file d'attente	نظرية صف الانتظار
Quick assets	avoirs liquides	اصول سائلة
Quick-disbursing aid	aide à débours rapide	معونة سريعة السحب
		مساعدة سريعة الأداء
Quick ratio	ratio de liquidité	مؤشر السيولة
Quid pro quo	contrepartie	مقابل
Quietus	quitus	مخالصة
Quintile	quintile	خميس
Quota	contingent	حصة – نصيب
	quota	
	quote-part	
Quota restrictions	contingentement	قيود حصصية – قيود حصية
	restrictions contingentaires	
Quota subscription	quote-part	مساهمة – حصة – نصيب
Quota system	système de contingentement	نظام الحصص
Quotation (*stock exchange*)	cote (*bourse*)	سعر (سوق الأوراق المالية)
	cours	تسعير
Quote, to	coter	سعَّر – ذكر سعراً
		سجّل بقائمة الأسعار
Quoted securities	valeurs cotées	سندات مسجلة
	valeurs inscrites	أوراق المقصورة

R

Racial discrimination	discrimination raciale	تمييز عنصري
Racial segregation	ségrégation raciale	فصل عنصري – عزل عنصري
Railroad network	réseau ferroviaire	شبكة السكك الحديدية
Railway network		
Railway traffic	trafic ferroviaire	نقل بالسكك الحديدية
	transport ferroviaire	حركة النقل بالسكك الحديدية
Rainfall	pluviosité	درجة سقوط الأمطار
Rainfed agriculture	culture sèche	زراعة مطرية
Raising capital	réunion du capital	جمع الرسمال
	mobilisation du capital	

Raising of funds	mobilisation de fonds	جمع أموال
Rally (*market*)	reprise (*marché*)	انتعاش (السوق)
Rally in prices	reprise des cours	انتعاش الأسعار
Random component	composante aléatoire	عنصر عشوائي
Random distribution	distribution aléatoire	توزيع عشوائي
Random disturbance	perturbations aléatoires	معكرات عشوائية
Random error	erreur aléatoire	خطأ عشوائي
Random factors	facteurs aléatoires	عوامل عشوائية
Random fluctuations	fluctuations accidentelles	تقلبات عشوائية
Random sample	échantillon aléatoire	عينة عشوائية
Random sampling	sondage probabiliste	سبر عشوائي – استبار عشوائي
	échantillonnage aléatoire	
Random selection	choix aléatoire	اختيار عشوائي
	choix au hasard	
Random variable	variable aléatoire	متغير عشوائي
Range	intervalle	مدى – تشكيلة
	gamme	
	écart	
Range of products	gamme de produits	أنواع المنتجات – تشكيلة المنتجات
Range of variation	intervalle de variation	مدى التغير
Rank coefficient	coefficient d'ordre	معامل الرتب
	coefficient de classement	
Rank correlation	corrélation par rangs de classement	ارتباط الرتب
	corrélation à rangs multiples	
	corrélation ordinale	
Ranking	classification	ترتيب
Ratchet effect	effet d'asymétrie	اثر اللاتوازي – أثر اللاتناسق
Rate	taux	سعر – معدل – رسم
	cours	ضريبة
	taxe	
Rate of capital turnover	taux de rotation du capital	معدل تدوير الرسمال
	vitesse de rotation du capital	
Rate of discount	taux de l'escompte	سعر الحسم – سعر الخصم
	taux d'actualisation	معدل الاحطاط
Rate of exchange	cours du change	سعر الصرف
Rate of growth	taux de croissance	معدل النمو
Rate of increase	taux d'accroissement	معدل الزيادة – معدل التزايد
Rate of inflation	taux d'inflation	معدل التضخم
Rate of interest	taux d'intérêt	سعر الفائدة
Rate of investment	taux d'investissement	معدل الاستثمار
Rate of profit	taux de profit	معدل الربح
Rate of return	taux de rentabilité	معدل العائد

Rate of saving	taux de l'épargne	معدل الادخار
Rate of taxation	taux d'imposition	معدل الضريبة
Rateable	imposable	خاضع للضريبة
Rateable contribution	contribution proportionnelle	مساهمة نسبية
Rateable value	valeur imposable	القيمة الضريبية
Rated bonds	obligations gradées	سندات مصنفة
	obligations notées	
Ratepayer	contribuable	ممول
Rating agency	établissement de gradation	مؤسسة تصنيف
	agence de notation	
Ratio	rapport	نسبة – معدل
	ratio	
	taux	
Ratio analysis	analyse des ratios	تحليل النسب
Rational choice	choix rationnel	خيار رشيد
Rationalisation	rationalisation	ترشيد
Rationalisation measures	mesures de rationalisation	تدابير الترشيد
Ration	ration	حصة
Rationed	rationné	محصص
Rationing	rationnement	الاحصاص
Raw data	données brutes	بيانات أصلية – بيانات خام
Raw materials	matières premières	مواد أولية – مواد خام
Raw material shortages	pénurie des matières premières	قصور المواد الأولية
Reactive approach (aid policy)	approche réactive (politique de l'aide)	منهج استجابي (السياسة الاعانية)
Ready money	argent liquide	نقد سائل – نقود حاضرة
Real assets	biens immobiliers	اصول عقارية
Real consumption	consommation réelle	استهلاك حقيقي
Real cost	coût réel	تكلفة حقيقية – كلفة حقيقية
Real domestic product	produit intérieur réel	الناتج المحلي الحقيقي
Real estate	immeubles	عقارات – عقار
Real estate credit	crédit immobilier	ائتمان عقاري
Real estate investments	investissements immobiliers	استثمارات عقارية
Real estate investment trust	société d'investissement immobilier	شركة استثمار عقاري
Real estate loan	prêt foncier – prêt immobilier	قرض عقاري
Real estate tax	impôt foncier	ضريبة عقارية
Real income	revenu réel	دخل حقيقي – دخل فعلي
Real interest rate	taux d'intérêt réel	سعر الفائدة الحقيقي
		سعر الفائدة الفعلي
Real per capita income	revenu réel par tête	الدخل الفردي الحقيقي
		متوسط الدخل الحقيقي
Real prices	prix réels	أسعار حقيقية – أثمان حقيقية
Real property	propriété immobilière	ملكية عقارية
Real wage rate	taux du salaire réel	معدل الأجر الحقيقي
Realisable assets	avoirs réalisables	اصول قابلة للتصريف – اصول قابلة للبيع

Realisation	réalisation	تصريف - انجاز - تحقيق
Realisation problem	problème de la réalisation	مشكلة التصريف
Realised capital gains	plus-value réalisée	أرباح رسمالية محصلة - نماء محصل
Realised profits	bénéfices réalisés	أرباح محققة - أرباح محصلة
Realised value	valeur réalisée	قيمة محققة - قيمة محصلة
Reallocation of resources	réallocation des ressources	اعادة توزيع الموارد
Rebate	rabais	حطيطة - خصم - تخفيض
	escompte	
Receipt	reçu - quittance - récépissé	ايصال
Receipts and expenditures	recettes et dépenses	ايرادات ومصروفات
Receipted invoice	facture acquittée	فاتورة خالصة - حسبونة مدفوعة
Receivables	créances échues	مستحقات - مبالغ مستحقة
	produits à recevoir	
Recession	récession	تراجع - انكماش
Recipient	bénéficiaire - donataire	مستفيد
	récipiendaire - receveur	
Recipient country	pays bénéficiaire - pays récepteur	دولة مستفيدة
	pays récipiendaire - pays receveur	
Reciprocal demand curve	courbe de demande réciproque	منحنى الطلب المتبادل
Reciprocal trade	commerce réciproque	تجارة متبادلة
Reciprocity of treatment	réciprocité de traitement	معاملة بالمثل
Reconnaissance survey	enquête préliminaire	مسح استطلاعي - دراسة استطلاعية
Reconstruction	reconstruction	اعادة التشييد - اعادة البناء - تعمير
Reconstruction loan	prêt de reconstruction	قرض تعمير - قرض اعادة تعمير
Record, to (accounting)	comptabiliser	قيّد (محاسبة)
Record output	production record	انتاج قياسي
Record price	prix record	ثمن قياسي - ثمن أقصى
Recoupment period	période de récupération	فترة الاسترداد
Recovery period		
Recovery	reprise	انتعاش - استرداد - تحصيل
	redressement	
	récupération	
	recouvrement	
Recovery of prices	redressement des cours	انتعاش الأسعار
Recovery of the market	reprise du marché	انتعاش السوق
Recreational activites	activités récréatives	نشاطات ترويحية
Recruitment	recrutement	توظيف - تشغيل
Recurrent expenditures	dépenses courantes	نفقات جارية - نفقات متجددة
Recycling	recyclage	اعادة استيعاب
Recycling mechanisms	mécanismes de recyclage	أساليب اعادة الاستيعاب
Redeem, to	rembourser	سدّد - استهلك
	amortir	
Redeemable bonds	obligations remboursables	سندات قابلة للسداد

Redemption	rachat remboursement	سداد ــ استرداد
Redemption at par	remboursement au pair	سداد سعر التعادل
Redemption fund	fonds d'amortissement	صندوق استهلاك ــ صندوق سداد
Redemption of a debt	amortissement d'une dette	سداد دين ــ قضاء دين
Redemption premium	prime de remboursement	علاوة سداد
Redemption price	prix de rachat prix de remboursement	سعر الاسترداد ــ سعر الشراء سعر السداد
Redemption table	tableau d'amortissement	جدول السداد
Redemption yield	rendement effectif	العائد النهائي ــ العائد الفعلي
Rediscount	réescompte	اعادة الخصم ــ اعادة الحسم
Rediscounting	réescompte	
Rediscount ceiling	plafond de réescompte	الحد الأعلى لاعادة الخصم الحد الأعلى لاعادة الحسم
Rediscount rate	taux de réescompte	سعر اعادة الخصم ــ سعر اعادة الحسم
Rediscountable	réescomptable	قابل لاعادة الخصم ــ قابل لاعادة الحسم
Redistribution of income	redistribution des revenus	اعادة توزيع الدخل
Reduced-form equations	équations à forme réduite équations réduites	معادلات مشتقة ــ معادلة مختزلة
Reduced-form parameters	paramètres à forme réduite paramètres réduits	ضوابط مشتقة ــ معاملات مشتقة ضوابط مختزلة ــ معاملات مختزلة
Reducing instalment depreciation	dépréciation dégressive	استهلاك متناقص ــ استهلاك بأقساط متناقصة
Reduction of capital	réduction de capital	تخفيض الرسمال
Re-export **Re-exportation**	réexportation	اعادة التصدير
Re-exports	réexportations	سلع معاد تصديرها
Reference currency	monnaie de référence	عملة الاسناد ــ عملة القياس
Reference price	prix de référence	سعر استرشادي ــ ثمن الاسناد ــ ثمن القياس
Refinancing	refinancement	اعادة التمويل
Refinery	raffinerie	مصنع تكرير
Reflation	relance reflation	انعاش
Reforestation	reboisement	اعادة التشجير
Reformism	réformisme	المذهب الاصلاحي ــ الاصلاحية
Refrigerating installations	installations frigorifiques	منشآت تثليج
Refrigerator vessel	navire congélateur	باخرة تثليج ــ سفينة تثليج
Refugee aid	aide aux réfugiés	اعانة اللاجئين ــ مساعدة اللاجئين
Refund	remboursement ristourne	سداد ــ رد
Refund, to	rembourser refinancer ristourner	سدّد ــ اعاد تمويل
Refunding	remboursement refinancement	سداد ــ اعادة تمويل

Regional administration	administration régionale	ادارة اقليمية
Regional agreement	accord régional	اتفاقية اقليمية
Regional analysis	analyse régionale	تحليل اقليمي
Regional aspect	aspect régional	الجانب الاقليمي
Regional centre	centre régional	مركز اقليمي
Regional cooperation	coopération régionale	تعاون اقليمي
Regional development	développement régional	تنمية اقليمية
Regional distribution	ventilation régionale	توزيع اقليمي
	ventilation par régions	
Regional economy	économie régionale	اقتصاد اقليمي
Regional preferences	préférences régionales	مزايا اقليمية – تفضيلات اقليمية
Regional grouping	groupement régional	تكتل اقليمي – كتلة اقليمية
		تجمع اقليمي
Regional inequalities	inégalités régionales	فروق اقليمية
Regional integration	intégration régionale	تكامل اقليمي
Regional integration scheme	système d'intégration régionale	برنامج تكامل اقليمي – نظام تكامل اقليمي
Regional market	marché régional	سوق اقليمي
Regional organizations	organisations régionales	منظمات اقليمية
Regional planning	planification régionale	تخطيط اقليمي
	aménagement du territoire	
Regional product	produit régional	الناتج الاقليمي
Regionalism	régionalisme	الاقليمية
Regionalization	régionalisation	تركّز اقليمي
Registered bond	obligation nominative	سند اسمي
Registered capital	capital nominatif	الرسمال المسجل
Registered office	siège social	المركز الرئيسي
Registered securities	titres nominatifs	أوراق مالية اسمية – سندات مسجلة
Registered trade-mark	marque déposée	ماركة مسجلة – علامة مسجلة – سمة مسجلة
Registration fees	droits d'enregistrement	رسوم قيد – رسوم تسجيل
Regression analysis	analyse de régression	تحليل الارتداد – تحليل الانحدار
Regression coefficient	coefficient de régression	معامل الارتداد
Regression curve	courbe de régression	منحنى الارتداد
Regressive tax	impôt régressif	ضريبة متناقصة
Regulated price	prix réglementé	سعر محدد
Regulation of production	contrôle de la production	تنظيم الانتاج
Rehabilitation	réorganisation	اعادة تنظيم – اصلاح – تجديد
	assainissement	
Rehabilitation plan	plan d'assainissement – plan de	خطة اصلاح
	réorganisation	
Reification	réification	تشيئة
Reimburse, to	rembourser	سدّد
Reimbursement	remboursement	سداد – تسديد

Reimportation	réimportation	اعادة استيراد
Reinflation	reflation	انعاش
Reinsurance	réassurance	اعادة التأمين
Reinvestment	réinvestissement	اعادة الاستثمار
Relations of production	rapports de production	علاقات الانتاج
Relative factor shares	parts relatives des facteurs	الأنصبة النسبية لعوامل الانتاج
Relative prices	prix relatifs	أسعار نسبية – أثمان نسبية
Relative rent	rente relative	ريع نسبي
Release of funds	déblocage de fonds	تحرير أموال – اطلاق أموال
		افراج عن أموال
Relending	refinancement	اعادة اقراض
Relief fund	caisse de secours	صندوق اعانة – صندوق اسعاف
		صندوق اغاثة
Relocation of industry	relocalisation industrielle	اعادة توطين الصناعة
	redéploiement industriel	اعادة التوطين الصناعي
Remission of a debt	remise d'une dette	اعفاء من دين – ابراء من دين
Remittances	remises	مدفوعات – تحويلات
	versements	
Remuneration	rémunération	مكافأة – أجر – جزاء
Remunerative price	prix rémunérateur	سعر مجزي – ثمن مجزي
Renewable resources	ressources renouvelables	موارد متجددة
Renewal bonds	obligations de reconduction	سندات تجديد
Renewal of a loan	prorogation d'un emprunt	تجديد قرض
	renouvellement d'un emprunt	
	reconduction d'un prêt	
Rent	rente	ريع – ايجار
Rental	loyer	
Rent, to	louer	أجّر
Rent control	contrôle des loyers	تقييد الايجارات – تحديد الايجارات
Rental vacancy rate	taux de vacance locative	معدل الخلو الايجاري – معدل خلو المساكن
Rental value	valeur locative	قيمة ايجارية
Rentier	rentier	صاحب دخل – صاحب أملاك
Renting	location	تأجير
Reorganisation of finances	assainissement des finances	علاج الوضع المالي – اصلاح مالي
Reorientation of the plan	réorientation du plan	اعادة توجيه الخطة
Repairs and maintenance	réparations et entretien	اصلاح وصيانة
Repatriation of capital	rapatriement du capital	استرجاع الرسمال
		اعادة تحويل الرسمال (إلى الوطن)
Repatriation of export proceeds	rapatriement des recettes d'exportation	استرجاع حصيلة الصادرات
Repayment	remboursement	سداد – وفاء
Repayment capacity	capacité de remboursement	قدرة السداد
Repayment option	option de remboursement	خيار السداد

Repayment schedule	tableau d'amortissement	جدول السداد
	calendrier d'amortissement	
	échéancier	
Repeater loan	prêt répétitif	قرض مكرر – قرض تكميلي
Repeater project	projet répétitif	مشروع مكرر – مشروع تكميلي
Repetitive borrowing	emprunt répétitif	اقتراض مكرر
Repetitive lending	financement répétitif	اقراض مكرر
Replacement cost	coût de remplacement	تكلفة الاستبدال
Replacement value	valeur de remplacement	قيمة الاستبدال
Replenishable resources	ressources renouvelables	موارد متجددة
Replenishment	reconstitution	اعادة التزويد – ازادة
	réapprovisionnement	
Replenishment of capital	reconstitution du capital	ازادة الرسمال
Replenishment of resources	reconstitution des ressources	اعادة التزويد بالموارد – ازادة الموارد
Repressed inflation	inflation refoulée	تضخم مكبوت
Reproducible goods	biens reproductibles	سلع متجددة الانتاج – منتجات متجددة
Reproducible tangible wealth	richesse matérielle reproductible	الثروة المادية المتجددة
Reproduction	reproduction	اعادة الانتاج
Reproduction rate (*demography*)	taux de reproduction (*démographie*)	معدل التناسل (سكان)
Repudiation of a debt	répudiation d'une dette	الغاء دين – نبذ دين
Repurchase	rachat	اعادة شراء
Repurchase agreement	accord de rachat	اتفاق اعادة شراء
Repurchase obligation	obligation de rachat	التزام اعادة الشراء – التزام الاسترداد.
Request for assistance	demande d'assistance	طلب معونة – طلب مساعدة
Required reserves	réserves obligatoires	احتياطي اجباري
Requited payments	paiements avec contrepartie	مدفوعات تبادلية – مدفوعات بمقابل
		مدفوعات عوضية
Requirements	besoins	حاجات – احتياجات
Requited transfers	transferts avec contrepartie	تحويلات عوضية–تحويلات تبادلية
		تحويلات بمقابل
Resale value	valeur de revente	قيمة اعادة البيع
Rescheduling of debt	révision de l'échéancier d'une dette	اعادة جدولة الدين
	révision du tableau d'amortissement	تعديل جدول السداد
Rescission right	droit d'annulation	حق الالغاء – حق الفسخ
	droit de résiliation	
Research and development	recherche et développement	البحث والتطوير
Researchist	recherchiste	اخصائي ابحاث
Reservation price	prix de rétention	سعر الحجز – ثمن الامتناع – سعر الحفظ
Reserve	réserve	احتياطي – مخصص
	provision	
Reserve assets	réserves monétaires	أرصدة نقدية احتياطية
	avoirs de réserve	أرصدة احتياطية
Reserve creation	création de réserves	خلق أرصدة احتياطية

Reserve currency	monnaie de réserve	عملة احتياطية – عملة رصيد
Reserve deposit	dépôt de couverture	وديعة غطاء – وديعة تغطية
Reserve for contingencies	réserve de prévoyance	مخصص طوارىء
	réserve d'imprévus	
Reserve for depreciation	provision pour dépréciation	مخصص الاستهلاك
Reserve for doubtful debts	provision pour créances douteuses	مخصص الديون المشبوهة
Reserve fund	fonds de réserve	مال احتياطي
Reserve position	situation des réserves	الوضع الرصيدي – حالة الأرصدة النقدية
Reserve ratio (*banking*)	taux de couverture (*banque*)	نسبة الاحتياطي – معدل الغطاء
	coefficient de liquidité	معامل السيولة (بنوك)
Reserve requirements	obligations de couverture	التزامات الغطاء
Resettlement	ré-installation	اعادة توطين
Resident population	habitants	المقيمون – السكان المقيمون
	population résidante	
Residential construction	construction résidentielle	بناء سكني – تشييد سكني – بناء المساكن
Residential property	immeubles résidentiels	عقارات سكنية
Residual factor	facteur résiduaire	العامل المتبقي – العامل الفائض
Residual value	valeur résiduaire – valeur résiduelle	القيمة المتبقية
		القيمة الفائضة
Resource	ressource	مورد
Resource allocation	répartition des ressources	تخصيص الموارد – توزيع الموارد
	affectation des ressources	
Resource availability	disponibilité des ressources	توفر الموارد
Resource conservation	conservation des ressources	حفظ الموارد
Resource development	mise en valeur des ressources	تنمية الموارد – استغلال الموارد
Resource economics	économie des ressources	اقتصاديات الموارد
Resource flows	flux de ressources	تدفق الموارد
Resource gap	déficit de ressources	عجز الموارد
Resource inventory	inventaire des ressources	جرد الموارد
Resource survey		
Resource mobilisation	mobilisation des ressources	حفز الموارد
Resource rent	rente de ressources	ريع الموارد
Resource transfer	transfert de ressources	نقل الموارد – تحويل الموارد
Respite	sursis	ارجاء – امهال – انظار
	délai	
	différé	
Restocking	restockage	اعادة تكوين المخزون – تجديد الكداس
	reconstitution des stocks	
Restraint of trade	restriction au commerce	قيد على المبادلات
	restriction des échanges	قيد على النشاط الاقتصادي
Restrictive measures	mesures restrictives	تدابير تقييدية – قيود
Restrictive monetary policy	politique monétaire restrictive	سياسة نقدية انكماشية
Restrictive practices	pratiques restrictives	أساليب تقييدية
Restructuring of the economy	restructuration de l'économie	اعادة هيكلة الاقتصاد القومي

Retail dealer	détaillant	تاجر تجزئة
Retailer		
Retail price	prix de détail	سعر التجزئة
Retail sales	ventes au détail	بيع بالتجزئة
Retail trade	commerce de détail	تجارة التجزئة
Retailing		
Retained earnings	bénéfices non-distribués	أرباح محتجزة – أرباح غير موزعة
Retained profits		
Retaliatory duties	droits de représailles	رسوم ثأرية
Retaliatory tariff	tarif de représailles	تعرفة ثأرية
Retention money	retenue de garantie	مبلغ ضمان الأداء – ضمان الأداء
Retirement	retraite	ترك الخدمة – معاش – سحب
	retrait	
Retirement of a bill	retrait d'un effet	سحب ورقة تجارية
Retirement of a debt	remboursement d'une dette	سداد دين – قضاء دين
Retirement of bonds	remboursement d'obligations	سداد السندات
Retraining	recyclage	اعادة تدريب
Retroactive finance	financement rétroactif	تمويل رجعي
Retrogression	recul	تقهقر
Return	rendement	عائد – ايراد – غلة
	rapport	
	recette	
Return-on-equity ratio	rentabilité des capitaux propres	نسبة ارحية الرسمال الذاتي
Return on investment	rendement de l'investissement	عائد الاستثمار
Return per hectare	rendement à l'hectare	العائد للهكتار
Returned cheque	chèque retourné – chèque refusé	شيك مرتجع – شيك مردود
Returns to scale	rendements d'échelle	عوائد الحجم
Revaluation	revalorisation	اعادة التقييم
	réévaluation	
Revealed preference	préférence révélée	تفضيل مجهر – تفضيل معلن
Revenue	revenu – recettes	ايراد – ايرادات
Revenue duty	droit fiscal	رسم مالي
Revenue-earning project	projet rentable	مشروع مربح – مشروع مدر لدخل
Reverse dumping	dumping inversé	اغراق عكسي – اغراق معكوس
	dumping inverse	
Reverse capital flows	flux inverses de capitaux	تدفقات عكسية للرسمال – تدفقات رسمالية عكسية
Reverse deposit	dépôt inverse	وديعة عكسية
Reverse engineering	ingénierie inversée – ingénierie à	هندسة عكسية
	rebours	
Reverse preferences	préférences inverses	مزايا عكسية – امتيازات عكسية
Reverse transfer of technology	transfert inverse de technologie	النقل المعاكس للقدرات الفنية
	transfert de technologie à rebours	
Revised costs	coûts révisés	تكاليف معدلة

Revocable credit	crédit révocable	ائتمان قابل للفسخ
		ائتمان غير نهائي
Revolving credit	crédit renouvelable	ائتمان مجدد – اعتماد متجدد
	crédit rotatif	
Revolving fund	fonds de roulement	رصيد متجدد – صندوق متجدد الموارد
Rice plantation	rizière	مرزة
Rigging of prices (*stock market*)	manipulation des cours (*bourse*)	تلاعب في الأسعار (أسواق مالية)
Right to strike	droit de grève	حق الاضراب
Riparian country	pays riverain	دولة سيفية – دولة ساحلية
Rising market	marché orienté à la hausse	سوق صاعد
Risk	risque	مخاطرة – خطر
Risk analysis	analyse des risques	تحليل المخاطر
Risk appraisal	appréciation des risques	تقدير المخاطر
Risk assessment	évaluation des risques	تقدير المخاطر
Risk aversion	aversion aux risques	ابلة المخاطر – كراهة المخاطر
	répugnance aux risques	
Risk avoider	éviteur de risque	آبل المخاطر – متقي المخاطر
Risk bearer	preneur de risque	مخاطر – متحمل المخاطر
Risk capital	capital propre	رسمال ذاتي
Risk element	élément de risque	عنصر المخاطرة
Risk factor	facteur-risque	عامل المخاطرة
Risk-indifference strategy	stratégie d'indifférence au risque	سياسة اهمال المخاطر
Risk premium	prime de risque	علاوة مخاطرة
Risk-return analysis	analyse risques-rendements	تحليل المخاطر والعوائد
Risk sharing	partage des risques	اقتسام المخاطر
Risk shifting	déplacement du risque	نقل المخاطر
Risk spreading	étalement des risques	توزيع المخاطر
Risk taker	preneur de risque	مخاطر
Risk taking	prise de risque	مخاطرة
River basin	bassin fluvial	حوض النهر
River control	régularisation fluviale	ضبط الأنهر
River navigation	navigation fluviale	ملاحة نهرية
River pollution	pollution des rivières	تلويث الأنهر
River transportation	transports fluviaux	نقل نهري
Road capacity	capacité routière	طاقة الطرق – طاقة استيعاب الطرق
Road development	développement routier	تنمية الطرق
Road maintenance	entretien du réseau routier	صيانة الطرق
Road network	réseau routier	شبكة الطرق
Road system		
Road planning	planification de la construction routière	تخطيط الطرق
Road policy	politique routière	سياسة الطرق
Road traffic	trafic routier	حركة النقل البري

Road transportation	transports terrestres	نقل بري
Road use	utilisation des routes	استخدام الطرق
Road user charges	péages	رسوم الطرق
Rolling plan	plan continu	خطة متجددة – خطة متحركة
	plan renouvelable	
Roll-over credit	crédit renouvelable (à intérêt ajustable)	قرض متجدد (بفائدة متغيرة)
Roll-over of debt	renouvellement de la dette	تجديد الدين
Rotating strike	grève tournante	إضراب دوري
Rotation of crops	assolement	دورة فلاحية – تناوب الحاصلات
Round figures	chiffres ronds	أرقام مقربة – أرقام مجبورة – أرقام مدورة
Round lot (*securities*)	paquet ordinaire (*titres*)	رزمة عادية (أوراق مالية)
	paquet standard	
Roundabout production	production indirecte	انتاج غير مباشر
Royalties	redevances	عوائد – فرائض
Rubber industry	industrie du caoutchouc	صناعة المطاط
Ruling classes	classes dirigeantes	طبقات حاكمة
Ruling price	prix courant	الثمن السائد – السعر الجاري
Run on a currency	mouvement spéculatif contre une monnaie	مضاربة ضد عملة معينة
Run on the banks	panique bancaire	ذعر مصرفي
Run-away industries	industries mobiles	صناعات قابلة للانتقال – صناعات لاجئة
	industries réfugiées	
Run-away inflation	inflation galopante	تضخم ضارم – تضخم راكض
	inflation débridée	
Running account	compte courant	حساب جاري – حساب جار
Running costs	dépenses courantes	نفقات جارية
Running expenses	frais d'exploitation	
Running-in period	période de rodage	فترة البدء – فترة البدى
	phase d'adaptation	
Running yield	rendement courant	عائد جاري – عائد جار
Rural	rural	ريفي
Rural development	développement rural	تنمية ريفية
Rural commune	commune rurale	جماعة ريفية – مجمعة ريفية
Rural economy	économie rurale	اقتصاد ريفي
Rural electrification	électrification rurale	كهربة ريفية
Rural exodus	exode rural	هجرة الريف – ترك الريف
Rural industry	industrie rurale	صناعة ريفية
Rural market	marché rural	أسواق ريفية
Rural migration	migration rurale	هجرة ريفية
Rural planning	planification rurale	تخطيط ريفي
Rural population	population rurale	سكان الريف
Rural settlement	agglomération rurale	قرية – مستعمرة ريفية
	colonie rurale	

Rural sociology	sociologie rurale	علم الاجتماع الريفي
Rural welfare	bien-être rural	رفاهية الريف
Rhythm of industrial activity	rythme de la vie industrielle	معدل النشاط الصناعي
	rythme de l'activité industrielle	

Sacrifice prices	prix sacrifiés	أسعار تصفية–أثمان تصفية
Safe investments	placements sûrs	استثمارات مأمونة
Safeguard clause	clause de sauvegarde	شرط نحوط – نص نحوط
Safekeeping fee	droits de garde	رسوم ايداع – رسوم حفظ
Safety net	filet de sécurité	شبكة أمان
Salary	salaire	أجر – مرتب
	appointments	
	traitement	
Salary system	salariat	نظام الأجر– نظام الاجراء
	système salarial	
Sale	vente	بيع – تخفيضات
	soldes	
	mise en vente	
Sale by auction	vente à la criée	بيع بالمزاد – مزايدة
	vente aux enchères	
Sale from portfolio	vente de valeurs en portefeuille	بيع من الحافظة
Sale of loan maturities	cession de portions de prêts	بيع شرائح قروض – بيع استحقاقات
Sale price	prix de vente	ثمن البيع
Sales engineering	technique de vente	تدير المبيعات
Salesman	vendeur	بائع
Sales proceeds	recettes de vente	ايرادات البيع – ايرادات المبيعات
Sales revenues	produit des ventes	حصيلة البيع
Sales promotion	campagne de vente	ترويج المبيعات – تشجيع المبيعات – حملة مبيعية
	promotion des ventes	
Sales tax	impôt sur le chiffre d'affaires	ضريبة المبيعات
Sales turnover	chiffre d'affaires	رقم الأعمال – حجم المبيعات
Sales volume		
Saleable value	valeur marchande	قيمة سوقية
Sale value		
Salvage value	valeur de récupération	القيمة المتخلفة – القيمة المتبقية – قيمة التخلص
Sample	échantillon	عينة
Sample census	recensement par sondage	احصاء بالعينات – احصاء استباري
Sample checking	vérification par échantillons	تدقيق بالعينات – تدقيق استباري

Sample mean	moyenne des échantillons	متوسط العينات
Sample period	période de sondage	فترة السبر – فترة الاستبار
Sample survey	enquête par sondage	مسح بالعينات – مسح استباري
Sample unit	unité d'échantillonnage	وحدة العينات
Sample variance	variance des échantillons	تغاير العينات – تباين العينات
Sampling	sondage échantillonnage	استبار – أخذ العينات –– سبر
Sampling distribution	distribution des échantillons	توزيع العينات
Sampling error	erreur d'échantillonnage	خطأ الاستبار – خطأ السبر
Samurai bonds	obligations samuraïs	سندات دولية يابانية–سندات «ساموري»
Sanitary services	services de la santé	خدمات صحية
Satiability of wants	satiabilité des besoins	قابلية الحاجات للاشباع
Satisfaction of a need	satisfaction d'un besoin	اشباع حاجة
Satisficing model	modèle de satisfaction	نموذج ارضائي – نموذج رضوي
Saturation point	point de saturation	حد التشبع
Save, to	épargner	ادخر – اقتصد
Saver	épargnant	مدخر
Saving (s)	épargne	ادخار–مدخرات
Savings account	compte d'épargne	حساب ادخار – حساب توفير
Savings and loan association	société d'épargne et de prêt (immobilier)	شركة ادخار واقراض (عقاري)
Savings bank	caisse d'épargne	بنك ادخار – صندوق ادخار
Savings bond **Saving certificate**	bon d'épargne	سند ادخار
Savings book	livret d'épargne	دفتر توفير
Savings deposit	dépôt d'épargne	حساب توفير – حساب ادخار وديعة ادخار
Saving plan	plan d'épargne	برنامج ادخار
Saving potential	capacité d'épargne	طاقة ادخارية
Savings ratio	taux d'épargne	معدل الادخار
Scale factor	facteur d'échelle	عامل الحجم
Scale of output	volume de production niveau de production	حجم الانتاج – مستوى الانتاج
Scale of preference	échelle de préférence	سلم التفضيل – جدول التفضيل
Scale of prices	gamme des prix échelle des prix	جدول الأسعار
Scale of production	volume de production échelle de production	حجم الانتاج – مستوى الانتاج
Scarce currency	monnaie rare	عملة صعبة
Scarce resources	ressources limitées	موارد محدودة
Scarcity	rareté	ندرة
Scarcity in skills	pénurie de compétences	ندرة الكفاءات
Scarcity of capital	pénurie de capitaux	شح الرسمال – قصور الرسمال

Scarcity of money	rareté de la monnaie	ندرة النقود
Scarcity rent	rente de rareté	ريع الندرة
Scarcity value	valeur de rareté	قيمة الندرة
Scatter	dispersion	تشتت
Scatter coefficient	coefficient de dispersion	معامل التشتت
Scatter diagram	diagramme de dispersion	رسم تشتت
Scenario	scénario	صوار – وضع افتراضي
Schedular taxes	impôts cédulaires	ضرائب نوعية
Schedule taxes		
Scheduled taxes		
Schedule of implementation	programme d'exécution	جدول التنفيذ
Schedule of par values	tableau des parités	جدول أسعار التعادل
Schedule of repayment	échéancier	جدول السداد
	tableau d'amortissement	
Schedule of withdrawal of loan proceeds	tableau relatif au retrait des fonds empruntés	جدول السحب من القرض
Scheduling	programmation	برمجة – جدولة
Scheme	projet – plan – système	برنامج – مشروع – نظام
Science intensive technology	technologie basée sur la science	تكنولوجية قائمة على العلوم – تكنولوجية علمية
Scientific and technological potential	potentiel scientifique et technologique	الطاقة العلمية والتكنولوجية
Scrap value	valeur-rebut	قيمة التخلص
	valeur de casse	
	valeur-ferraille	
Screening of projects	filtrage des projets	فرز المشاريع
	pré-sélection des projets	
Scrip	titres – certificats	سندات – شهادات – شهادات مؤقتة
	certificats provisoires	
Scrip certificate	certificat d'actions	شهادة أسهم – شهادة اكتتاب
	certificat de souscription	
Scrip issue	émission d'actions gratuites	توزيع أسهم مجانية
	émission de titres	اصدار أوراق مالية
Sea-bed resources	ressources sous-marines	موارد قاع البحار
Sea navigation	navigation maritime	ملاحة بحرية
Sea transportation	transports maritimes	نقل بحري
Seasonal credit	crédit saisonnier	ائتمان موسمي
Seasonal fluctuations	variations saisonnières	تقلبات موسمية – تغيرات موسمية
	fluctuations saisonnières	
Seasonal irrigation	irrigation saisonnière	ري موسمي
Seasonal migration	migration saisonnière	هجرة موسمية
	déplacement saisonnier	
Seasonal movements	mouvements saisonniers	تغيرات موسمية – حركات موسمية
Seasonal variations	variations saisonnières	
Seasonal unemployment	chômage saisonnier	بطالة موسمية

Seasonal work	travail saisonnier	عمل موسمي
Seasonal workers	travailleurs saisonniers	عمال موسميون
Seasonally-adjusted figures	chiffres corrigés pour variations saisonnières	أرقام معدلة موسمياً
Second-best	second-best	الثنيان
Second-hand equipment	matériel d'occasion	أجهزة مستعملة
Second-hand goods	biens d'occasion	سلع مستعملة
Second-hand market	marché d'occasion	سوق الأشياء المستعملة – سوق المستعمل
Second-rate shares	actions de second rang	أسهم من الدرجة الثانية
Secondary benefits	avantages secondaires – avantages indirects	منافع ثانوية – منافع غير مباشرة
Secondary industries	industries secondaires	صناعات ثانوية
Secondary liquidities	liquidités secondaires	سيولة ثانوية
Secondary market	marché secondaire	سوق التداول
Secondary sector	secteur secondaire	القطاع الثاني
Secret partner	commanditaire	شريك موصي
Secret reserves	réserves occultes	احتياطي خفي – احتياطي مستتر
Sector loan	prêt sectoriel	قرض قطاعي
Sector study Sectoral study	étude sectorielle	دراسة قطاعية – مسح قطاعي
Sectoral distribution	ventilation sectorielle ventilation par secteurs	توزيع قطاعي
Sectoral plan	plan sectoriel	خطة قطاعية
Sectoral planning	planification sectorielle	تخطيط قطاعي
Secular growth	croissance séculaire croissance à long terme	نمو طويل الأجل – نمو طويل المدى
Secular stagnation	stagnation séculaire	ركود طويل الأجل
Secular trend	tendance séculaire tendance à long terme	اتجاه طويل الأجل
Secured debt	dette garantie	دين مضمون – دين مكفول
Secured loan	emprunt garanti	قرض مضمون – قرض مكفول
Securities	titres	أوراق مالية – صكوك مالية – سندات
Securities account	compte de titres	حساب ايداع أوراق مالية
Securities market	marché des valeurs	سوق الأوراق المالية – سوق الأسهم والسندات
Security (guarantee)	garantie caution	ضمان
Security account	dossier-titres compte-titres	حساب سندات – حساب أوراق مالية
Security assistance	assistance de sécurité	معونة أمان – معونة أمنية
Security holding	portefeuille-titres	حافظة سندات – حافظة أوراق مالية
Security of supply	sécurité de l'approvisionnement	ضمان التزويد – ضمان التزود ضمان الامداد
Sedentarisation	sédentarisation	توطين – اقرار – قنطرة

Sedentary population	population sédentaire	السكان المستقرون
Seignioriage	seigneuriage	رسم السك
	droits de monnayage	
Seizure	saisie	حجز – استيلاء
Selection of projects	choix des projets	اختيار المشاريع – تخير المشاريع
Selective credit control	contrôle sélectif du crédit	الرقابة الكيفية على الائتمان
Selective market	marché sélectif	سوق تخيري
Selective tender	adjudication restreinte	مناقصة محدودة – مناقصة خاصة
Self-consumption	auto-consommation	استهلاك ذاتي
Self-determination	auto-détermination	حق تقرير المصير
Self-development	développement autonome	تنمية ذاتية
Self-employed	travailleur indépendant	عامل مستقل – حرفي
Self-employment	travail indépendant	عمل مستقل
Self-financing	auto-financement	تمويل ذاتي
Self-help	efforts propres	جهود ذاتية – مساعدة ذاتية
	auto-assistance	اعتماد على النفس
Self-help institutions	institutions d'auto-assistance	مؤسسات المساعدة الذاتية
		مؤسسات الاعتماد على النفس
Self-interest	intérêt personnel	المصلحة الذاتية
Self-liquidating loan	prêt auto-amortissable	قرض مستصفي
Self-liquidating project	projet auto-amortissable	مشروع مغط لتكاليفه – مشروع مستصفي
	projet auto-liquidant	
Self-managed enterprise	entreprise auto-gérée	مشروع مسير ذاتياً – مشروع مسير عمالياً
	entreprise à gestion ouvrière	
Self-management	auto-gestion	تسيير ذاتي
Self-reliance	efforts propres	جهود ذاتية – اعتماد على النفس
	autonomie – autodétermination	
Self-service	libre-service	خدمة ذاتية
Self-sufficiency	autarcie	اكتفاء ذاتي
	auto-suffisance	
Self-sufficient economy	économie fermée	اقتصاد مغلق – اقتصاد مكتف ذاتياً
	économie autarcique	اقتصاد مستكف
Self-sustained growth	croissance auto-entretenue	نمو تلقائي – نمو ذاتي
Sell, to	vendre	باع
Sell forward, to	vendre à terme	باع لأجل
Sell off, to	liquider	صفي
Sell short, to	vendre à découvert	باع على المكشوف – ضارب على النزول
Seller	vendeur	بائع
Sellers' inflation	inflation des vendeurs	تضخم البائعين
Sellers' market	marché-vendeurs	سوق البائعين
Selling arrangements	dispositions concernant la vente	ترتيبات البيع
Selling costs	frais de vente	تكاليف البيع
Selling group	syndicat de placement	حلقة التصريف – دارة البيع

Selling price	prix de vente	سعر البيع – ثمن البيع
Selling rate	cours-vendeur	سعر البيع
Semi-annual coupon	coupon semestriel	قسيمة نصف سنوية
Semi-annual instalments	versements semestriels	أقساط نصف سنوية
Semi-arid agriculture	agriculture des régions semi-arides	زراعة المناطق شبه الجافة
Semi-durable goods	biens semi-durables	سلع شبه معمرة
Semi-finished products	produits semi-finis	سلع شبه تامة
Semi-logarithmic chart	diagramme semi-logarithmique	رسم نصف لوغاريتمي – لوحة نصف لوغاريتمية
Semi-manufactured product Semi-processed goods	produits semi-ouvrés	سلع شبه مصنعة
Semi-skilled manpower	main d'oeuvre semi-qualifiée	عمال شبه متخصصين قوة عاملة شبه متخصصة
Senior capital	capital privilégié	رسمال ممتاز
Senior debt	dette privilégiée	دين ممتاز – دين مقدم
Senior partner	associé principal	شريك أول – شريك رئيسي
Sensitivity analysis	analyse de sensibilité	تحليل استجابي – تحليل الاستجابة
Separate development	développement séparé	نمو منفصل
Separation of ownership and control	dissociation de la propriété et du contrôle	فصل الملكية عن الادارة انفصام التملك والادارة
Sequential analysis	analyse séquentielle	تحليل تعاقبي
Serf	serf	قن – عبد (الاقطاع)
Serfdom	servage	نظام العبودية – نظام القنانة (الاقطاع)
Serial bonds	obligations remboursables par séries obligations sérielles	سندات مسلسلة
Serial correlation	corrélation caténaire corrélation sérielle	ارتباط تتابعي – ارتباط مسلسل
Sericulture	sériculture	انتاج الحرير
Services	services	خدمات
Service charge	commission de service frais d'administration frais de gestion	رسم خدمات – رسم اداري
Service contract	marché de prestation de services contrat de services	عقد أداء خدمات – عقد خدمات
Service industries	industrie des services	قطاع الخدمات
Service of the loan	service de l'emprunt	خدمة القرض
Service-oriented economy	économie à dominante-services	اقتصاد خدمات
Service payments	paiements du service de l'emprunt	مدفوعات خدمة القرض
Servicing facilities	services d'entretien	خدمات صيانة – خدمات جارية
Set-aside programme	programme de la jachère	برنامج الاستحال – برنامج الأرض المستحالة
Set of prices	série de prix	مجموعة أسعار
Settlement	colonie colonisation installation	مستوطنة – مستعمرة – توطن – اقرار

Settlement (*of a debt, etc.*)	règlement (*d'une dette, etc.*) liquidation	تسوية – تصفية – دفع (دين..الخ)
Settlement (*of disputes*)	solution de ... règlement de litiges	تسوية المنازعات
Settlement account	compte de liquidation	حساب تصفية
Settlement price	cours de résiliation	سعر الفسخ
Settlers	colons	وضائع – مستوطنون – معمرون
Settling date	date de liquidation	تاريخ الدفع – تاريخ التسوية
Sexual discrimination	discrimination sexuelle	تمييز جنسي
Shadow exchange rate	taux de change comptable	سعر صرف اعتباري سعر صرف محاسبي
Shadow prices	prix comptables prix de référence	سعر اعتباري – ثمن محاسبي
Shadow pricing	emploi des prix de référence	تسعير اعتباري – تسعير محاسبي
Shadow wage rate	taux de salaire comptable salaire de référence	معدل الأجر الاعتباري معدل الأجر المحاسبي
Sham dividends	dividendes fictifs	أرباح وهمية
Shanty-town	bidonville	عشيش – مدينة عشيش
share	action – quote-part part – titre	سهم – نصيب – سند
Share capital	capital-actions capital social	رسمال سهمي – رسمال المساهمين
Share certificate	titre d'action	سهم مؤقت – شهادة مساهمة
Share-cropper **Share-farmer** **Share-tenant**	métayer	مؤاكر – مزارع
Share-cropping	métayage	مؤاكرة – مزارعة
Share prices	cours des actions	سعر الأسهم
Share split	fractionnement d'actions	تقسيم الأسهم
Shareholder	actionnaire	مساهم
Shareholder's equity	participation nette des sociétaires	صافي مساهمة المساهمين
Sheep breeding	élevage de moutons élevage ovin	تربية الأغنام
Sheltered industry	industrie protégée	صناعة محمية
Shifting of tax	transfert de l'impôt	نقل عبء الضريبة – نقل الضريبة
Shiftwork	travail par équipes	عمل الورديات
Shipbuilding and repairing industry	construction et réparations navales	صناعة بناء واصلاح السفن
Ship-load	cargaison fret	حمولة
Shipment	expédition chargement	شحنة – شحن

Shipment on consignment	envoi en consignation	شحن تحت الايداع
Shipping	transport maritime	ملاحة – نقل بحري
Shipper	chargeur	شاحن
Shipping line	ligne de navigation voie maritime	خط ملاحي – خط بحري
Shipping documents	documents d'expédition	مستندات الشحن – وثائق الشحن
Shipyard	chantier de construction navale	ترسانة بحرية – ترسانة بناء سفن
Shopping center	centre commercial	مركز تجاري
Short-fall in export earnings	déficit des recettes d'exportation	عجز في ايرادات التصدير
Short-fall in export proceeds	insuffisance des recettes d'exportation	نقص ايرادات التصدير
Short list	liste de pré-sélection	قائمة المرشحين
Short sale	vente à découvert	بيع على المكشوف
Short-seller	vendeur à découvert	بائع على المكشوف
Short term	court terme	قصير الأجل – الأجل القصير
Short-term bills	effets à court terme	أوراق تجارية قصيرة الأجل
Short-term capital	capitaux à court terme	رسمال قصير الأجل
Short-term claims	créances à court terme	حقوق قصيرة الأجل
Short-term credit	crédit à court terme	ائتمان قصير الأجل
Short-term funds	fonds à court terme	أموال قصيرة الأجل
Short-term liabilities	dettes à court terme	ديون قصيرة الأجل
Shortage	déficit pénurie manque	عجز – نقصان – ندرة
Shortage of capital	pénurie de capital	شح الرسمال – ندرة الرسمال – قصور الرسمال
Shortage of food	pénurie de produits alimentaires	نقص المواد الغذائية – قصور المواد الغذائية
Shortage of labour	pénurie de main-d'oeuvre	قصور الأيدي العاملة
Showroom	salle d'exposition	صالة العرض
Shunting	arbitrage commerce triangulaire	موازنة – تجارة ثلاثية
Shutdown point	seuil de fermeture – seuil d'arrêt	حد الغلق – حد الاغلاق
Side effects	effects secondaires	آثار جانبية
Sight assets	avoirs à vue	اصول معجلة
Sight debt	dette à vue	دين معجل
Sight deposits	dépôts à vue	ودائع معجلة – ودائع تحت الطلب
Sight bill Sight draft	traite à vue	كمبيالة معجلة – سند اذني معجل
Sight credit	crédit à vue	اعتماد تحت الطلب
Significant level	seuil de signifiance	حد الدلالة – مستوى الدلالة
Significance test	test de signifiance	اختبار الدلالة
Silent partner	commanditaire	شريك موصى
Silo	silo	صومعة غلال – صومعة حبوب – مطمر

Silting	envasement	ترسب
Silver standard	étalon-argent	قاعدة الفضة
Silviculture	sylviculture	زراعة الأشجار
Simple commodity production	production marchande simple	الانتاج السلعي البسيط
Simple interest	intérêt simple	فائدة بسيطة
Simple reproduction	reproduction simple	اعادة الانتاج البسيط
Simplex method	méthode du simplex	منهج البسيط
Simulation model	modèle de simulation	نموذج ارمازي – نموذج محاكاة
Single-crop economy	économie de monoculture	اقتصاد المحصول الواحد
Single-crop farming	monoculture	زراعة المحصول الواحد
Single entry accounting	comptabilité simple comptabilité en partie simple	محاسبة القيد المفرد
Single factorial terms of trade	termes de l'échange uni-factoriel	معدل التبادل العواملي البسيط
Single tax system	système de l'impôt unique	نظام الضريبة الواحدة
Single tender	marché de gré à gré	ممارسة
Sinking fund	fonds d'amortissement caisse d'amortissement	صندوق استهلاك – صندوق سداد
Site of a project	chantier du projet emplacement du projet	مكان المشروع – موقع المشروع
Site rent	rente d'emplacement rente de situation	ريع الموقع
Sites and services project	projet de trames d'accueil	مشروع تقسيم أراضي
Siting of a project	localisation d'un projet	توطين المشروع – تحديد موقع المشروع
Size of the enterprise	dimension de l'entreprise taille de l'entreprise	حجم المؤسسة – حجم المشروع
Size of the market	dimension du marché étendue du marché taille du marché	حجم السوق – نطاق السوق
Skewness of a curve	dissymétrie de la courbe	اعوجاج المنحنى – التواء المنحنى
Skilled labour Skilled manpower	main-d'oeuvre qualifiée	عمل مؤهل – قوة عاملة مؤهلة
Skilled workman	ouvrier spécialisé	عامل متخصص
Slack season	morte-saison	موسم الكساد
Slack variable	variable d'écart	مكمل – متغير مكمل
Slackening	ralentissement	تباطؤ – فتور
Slackening of demand	ralentissement de la demande	تقاعس الطلب
Slave system	système esclavagiste	نظام الرق – نظام العبودية
Sleeping partner	commanditaire	شريك موصى
Sliding-scale clause	clause d'échelle mobile	نص المستوى المتحرك – نص السلم المتحرك
Sliding tariff	tarif douanier mobile	تعرفة جمركية متحركة
Sliding wage scale	échelle mobile des salaires	السلم المتحرك للاجور
Slope of a curve	pente d'une courbe	انحدار المنحنى – ميل المنحنى
Slowdown	ralentissement grève perlée	تباطؤ – فتور – ابطاء العمل

Sluggish growth	croissance lente	نمو متثاقل
	croissance hésitante	
Sluggish market	marché déprimé	سوق راكد – سوق كاسد – سوق متثاقل
Slump	dépression	آزبة – انهيار – كساد
	effondrement	
Small business	petites entreprises	مشروعات صغيرة
Small change	monnaie d'appoint	نقود مساعدة
Small crafts	artisanat	الحرفية
Small farm	petite exploitation	حيازات صغيرة – استغلالات صغيرة
Small holding	petite propriété	وحدات زراعية صغيرة
Small holder	petit exploitant	مزارع صغير
Small saver	petit épargnant	مدخر صغير
Small-scale industry	petite industrie	صناعة صغيرة
Smuggled goods	marchandises de contrebande –	سلع مهربة – سلع تهريب
	articles de contrebande	
Smuggling	contrebande	تهريب
"Snake in the tunnel" system	système de la flexibilité contrôlée	نظام الصرف المرن المحدد
	serpent communautaire – serpent	الثعبان النقدي
	monétaire	
Social accounting	comptabilité nationale	محاسبة قومية
Social accounts	comptes nationaux	حسابات قومية
Social benefits	prestations sociales	اعانات اجتماعية – مساعدات اجتماعية
	avantages sociaux	منافع اجتماعية – فوائد اجتماعية
Social capital	capital social	رسمال اجتماعي
Social change	changement social	تغير اجتماعي – تغيير اجتماعي
Social class	classe sociale	طبقة اجتماعية
Social compact	contrat social	عقد اجتماعى
Social contract		
Social conflicts	conflits sociaux	نزاعات اجتماعية – صراعات اجتماعية
Social costs	coûts sociaux	تكاليف اجتماعية – كلف اجتماعية
Social democracy	social-démocratie	الاشتراكية الديمقراطية
Social development	développement social	تنمية اجتماعية – نمو اجتماعي
Social discount rate	taux social d'actualisation	المعدل الاجتماعي للاحطاط
Social dividend	dividende social	عائد اجتماعي – دخل اجتماعي
Social division of labour	division sociale du travail	التقسيم الاجتماعي للعمل
Social environment	milieu social	بيئة اجتماعية
Social framework	cadre social	اطار اجتماعي – هيكل اجتماعي
	structure sociale	
Social indicators	indices sociaux	مؤشرات اجتماعية
Social inequalities	inégalités sociales	فوارق اجتماعية
Social infrastructure	infrastructure sociale	بنية أساسية اجتماعية
Social institutions	institutions sociales	نظم اجتماعية

Social insurance	assurances sociales	تأمينات اجتماعية
Social insurance benefits	prestations de la sécurité sociale	اعانات التأمين الاجتماعي
Social integration	intégration sociale	تكامل اجتماعي – تآلف اجتماعي
Social investment	investissements sociaux	استثمارات اجتماعية
Social justice	justice sociale	عدالة اجتماعية
Social mobility	mobilité sociale	سيولة اجتماعية
Social order	ordre social	نظام اجتماعي
Social overhead capital	infrastructure sociale	بنية أساسية اجتماعية
Social planning	planification sociale	تخطيط اجتماعي
Social product	produit social	ناتج اجتماعي
Social profitability	rentabilité sociale	ارحية اجتماعية
Social progress	progrès social	تطور اجتماعي
Social project	projet social	مشروع اجتماعي
Social reform	réforme sociale	اصلاح اجتماعي
Social relations of production	rapports sociaux de production	علاقات الانتاج الاجتماعية
Social returns	rendements sociaux	عوائد اجتماعية – منافع اجتماعية
Social scale	échelle sociale	سلم اجتماعي – مراتب اجتماعية
Social sciences	sciences sociales	علوم اجتماعية
Social security	sécurité sociale	تأمين اجتماعي
Social security benefits	allocations de la sécurité sociale	اعانات التأمين الاجتماعي
Social security contributions	cotisations de la sécurité sociale	مساهمات التأمين الاجتماعي
Social services	services sociaux	خدمات اجتماعية
Social status	situation sociale rang social	مركز اجتماعي
Social strata	couches sociales	فئات اجتماعية – طبقات اجتماعية
Social stratification	stratification sociale	تقسيم اجتماعي – سلم اجتماعي
Social surplus	plus-value sociale	فائض اجتماعي
Social system	système social	نظام اجتماعي
Social technology	technologie sociale	التكنية الاجتماعية – التكنولجية الاجتماعية
Social utility	utilité sociale	منفعة اجتماعية – نفع اجتماعي
Social value	valeur sociale	القيمة الاجتماعية
Social welfare	sécurité sociale services sociaux bien-être social	خدمات اجتماعية – تأمين اجتماعي رفاهة اجتماعية
Social welfare function	fonction sociale de bien-être	دالة الرفاهة الاجتماعية
Socialism	socialisme	الاشتراكية
Socialist economy	économie socialiste	اقتصاد اشتراكي
Socio-economic development	développement socio-économique	التنمية الاجتماعية الاقتصادية
Socio-economic indicators	indicateurs socio-économiques	مؤشرات اجتماعية اقتصادية
Socio-political variable	variable socio-politique	متغير سياسي اجتماعي
Sociology of development	sociologie du développement	اجتماعيات التنمية – علم الاجتماع الانمائي
Soft currency	monnaie faible	عملة سهلة
Soft funds	fonds concessionnels	أموال ميسرة

Soft loan	prêt concessionnel	قرض ميسر
Soft terms	conditions de faveur – conditions libérales	شروط ميسرة
Software	composante immatérielle – composante logicielle	عنصر الفكر – عنصر غير مادي
Soft window	volet concessionnel guichet concessionnel	طاقة ميسرة
Soil conservation	conservation du sol	حفظ التربة
Soil erosion	érosion du sol	تعرية التربة – سحل التربة
Soil exhaustion	épuisement du sol	انجاع الأرض – انهاك التربة
Soil improvement	amélioration des sols	تحسين التربة
Soil science	science du sol pédologie	علم التربة
Soil survey	étude des sols étude pédologique	دراسة التربة
Solar energy	énergie solaire	طاقة شمسية
Sole distributor	agent exclusif	وكيل وحيد
Solidarity	solidarité	تضامن
Solidarity strike	grève de sympathie	اضراب تضامني
Solvency Solvability	solvabilité	ملاءة مالية – ملاءة
Solvent debtor	débiteur solvable	مدين مليء
Sophisticated techniques Sophisticated technology	techniques sophistiquées technologie sophistiquée	فن انتاجي معقد تكنية متقدمة
Sound project	projet valable	مشروع سليم
Sounding	sondage	سبر – استبار
Source country	pays d'origine	دولة الأصل
Source enterprise	entreprise d'origine	مؤسسة الأصل – المؤسسة الأصلية
Source of energy	source d'énergie	مصدر طاقة
Source of finance	source de financement	مصدر تمويل
Source of funds	source de financement origine des fonds	مصدر تمويل – مصدر الأموال
Sources and applications of funds	sources et emplois des fonds	مصادر واستخدامات التمويل
Sourcing	détermination de la source d'approvisionnement	تحديد مصدر التزود – تحديد مصدر الشراء
Sovereign risk	risque politique risque étatique	مخاطر سيادية – مخاطر سياسية
Sovereignty over natural resources	souveraineté sur les ressources naturelles	السيادة على الموارد الطبيعية
Sovkhose (USSR)	*sovkhose* (URSS)	مزرعة حكومية (الاتحاد السوفيتي)
Space industry	industrie spatiale	صناعة الفضاء
Space-ship economy	économie de vaisseau spatial	اقتصاد سفينة الفضاء
Spare parts	pièces de rechange	قطع غيار

Spatial economics	économie spatiale économie des espaces	اقتصاديات المناطق – اقتصاديات المكان
Spatial factor	facteur spatial	عامل مكاني – عامل المكان
Spatial-temporal analysis	analyse spatio-temporelle	تحليل زماني مكاني
Special budget	budget spécial	موازنة خاصة – ميزانية خاصة
Special drawing rights (SDRs)	droits de tirage spéciaux (DTS)	حقوق السحب الخاصة
Special fund	fonds spécial	صندوق خاص
Special majority	majorité qualifiée	أغلبية خاصة
Specialisation	spécialisation	تخصص
Specialised agencies	institutions spécialisées	وكالات متخصصة
Specialised credit institution	établissement de crédit spécialisé	مؤسسة ائتمانية متخصصة – مصرف متخصص
Specialised fund	fonds d'investissement spécialisé	صندوق استثمار متخصص
Specie	pièces de monnaie	مسكوكات – سكة
Specific (*customs*) duty	droit (*de douane*) spécifique	رسم (جمركي) نوعي
Specific project	project spécifique	مشروع محدد
Specifications of a project	état descriptif du projet devis descriptif du projet	مواصفات المشروع
Speculate, to	spéculer	ضارب
Speculation	spéculation	مضاربة
Speculative funds	fonds spéculatifs	أموال مضاربة
Speculative motive	motif de spéculation	دافع المضاربة
Speculative shares	titres spéculatifs valeurs spéculatives	أسهم مضاربة
Speculator	spéculateur	مضارب
Spend, to	dépenser	انفق
Spendable income	revenu disponible	دخل متاح – دخل قابل للانفاق
Spending	dépense	انفاق
Spending agency	organisme dépenseur	جهاز الانفاق
Sphere of influence	sphère d'influence	منطقة نفوذ
Spill-over effects	effets indirects effet secondaires	آثار غير مباشرة
Split exchange market	double marché des changes	سوق صرف مزدوج
Split-level trust	fonds d'investissement à deux volets fonds d'investissement bivalent	صندوق استثمار مزدوج
Sponsor	promoteur parrain	مروج – مؤسس – كفيل – راع
Sponsor, to	promouvoir – parrainer	روّج – كفل – تبنى – رعى
Spot delivery	livraison immédiate	تسليم فوري
Spot exchange operation	opération de change au comptant	عملية صرف معجلة – عملية صرف فوري
Spot market	marché du comptant	سوق المعجل
Spot payment	paiement immédiat	دفع فوري
Spot rate	cours au comptant	سعر العمليات المعجلة – سعر فوري سعر المعجل

Spot transactions	opérations au comptant	عمليات معجلة
Spread	marge – écart – fourchette	هامش – فرق – مدى
Spread effect	effet de propagation	أثر الانتشار
	effet de diffusion	
Spreading of risks	répartition des risques	توزيع المخاطر
Sprinkler irrigation	aspersion	ري بالرش
	aspersage	
Spurious correlation	corrélation illusoire	ارتباط وهمي
	fausse corrélation	
Squatter settlements	bidonvilles	عشيش
Stabilisation fund	fonds de stabilisation	صندوق تثبيت
Stabilisation of commodity prices	stabilisation du prix des produits	تثبيت أسعار السلع
		تثبيت أثمان المنتجات
Stabilisation of export earnings	stabilisation des recettes d'exportation	تثبيت ايرادات التصدير
Stabilisation plan	plan de stabilisation	خطة تثبيت
Stabilisation policy	politique de stabilisation	سياسة التثبيت
Stabilisation program	programme de stabilisation	برنامج تثبيت
Stability	stabilité	ثبات – استقرار
Stability of prices	stabilité de prix	ثبات الأسعار – استقرار الأثمان
Stability of trade	stabilité des échanges	استقرار المبادلات
Stable currency	monnaie stable	عملة ثابتة
Stable equilibrium	équilibre stable	توازن مستقر – توازن ثابت
Stable exchange rates	taux de change stables	أسعار صرف ثابتة
Stable growth	croissance continue	نمو مطرد – نمو متوازن
	croissance équilibrée	
Stable market	marché stable	سوق مستقر
Stable money	monnaie stable	نقد ثابت القيمة – عملة ثابتة
Stable prices	prix stables	أسعار ثابتة – أثمان مستقرة
Staff member	membre du personnel	عضو الجهاز الفني
Stag	spéculateur à la souscription	مضارب اكتتاب
Stage by stage development	évolution par étapes	نمو مرحلي – نمو تدريجي
	développement par étapes	
Stage of development	étape du développement	مرحلة النمو – مرحلة التطور
	stade de développement	
Stage of economic growth	étape de l'évolution économique	مرحلة التطور الاقتصادي
		مرحلة النمو الاقتصادي
Stagflation	stagflation	كساد تضخمي – تضخم كسادي – تكسدم
Staggered payments	paiements échelonnés	مدفوعات متوالية
Stagnant economy	économie stagnante	اقتصاد راكد
Stagnation	stagnation	ركود
	marasme	
Stamp duty	timbre fiscal	رسم دمغة – دمغة
Stamp fee	droit de timbre	

Stand-by agreement	accord de confirmation – accord de stand-by accord d'aide éventuelle	اتفاق موازرة – اتفاق توفير ائتمان
Stand-by capacity	capacité disponible	طاقة متاحة
Stand-by credit	crédit stand-by – prêt conditionnel ligne de crédit	اعتماد متاح – ائتمان موازر
Standard basket of currencies	panier-type de monnaies	سلة نقدية مختارة – سلة نقدية نمطية
Standard-basket of goods	panier-type de biens	سلة سلعية مختارة – سلة سلعية نمطية
Standard costs	coûts standards normes de coûts	تكاليف نمطية – تكاليف نموذجية
Standard deviation	écart-type	انحراف معياري
Standard error	erreur-type	خطأ معياري
Standard of living	niveau de vie	مستوى المعيشة
Standards of project appraisal	critères d'évaluation des projets	معايير تقييم المشاريع
Standard of value	étalon de valeur	مقياس للقيم
Standard specifications	normes descriptives spécifications standardisées	مواصفات نمطية – مواصفات نموذجية
Standardisation	normalisation standardisation	تنميط
Standardisation of agricultural produce	normalisation des produits agricoles	تنميط المنتجات الزراعية
Standardised products	produits standardisés	منتجات نمطية
Stand-still agreement	accord moratoire	اتفاق مكابلة
Staple food	aliment principal	غذاء أساسي – غذاء رئيسي
Staple product	produit principal produit de base	سلعة رئيسية – ناتج أساسي
Start-up costs	frais de démarrage – frais de mise en train	تكاليف البدء
Start-up period	période de démarrage période de rodage période de mise en train	فترة البدء – فترة البدى
State bourgeoisie	bourgeoisie d'Etat	بورجوازية الدولة
State capitalism	capitalisme d'Etat	رسمالية الدولة
State control	contrôle de l'Etat	اشراف حكومي – اشراف الحكومة
State economy	économie étatique	اقتصاد حكومي
State enterprise	entreprise étatique	مشروع حكومي – مشروع عام
State farm	*sovkhose* – ferme étatique	مزرعة حكومية
State guarantee	garantie de l'Etat	ضمان حكومي – ضمان الدولة
State intervention	intervention de l'Etat	تدخل الدولة
State monopoly	monopole d'Etat	احتكار حكومي
State monopoly capitalism	capitalisme monopoliste d'Etat	نظام احتكارية الدولة
State of technology	état de la technologie	الأوضاع الفنية – الأوضاع التكنية
State of the arts	niveau de la technique	

State-owned bank	banque d'Etat	مصرف حكومي – بنك حكومي
State property	propriété publique	ملكية عامة – ملك حكومي
	propriété de l'Etat	
State sector	secteur étatique	القطاع الحكومي – القطاع العام
	secteur public	
State socialism	socialisme d'Etat	اشتراكية الدولة
State trading	commerce d'Etat	اتجار الدولة – تجارة حكومية
State-trading countries	pays à commerce d'Etat	دول ذات تجارة حكومية
Stated capital	capital déclaré	رسمال مقرر
Stateless money	monnaie apatride	أموال نقيلة – أموال مفرجة
Statement of account	relevé de compte	كشف حساب
	extrait de compte	
Static equilibrium	équilibre statique	توازن ساكن – توازن سكوني
Stationary economy	économie stationnaire	اقتصاد ساكن – اقتصاد راكد
Stationary population	population stationnaire	عدد سكان ثابت
Stationary state	état stationnaire	مجتمع ساكن – مجتمع لا حركي
Statistical analysis	analyse statistique	تحليل احصائي
Statistical association	association statistique	توافق احصائي
Statistical discrepancy	écart statistique	فرق احصائي
Statistical indicators	indicateurs statistiques	مؤشرات احصائية
Statistical information	information statistique – données	بيانات احصائية
	statistiques	
Statistical methods	méthodes statistiques	أساليب احصائية
Statistical observations	observations statistiques	مشاهدات احصائية
Statistical population	population statistique	مجتمع احصائي
Statistical survey	enquête statistique	دراسة احصائية – مسح احصائي
Statistical tables	tableaux statistiques	جداول احصائية
Statistical test	test statistique	اختبار احصائي
Statistician	statisticien	احصائي
Statistics	statistique	الاحصاء – بيانات احصائية
	statistiques	
Status quo	*status quo*	الوضع الراهن
Status quo ante	*status quo ante*	الوضع السابق
Status of subscriptions	état des souscriptions	وضع المساهمات
Statutory reserve	réserve statutaire	احتياطي نظامي
Stay-in strike	grève sur le tas	اضراب ماكت – اعتصام
Steady growth	croissance soutenue	نمو ثابت – نمو متواصل – نمو منتظم
	croissance régulière	
Steady market	marché soutenu	سوق متماسك
Steel complex	complexe sidérurgique	مجمع صلب – مجمع فولاذي
Steel mill	aciérie	مصنع صلب – مصنع فولاذ
Steppe	steppe	سباسب
Sterilisation of gold	stérilisation de l'or	تعقيم الذهب

Sterling area	zone sterling	منطقة الاسترليني – المنطقة الاسترلينية
Sterling bloc	bloc sterling	كتلة الاسترليني – الكتلة الاسترلينية
Stochastic equation	équation stochastique	معادلة احتمالية
Stochastic model	modèle stochastique	نموذج احتمالي
Stochastic variable	variable aléatoire	متغير عشوائي – متغير احتمالي
Stock (*goods*)	stock (*biens*)	مخزون – كداس (سلع)
	inventaire	
Stock (*capital*)	capital	رسمال
Stocks	titres	أسهم – أوراق مالية
	actions	
Stocks and flows	stocks et flux	أرصدة وتدفقات
Stockage	stockage	تخزين – تكديس – اركام
Stock-broker	courtier	سمسار (مالي)
	agent de change	
Stock certificate	certificat d'action	شهادة أسهم
	certificat représentatif de titres	
Stock clearance	liquidation des stocks	تصفية المخزون
Stock company	société par actions	شركة مساهمة
Stock concept	concept de stock	مفهوم رصيدي
Stock dividend	dividende sous forme d'actions	أرباح في صورة أسهم
		أرباح سهمية
Stock exchange	bourse des valeurs	سوق الأوراق المالية
Stock market	marché des valeurs	
Stock exchange transactions	opérations de bourse	عمليات السوق المالية
	transactions boursières	
Stock farmer	éleveur	مربي ماشية – مواش
Stock-holder	actionnaire	مساهم – حامل أسهم
Stock issue	émission d'actions	اصدار أسهم
Stock of gold	stock d'or	رصيد الذهب
Stock option	option de souscription	حق اكتتاب – خيار اكتتاب
Stock price quotations	cours des actions – cotation des	أسعار الأسهم – أثمان الأوراق المالية
	actions	
Stock-taking	inventaire	جرد
Stock-turnover	rotation des stocks	دورة المخزون – تدوير الكداس
Stockpiling	constitution de stocks	تكوين مخزون – تكديس
Stockbuilding		
Stockpiling cycle	cycle d'inventaire	دورة كداسية
Stop-and-go strike	grève intermittente	اضراب متقطع
Stop-gap loan	crédit transitoire	قرض مؤقت – قرض طوارئ
Storage and warehousing	entreposage	تخزين
	emmagasinage	
Storage (*electronics*)	mémoire (*électronique*)	ذاكرة (الكترونيات)
Store of value	réserve de valeur	وعاء لحفظ القيمة – وسيلة ادخار
Stored-up labour	travail congelé	عمل مجسم

Straight bond	obligation classique	سند تقليدي – سند بحت
Straight-line depreciation	dépréciation linéaire	استهلاك خطي
Straight-line trend	trend linéaire	اتجاه خطي
	tendance linéaire	
Strategic raw materials	matières premières stratégiques	مواد أولية أساسية
		مواد أولية حاسمة
Strategic sector	secteur clé	قطاع أساسي – قطاع حاسم
Streams of costs and benefits	flux des coûts et des avantages	سلسلة التكاليف والمنافع
Strike	grève	اضراب
Strike fund	fonds de grève	صندوق اضراب
Strong market	marché soutenu	سوق رائج – سوق رائجة
	marché ferme	
Structural analysis	analyse structurelle	تحليل هيكلي
Structural change	changement structurel	تغير هيكلي – تغير بنياني
Structural deficiency	déficience structurelle	نقص هيكلي – عيب هيكلي
Structural development	développement structurel	نمو هيكلي – انماء هيكلي
Structural disequilbrium	déséquilibre structurel	اختلال هيكلي
Structural equations	équations structurelles	معادلات هيكلية
Structural inflation	inflation structurelle	تضخم هيكلي
Structural parameters	paramètres structurels	ضوابط هيكلية
Structural planning	planification structurale	تخطيط هيكلي
	planification structurelle	
Structural reforms	réformes des structures	اصلاحات هيكلية
Structural transformation	transformation structurale	تغير هيكلي
	transformation structurelle	
Structural unemployment	chômage structurel	بطالة هيكلية
Structure of maturities	agencement des échéances	نمط الإستحقاقات
Structure of the market	structure du marché	هيكل السوق
Sub-contracting	sous-traitance	ابطان – تعاقد من الباطن
Sub-contractor	sous-traitant	بطين – مقاول من الباطن
Sub-loan	sous-prêt	قرض فرعي – قرض مشتق
Sub-marginal	sous-marginal	دون الحدى
Sub-marginal land	terre sous-marginale	أرض دون حدية
Sub-optimisation model	modèle de sous-optimisation	نموذج دون الامثال
Sub-optimum	sous-optimum	دون الأمثل
Sub-project	sous-projet	مشروع فرعي
Sub-regional grouping	groupement sous-régional	مجموعة شبه اقليمية
Sub-sample	sous-échantillon	عينة فرعية
Sub-underwriting	sous-garantie	ضمان الضمان
Subordinated loan	prêt subordonné	قرض متأخر المرتبة
Subscribed capital	capital souscrit	رسمال مكتتب
Subscriber	souscripteur	مكتتب
Subscription	souscription	اكتتاب
Subscription agreement	contrat de prise ferme	عقد اكتتاب
	contrat de placement	

Subscription period	période de souscription	فترة الاكتتاب
Subscription price	prix de souscription	سعر الاكتتاب
Subscription rights	droits de souscription	حقوق الاكتتاب
Subsidiary company	filiale	شركة تابعة
Subsidiary loan	prêt subsidiaire	قرض فرعي
Subsidies	subventions	منح – اعانات
Subsidise, to	subventionner	اعان
Subsidised industry	industrie subventionnée	صناعة معانة
Subsidised price	prix subventionné	سعر مدعم – ثمن مدعم
Subsidy	subside	اعانة
Subsistence agriculture	agriculture de subsistance	زراعة معيشية
Subsistence economy	économie de subsistance	اقتصاد كفاف – اقتصاد معيشي
Subsistence farming	culture de subsistance production agricole de subsistance	فلاحة معيشية
Subsistence production	production de subsistance	انتاج معيشي
Subsistence wage	salaire de subsistance	أجر الكفاف
Subsoil	sous-sol	جوف الأرض
Sub-soil resources	ressources du sous-sol	موارد جوفية
Substitutability	substitutabilité	قابلية للاستبدال
Substitute products	produits de substitution produits de remplacement	سلع بديلة
Substitute trade flows	flux commerciaux de substitution	تيارات تجارية استبدالية
Substitution effect	effet de substitution	عامل الاحلال – عامل الاستبدال
Substitution product	produit de substitution	سلعة بديلة
Subvention	subvention	اعانة
Succession tax	droits de succession impôt de succession	ضريبة الارث – ضريبة الميراث
Sugar mill	usine de sucre	مصنع سكر
Sumptuary tax	impôt somptuaire	ضريبة على السلع الترفية
Sundry debtors	débiteurs divers	مدينون متنوعون
Sundry expenses	frais divers	نفقات متنوعة
Sundry receipts	recettes diverses	ايرادات متنوعة
Sunk costs	coûts investis – coûts engagés	تكاليف مستثمرة – تكاليف متكبدة
Supermarket	supermarché	مجمع تجاري
Supervised credit	crédit contrôlé	ائتمان موجه
Supervision of projects	contrôle de l'exécution des projets supervision des projets	متابعة تنفيذ المشاريع الاشراف على المشاريع
Supervision of works	supervision des travaux	الاشراف على الأعمال
Supplemental credit	crédit supplémentaire	ائتمان تكميلي – قرض تكميلي
Supplementary budget	budget annexe	موازنة ملحقة
Supplementary finance	financement supplémentaire	تمويل تكميلي – تمويل مكمل
Supplier	fournisseur	مورّد
Suppliers' credit	crédit-fournisseur	ائتمان الموردين

Supply	offre	عرض – تزويد – توريد
	fourniture	
	approvisionnement	
Supply and demand	offre et demande	العرض والطلب
Supply contract	marché de fournitures	عقد توريد
Supply curve	courbe d'offre	منحنى العرض
Supply management	gestion de l'approvisionnement	ادارة التوريدات – ادارة التزويد
	gestion de l'offre	
Supply price	prix de l'offre	ثمن العرض
	prix d'offre	
Supply schedule	tableau de l'offre	جدول العرض
Supplying country	pays fournisseur	دولة موردة
Support price	prix de soutien	سعر الدعم
Suppressed inflation	inflation refoulée	تضخم مكبوت – تضخم كامن
Supra-national enterprise	entreprise supra-nationale	مشروع دولي – مشروع عبر دولي
	entreprise transnationale	
Surcharge	surtaxe	ضريبة اضافية – رسم اضافي
Surtax	taxe supplémentaire	
Surety	garantie	ضمان
	caution	
Surety bond	cautionnement	ضمان – كفالة
Surface irrigation	irrigation gravitaire – irrigation de	ري سطحي – ري جاذبي
	surface	
Surplus	surplus – excédent	فائض
Surplus agricultural commodities	excédents agricoles	فائض المنتجات الزراعية – فائض زراعي
Surplus country	pays excédentaire – pays à surplus	دولة فائضة – دولة ذات فائض
Surplus funds	fonds excédentaires	أموال فائضة
Surplus labour	surtravail	فائض عمل
Surplus production	production excédentaire	فائض الانتاج – انتاج فائض
	surproduction	
Surplus-value	plus-value	فائض القيمة
Survey mission	mission d'étude	بعثة استطلاعية
Survey of resources	inventaire des ressources	مسح الموارد – جرد الموارد
Surveyor	expert géomètre	مساح – خبير هندسي
Surveyor of taxes	inspecteur des contributions directes	مفتش ضرائب
Suspense account	compte de transition – compte	حساب مؤقت – حساب انتقالي
	provisoire	
Suspension of disbursements	suspension des déboursements	ايقاف السحب – ايقاف الصرف
Suspension of payments	cessation de paiement	توقف عن الدفع – ايقاف الدفع
Sustained growth	croissance continue	نمو متواصل
Swap	troc	مبادلة – مقايضة
	échange	
Swap arrangement	accord de crédit croisé	اتفاق ائتمان متبادل

Swap credit	crédit croisé	ائتمان متبادل
Swap facilities	facilités de crédit croisé	تسهيلات ائتمانية متبادلة
Swing credit	marge de crédit réciproque	هامش ائتمان متبادل
Switch (*foreign exchange*)	change triangulaire	صرف ثلثي
Symbolic modernisation	modernisation symbolique	تحديث رمزي – تحديث مظهري
Symmetallism	symmétallisme	نظام المعدن المختلط
Syndicalism	syndicalisme	النقابة
Syndicate	syndicat	نقابة – حلقة
Syndicated loan	prêt syndiqué prêt consortial	قرض حلقي
Syndicated finance	financement syndiqué financement consortial	تمويل حلقي
Synthetic fibres	fibres synthétiques	خيوط صناعية – ألياف صناعية
Synthetic products	produits synthétiques	منتجات تركيبية
System	système – structure régime	نظام – منظوم – هيكل
Systems analysis	analyse de systèmes	تحليل هيكلي – تحليل نظمي
System of accounts	système comptable	نظام محاسبي – نظام الحسابات
System of communication	système de communication	نظام المواصلات
System of education	système d'éducation	نظام التعليم – نظام تعليمي
System of irrigation	système d'irrigation	نظام الري
System of price formation	système de la formation des prix	نظام تحديد الأسعار – نظام تكوين الأثمان
System of taxation	régime fiscal système fiscal	نظام الضرائب – النظام الضريبي
Systemic planning	planification systématique planification systémique	تخطيط نظمي

Take-home pay	salaire net	صافي الأجر
Take-off	décollage démarrage	انطلاق – نهوض – نهض
Take-over bid	offre publique d'achat	عرض شراء علني
Take stock, to	faire l'inventaire	جرد
Tangible assets	biens corporels	اصول مادية
Tanker	bateau-citerne pétrolier	تنكر–ناقلة نفط
Tantième	tantième	نسبة أرباح أعضاء مجالس الادارة
Tap issues	émissions ouvertes – émissions à guichets ouverts	اصدارات مفتوحة

Targets of development	objectifs du développement	أهداف التنمية – مستهدفات التنمية
Target rate of growth	taux-objectif de croissance	المعدل المستهدف للنمو
Target variable	variable-but variable-objectif	متغير هدفي – متغير مستهدف
Tariff	tarif	تعرفة – تعريفة
Tariff agreement	accord tarifaire	اتفاقية تعرفة
Tariff barriers Tariff walls	barrières douanières	عوائق جمركية – حواجز جمركية
Tariff concessions	concessions tarifaires	تيسيرات جمركية
Tariff cut	baisse de tarif	خفض الرسوم الجمركية
Tariff harmonisation	coordination des tarifs	تنسيق التعرفات الجمركية
Tariff legislation	législation douanière	تشريع جمركي
Tariff negotiations	négociations tarifaires	مفاوضات تعرفية
Tariff nomenclature	nomenclature douanière	تصنيف جمركي
Tariff policy	politique douanière politique tarifaire	سياسة جمركية
Tariff preferences	préférences tarifaires	مزايا جمركية – تفضيلات تعرفية
Tariff protection	protection douanière	حماية جمركية
Tariff quota	contingent tarifaire	حصة تعرفية
Tariff schedule	liste tarifaire tarif	جدول التعرفة
Tariff system	système tarifaire	نظام جمركي
Tariff war	guerre tarifaire	حرب جمركية
Tax	impôt – taxe	رسم – ضريبة
Tax, to	imposer	فرض ضريبة
Tax accounting	compatibilité fiscale	محاسبة ضريبية
Tax-adjusted yield	rendement après impôt	العائد بعد الضريبة
Tax administration	administration fiscale	الادارة الضريبية
Tax agreement	accord fiscal	اتفاقية ضريبية
Tax allowance	dégrèvement fiscal	خصم ضريبي – خفض ضريبي
Tax arrears	arriérés d'impôt	متأخرات ضريبية
Tax assessment	calcul de l'impôt établissement de l'impôt	تقدير الضريبة – حساب الضريبة
Tax authorities	autorités fiscales	السلطات الضريبية
Tax avoidance	esquive fiscale évasion fiscale	افلات ضريبي
Tax barriers	barrières fiscales	عوائق ضريبية – حواجز ضريبية
Tax base	matière imposable assiette de l'impôt	وعاء الضريبة – محل الضريبة
Tax burden	pression fiscale charge fiscale	عبء الضرائب
Tax collecting machinery	appareil de perception des impôts	جهاز تحصيل الضرائب

Tax collection	recouvrement des impôts perception des impôts	تحصيل الضرائب
Tax collector	percepteur	محصل الضرائب
Tax concession	concession fiscale	تيسير ضريبي
Tax consultant	conseiller fiscal	خبير ضرائب – مستشار ضرائب
Tax convention	convention fiscale	معاهدة ضريبية
Tax credit	crédit d'impôt remise d'impôt	خصم ضريبي
Tax deductible	déductible de l'impôt	قابل للخصم من الضرائب
Tax discrimination	discrimination fiscale	تمييز ضريبي
Tax dodging·	évasion fiscale	افلات ضريبي
Tax equity	justice fiscale	عدالة ضريبية
Tax evasion	évasion fiscale fraude fiscale	تهرب ضريبي
Tax exemption	exonération d'impôt exemption d'impôt	اعفاء ضريبي
Tax farming	affermage des impôts	الزام الضرائب
Tax free	exempt d'impôt	معفى من الضرائب
Tax free income	revenu exempté	دخل معفى من الضريبة
Tax harmonisation	harmonisation fiscale	تنسيق ضريبي
Tax haven	paradis fiscal havre fiscal	ملجأ ضريبي
Tax holiday	exonération fiscale temporaire – trève fiscale	فترة اعفاء ضريبي – عطلة ضريبية
Tax immunities	immunités fiscales	حصانات ضريبية
Tax incentives	stimulants fiscaux	حوافز ضريبية
Tax incidence	incidence de l'impôt	رجعية الضريبة – وقع الضريبة مسقط الضريبة
Tax law	loi fiscale – droit fiscal	قانون ضريبي
Tax levied	impôt perçu	ضريبة محصلة
Tax liabilities	impôts dus cotisations fiscales	التزامات ضريبية – ضرائب مستحقة
Tax load	charge fiscale	عبء ضريبي
Tax measures	mesures fiscales	اجراءات ضريبية
Tax morality	morale fiscale	الاخلاقيات الضريبية
Tax offence	délit fiscal	مخالفة ضريبية – جريمة ضريبية
Tax officer	percepteur—agent du fisc	مأمور ضرائب
Tax payer	contribuable	ممّول
Tax paying capacity	faculté contributive capacité contributive	قدرة ضريبية – طاقة ضريبية
Tax penalties	sanctions fiscales	عقوبات ضريبية
Tax policy	politique fiscale	سياسة ضريبية
Tax privilege	avantage fiscal – privilège fiscal	ميزة ضريبية–مزية ضريبية–امتياز ضريبي

Tax proceeds	revenus fiscaux recettes fiscales	ايرادات ضريبية – حصيلة الضريبة
Tax rate	taux d'imposition	سعر الضريبة – معدل الضريبة
Tax receipts	recettes fiscales	ايرادات ضريبية
Tax reduction	réduction d'impôt dégrèvement d'impôt	خفض الضريبة – انقاص الضريبة – تخفيف الضريبة
Tax reform	réforme fiscale	اصلاح ضريبي
Tax refund	ristourne d'impôt remboursement d'impôt	استرداد ضريبي – استرداد ضرائب
Tax relief	dégrèvement fiscal allègement fiscal	تخفيف الضريبة
Tax revenue	revenus fiscaux	ايرادات ضريبية
Tax shelter	havre fiscal	ملجأ ضريبي
Tax shifting	transfert de l'impôt déplacement de l'impôt	نقل عبء الضريبة – نقل الضريبة
Tax specialist	expert fiscal	اخصائي ضرائب – خبير ضرائب
Tax structure	structure de l'impôt	هيكل الضريبة
Tax system Taxation system	système fiscal	نظام الضرائب – النظام الضريبي
Taxable	imposable taxable	خاضع للضريبة – قابل للخضوع إلى الضريبة
Taxable capacity	potentiel imposable	طاقة ضريبية
Taxable income	revenu imposable	دخل خاضع للضريبة
Taxation	taxation imposition	فرض الضرائب
Taxation schedule	tarif de l'impôt	جدول الضريبة
Taxes outstanding	arriérés d'impôts	متأخرات ضريبية
Taxing power	droit d'imposition	سلطة فرض الضرائب
Taxonomic approach	approche taxonomique	منهج تصنيفي
Technical assistance	assistance technique	معونة فنية
Technical assistance programme	programme d'assistance technique	برنامج معونة فنية
Technical breakthrough Technological breakthrough	percée technologique	فتح فني-فتح تكنولجي
Technical change	changement technique	تطور فني – تغير فني
Technical consultant	conseiller technique	مستشار فني
Technical cooperation	coopération technique	تعاون فني
Technical progress	progrès technique	تطور فني – تقدم فني
Technical shortcomings	lacunes techniques	أوجه القصور الفني
Techno-economic study	étude techno-économique	دراسة فنية اقتصادية – دراسة تكنية اقتصادية
Techno-economic variable	variable techno-économique	متغير فني اقتصادي – متغير تكني اقتصادي
Technocracy	technocratie	التكنوقراطية – حكم الفنيين
Technocrat	technocrate	فني
Technological capabilities	capacités technologiques – capacités techniques	قدرات تكنولجية – قدرات فنية

Technological constraint	contrainte technologique contrainte technique	قيد فني – قيد تكنولوجي
Technological dependence	dépendance technologique	تبعية فنية – تبعية تكنولوجية
Technological development	développement technologique	تنمية فنية – تنمية تكنية – تطوير فني – انماء تكنولوجي
Technological forecasting	prévisions technologiques	تنبؤات تكنولوجية
Technological gap	retard technologique écart technologique	تخلف فني – فجوة فنية – فجوة تكنية – فجوة تكنولوجية
Technological independence	indépendance technologique	استقلال فني – استقلال تكنولوجي
Technological innovations	innovations technologiques	ابتكارات فنية – ابتكارات تكنية
Technological obsolescence	obsolescence technologique	قدم فني – بلى فني – قدم تكني
Technological unemployment	chômage technologique	بطالة فنية – بطالة تكنية
Technology	technologie	تكنولوجيا – فنون الانتاج – تكنولوجية – تكنية
Technology assessment	évaluation de la technologie évaluation technologique	تقييم فنون الانتاج – تقييم التكنولوجية
Technostructure	classe des technocrates	طبقة المديرين – طبقة المدراء
Telecommunications	télécommunications	مواصلات سلكية ولاسلكية
Teller	caissier	صراف – خازن
Temporary admission	admission temporaire	ادخال مؤقت – دخول مؤقت سماح مؤقت
Ten-year plan	plan décennal	خطة عشرية
Tenant	locataire	مستأجر
Tenant-farmer	fermier	مزارع مستأجر
Tenant-farming	fermage	زراعة ايجارية – فلاحة ايجارية
Tender	soumission – offre appel d'offres	عطاء – عرض – مناقصة
Tender, to	soumissionner	قدم عطاء
Tender terms	cahier des charges	شروط المناقصة
Tenderer	soumissionnaire	مقدم عطاء – مناقص
Tendering	adjudication – appel d'offres	مناقصة – عطاء
Term	terme – délai échéance – durée	فترة – أجل – مدة
Terms and conditions of financing	modalités de financement	شروط التمويل
Terms and conditions of repayment	modalités de remboursement	شروط السداد – شروط الوفاء
Term bill	traite à terme	كمبيالة لأجل – كمبيالة آجلة
Term loan	prêt à terme	قرض آجل – قرض لأجل
Terms of aid	conditions de l'aide	شروط المعونة – شروط المساعدة
Terms of delivery	conditions de livraison	شروط التسليم
Terms of payment	conditions de paiement	شروط الدفع
Terms of redemption	tableau d'amortissement conditions d'amortissement	جدول السداد – شروط السداد
Terms of reference	mandat – cadre	عناصر المهمة – ضوابط المهمة

Terms of trade	termes de l'échange	معدل التبادل – نسبة التبادل
Term structure of interest rates	structure temporelle des taux d'intérêt	الهيكل الزمني لأسعار الفائدة
Termination clause	clause de résiliation	نص الفسخ
Tertiary sector	secteur tertiaire	القطاع الثالث – القطاع الثالي
Tertiary industries	industries tertiaires	صناعات ثالية
Test	essai	اختبار
	test	
Testing	testage	اختبار
Textile and wearing apparel industries	industries du textile et de l'habillement	صناعة المنسوجات والملابس
Textile factory	usine textile	مصنع منسوجات
Theorem	théorème	قانون
Theory	théorie	نظرية
Thermal power	énergie thermique	طاقة بخارية – طاقة حرارية
Third window (*IBRD*)	troisième guichet (BIRD)	الطاقة الثالثة (البنك الدولي)
Third world	tiers-monde	العالم الثالث
Three-year plan	plan triennal	خطة ثلاثية
Threshold countries	pays candidats	دول مرشحة–دول شبه مؤهلة
	pays quasi-qualifiés	
Thrift	épargne – économie	اقتصاد – ادخار
Tidal power	énergie marémotrice	طاقة جزرية
Tide power		
Tied aid	aide liée	معونة مقيدة
Tied loan	prêt lié	قرض مقيد
Tie-in sale	vente couplée	بيع مزدوج – بيع مزاوج
Tight credit policy	politique de resserrement du crédit	سياسة تضييق الائتمان
Tight money policy	politique d'argent cher	سياسة الحد من الائتمان
Till-money	encaisse	نقدية
Tillable land	terre cultivable	أرض قابلة للزراعة
Time deposit	dépôt à terme	وديعة لأجل – وديعة آجلة
Time draft	traite à terme	كمبيالة لأجل – كمبيالة آجلة – سند اذني لأجل
Time factor	facteur-temps	عامل الزمن – عنصر الوقت
Time horizon	horizon chronologique	افق زمني
Time intensity	intensité temporelle	كثافة زمنية
Time lag	décalage chronologique	فجوة زمنية – ثغرة زمنية
	écart temporel	
Time path	trajet temporel	مسار زمني
Time pattern	agencement temporel	نمط زمني
	structure temporelle	
Time preference	préférence temporelle	تفضيل زمني
Time series	séries chronologiques	سلاسل زمنية – سلس زمنية
Time sequence	séquence chronologique	تسلسل زمني
Time-table	calendrier	جدول زمني
Time wage	salaire au temps	أجر زمني

Timing of a project	choix temporel d'un projet	توقيت المشروع
Tithe	dîme	عشور
Token money	monnaie symbolique	نقود رمزيه
	monnaie fictive	
Token payment	paiement symbolique	دفع رمزي
Toll	péage	رسم مرور – رسم طريق
Toll road	route à péage	طريق فريض
Tombstone (issues)	pierre tombale (émissions)	الشاهدة (اصدارات)
Tonnage	tonnage	حمولة
	jauge	
Tools	outils	أدوات
Top-down planning	planification à partir du sommet	تخطيط من أعلى
Top management	direction supérieure	ادارة عليا
Total assets	total de l'actif	مجموع الاصول
Total costs	coût total	التكلفة الكلية – مجموع التكاليف
Total disbursements	somme des débours	مجموع السحوبات
	total des déboursements	
Total investment	investissement global	مجموع الاستثمار – الاستثمار الكلي
Total liabilities	passif total	مجموع الحصوم
Total life-time cost	coût total de durée utile	تكلفة كامل الاستخدام
Total loss	perte totale	مجموع الخسارة – الخسارة الكلية
Total profit	bénéfice total	مجموع الأرباح
Total receipts	recettes totales	مجموع الايرادات
Total revenue		
Total utility	utilité totale	المنفعة الكلية
Tourism	tourisme	سياحة
Tourist allowance	allocation touristique (de devises)	مخصص سياحي (من العملات الأجنبية)
Tourist centre	centre touristique	مركز سياحي
Tourist industry	industrie touristique	قطاع السياحة
Town and country planning	aménagement du territoire	تخطيط البيئة
Town planning	aménagement urbain	تخطيط المدن – التخطيط الحضري
Tractor	tracteur	جرار
Trade	commerce	تجارة
Trade acceptance	acceptation commerciale	قبول تجاري – قبالة تجارية
Trade agent	agent commercial	وكيل تجاري
Trade agreement	accord commercial	اتفاق تجاري – اتفاقية تجارية
	convention commerciale	
Trade balance	balance commerciale	ميزان تجاري – ميزان التجارة
Trade barriers	obstacles au commerce	حواجز تجارية – عوائق تجارية
	entraves au commerce	
Trade bill	papier commercial	ورقة تجارية
Trade paper		
Trade concessions	concessions commerciales	مزايا تجارية

Trade creation	création de commerce création d'échanges	خلق تبادل – خلق مبادلات
Trade credit	crédit commercial	ائتمان تجاري
Trade cycle	cycle économique	دورة اقتصادية
Trade deficit	déficit commercial	عجز تجاري – عجر الميزان التجاري
Trade development	développement des échanges	تنمية المبادلات
Trade discount	remise escompte commercial	حطيطة تجارية – خصم تجاري
Trade diversion	détournement des échanges dérivation du commerce	تحويل التجارة – تحويل مجرى المبادلات
Trade enterprise	entreprise commerciale – maison de commerce	مؤسسة تجارية – بيت تجاري
Trade exhibition	exposition commerciale	معرض تجاري
Trade fair	foire commerciale	
Trade flows	flux commerciaux	تيارات تجارية
Trade gap	déficit commercial	عجز تجاري
Trade-in value	valeur de reprise	قيمة الابدال
Trade liberalisation	libéralisation des échanges	تحرير التجارة – تحرير المبادلات
Trade-mark	marque commerciale marque de fabrique	علامة تجارية – سمة تجارية
Trade mart	expomarché	معرض تجاري – سوق تجاري
Trade mission	mission commerciale	بعثة تجارية
Trade monopoly	monopole du commerce	احتكار تجاري
Trade-name	nom commercial raison commerciale	اسم تجاري
Trade negotiations	négociations commerciales	مفاوضات تجارية
Trade-off	échange – troc	مبادلة – استبدال
Trade preferences	préférences commerciales	امتيازات تجارية
Trade promotion	promotion des échanges	تشجيع التجارة – حفز المبادلات التجارية
Trade promotion and marketing	développement du commerce et de la commercialisation	تنشيط التجارة والتسويق تشجيع التجارة والتسويق
Trade relations	relations commerciales	علاقات تجارية – روابط تجارية
Trade representative	agent commercial – délégué commercial	وكيل تجاري – ممثل تجاري
Trade sanctions	sanctions commerciales	عقوبات تجارية
Trade secret	secret commercial	سر تجاري
Trade surplus	balance commerciale favorable excédent commercial	فائض الميزان التجاري – فائض تجاري
Trade-union	syndicat ouvrier	نقابة عمالية – نقابة
Trade-unionism	syndicalisme	النقابية
Trade warfare	guerre commerciale	حرب تجارية
Trade-weighted exchange rates	taux de change pondérés par les échanges commerciaux	أسعار صرف مرجحة تجارياً

Traded goods	biens échangeables	سلع تبادل – سلع متبادلة
Trading account	compte d'exploitation	حساب المتاجرة – حساب التشغيل
Trading capital	capital engage	رسمال موظف رسمال مستثمر
Trading firm	maison de commerce	بيت تجاري
Trading floor	corbeille	المقصورة
Trading partners	partenaires commerciaux	أطراف التبادل
Trading profit	bénéfice d'exploitation	أرباح التشغيل – أرباح المتاجرة
Traditional donors	donneurs traditionnels	الدول العاطية التقليدية
Traditional elites	élites traditionnelles	النخب التقليدية
Traditional exports	exportations traditionnelles	صادرات تقليدية
Traditional sectors	secteurs traditionnels	قطاعات تقليدية
Traditional techniques	techniques traditionnelles	أساليب الانتاج التقليدية – التكنية التقليدية
Traditionalism	traditionalisme	المذهب السلفي – السلفية
Traffic volume	densité de la circulation	كثافة حركة المرور – كثافة المرور
Trainees	stagiaires	متدربون
Training	formation	تدريب
Training programme	programme de formation	برنامج تدريب – برنامج تدريبي
Trajectory of the economy	trajectoire de l'économie	مسار الاقتصاد القومي
Tramp ship	tramp	سفينة طوافة – طوافة
Tramping	tramping	طوف
Transaction	opération	عملية – صفقة
	transaction	
Transaction motive	motif de transactions	دافع التعامل – دافع المعاملات
Transactions basis, on	sur base-transactions	على أساس العمليات
Transactor	agent	متعامل
Transfer	transfert	تحويل
	virement	
Transfer charge	droits de transfert	رسم تحويل
Transfer fee	droits de transport	
Transfer cost	coût de transfert	كلفة التحويل – نفقة التحويل
Transfer in kind	transfert en nature	تحويل عيني
Transfer of funds	virement de fonds	تحويل أموال
Transfer of property	transfert de propriété	تحويل ملكية
Transfer of resources	transfert de ressources	تحويل الموارد
Transfer of technology	transfert de la technologie	نقل المعرفة الفنية – نقل فنون الانتاج
Transfer operations	opérations de transfert	عمليات تحويلية
Transfer payments	paiements de transfert	مدفوعات تحويلية
Transfer pricing	tarification de transfert	تسعير تحويلي
	fixation des prix de transfert	
Transferee	cessionnaire	محول إليه
Transferor	cédant	محول
Transformation curve	courbe de transformation	منحنى تحويل
Transformation industry	industrie de transformation	صناعة تحويلية

Transit	transit	مرور – عبور
Transit agent	transitaire	وكيل نقل – وكالة نقل
Transit agreement	accord de transit	اتفاقية مرور–اتفاقية عبور
Transit duties	droits de transit	رسوم مرور–رسوم عبور
Transit rights	droits de transit	حقوق مرور–حقوق عبور
Transit trade	commerce de transit	تجارة المرور–تجارة عبور
Transnational corporation	société transnationale	شركة عبر دولية – شركة دولية
		شركة متعددة الجنسيات
Transport	transport	نقل
Transportation		
Transport agent	commissionnaire de transports	وكيل نقل
Transport economics	économie des transports	اقتصاديات النقل
Transport industry	industrie des transports	صناعة النقل
Transport system	système des transports	نظام النقل
Transportation charges	frais de transport	تكاليف النقل
Transportation company	compagnie de transports	شركة نقل
Transportation equipment	matériel de transport	أجهزة النقل
Transportation facilities	facilités de transport	تسهيلات النقل
Transportation index	indice du transport	مؤشر النقل
Transportation insurance	assurance de transports	تأمين النقل
Transportation network	réseau des transports	شبكة النقل
Transportation of goods	transport de marchandises	نقل البضاعة – نقل البضائع
Transportation planning	planification des transports	تخطيط النقل
Transportation policy	politique des transports	سياسة النقل
Transportation problems	problèmes des transports	مشكلات النقل
Transportation rate	taux de fret	تعرفة النقل
Transportation services	services de transport	خدمات النقل
Transportation users	usagers des moyens de transport	المنتفعون بوسائل النقل
Traveller's checks	chèques de voyage	شيكات سياحية
Travelling exhibition	exposition itinérante	معرض متنقل
Treasurer	trésorier	خازن – صراف
Treasury	trésor	بيت المال – الخزانة
	trésorerie	
Treasury bills	bons du trésor	اذون الخزانة
Treasury bonds	obligations du trésor	سندات الخزانة
Treaty of commerce	traité de commerce	معاهدة تجارية
Trend	trend	اتجاه – اتجاه طويل الأجل
	tendance	
	orientation	
Trend component	composante de longue durée	عنصر الاتجاه
"Triage" policy	triage	سياسة الفرز
	politique de triage	
Trial balance	bilan de vérification	ميزان المراجعة

Trial well	puits expérimental	بئر تجريبية
Triangular project	projet triangulaire	مشروع ثلاثي
Triangular trade	commerce triangulaire	تجارة ثلاثية
Tribute	tribut	جزية – بقط
Trickle down theory	théorie de l'osmose	نظرية الرشح
Trilateral cooperation	coopération trilatérale	تعاون ثلاثي
Tropical agriculture	agriculture tropicale	الزراعة المدارية
Tropical crops	cultures de la zone tropicale	حاصلات مدارية – محاصيل مدارية
Tropical soil	sol tropical	تربة مدارية
Trough	creux	قاع – حضيض
Truck farming	culture maraîchère	زراعة الخضروات
Truck system	système du paièment en nature	نظام الأجر العيني
Trust	trust – fiducie	ترست – احتكار – امنة – أمانة – استئمان
Trust account	compte fiduciaire	حساب استئمان
Trust agreement	accord de fiducie	عقد استئمان – عقد امانة
Trust indenture		
Trust company	société fiduciaire	شركة استئمانية – شركة استئمان
Trust fund	fonds fiduciaire	صندوق استئمان
Trustee	fidéicommis – curateur représentant fiduciaire	امين
Turning points (*cycles*)	tournants (*cycles*)	فترات الانقلاب – فترات الدور (دورات)
Turnkey contract	contrat "clef en main"	عقد جهيز – عقد تسليم المفتاح
Turnkey project	projet "clef en main"	مشروع جهيز – مشروع «على المفتاح»
Turnover	chiffre d'affaires rythme de renouvellement	رقم الأعمال – معدل التجدد
Turnover tax	taxe sur le chiffre d'affaires	ضريبة على رقم الأعمال
Two-part tariff	tarif binôme	تعرفة مزدوجة
Two-tier market	marché double	سوق مزدوج – سوق مزدوجة
Two-tier price system	système de prix double	نظام أسعار مزدوج
		نظام أسعار مثنى

Ultimate consumer	consommateur final	المستهلك الأخير – المستهلك النهائي
Unbalanced entry	entrée non soldée	قيد مفرد
Unbankable paper	papier non-bancable	أوراق تجارية طالحة
Unbiased estimate	estimation non biaisée	تقدير غير متحيز
Unbiased sample	échantillon neutre – échantillon non biaisé	عينة غير متحيزة
Unbundling of imported technologies	démontage des technologies importées déglobalisation des technologies importées désagrégation des technologies importées	افضاض التكنولجيات المستوردة – تفضيض الفنون الانتاجية المستوردة

Uncalled capital	capital non appelé	رسمال غير مدعى
Uncertainties	aléas – incertitudes	احتمالات
Uncertainty	incertitude	اللايقين – الشك
Uncleared goods	marchandises non dédouanées	سلع غير مجمركة
Underconsumption	sous-consommation	قصور الاستهلاك
Under-capitalisation	sous-capitalisation	قصور الرسملة
Under-developed countries	pays sous-développés	دول متخلفة
Under-development	sous-développement	تخلف
Under-employment	sous-emploi	قصور العمالة – العمالة الناقصة
Under-employment equilibrium	équilibre de sous-emploi	توازن العمالة الناقصة
		توازن العمالة القاصرة
Underestimate, to	sous-estimer	بخس
Under-estimation	sous-estimation	ابخاس – بخس
Under-evaluation	sous-évaluation	
Underground water	eaux souterraines	مياه جوفية
Underground water utilization	utilisation des eaux souterraines	استخدام المياه الجوفية
Under-identification	sous-identification	قصور التعيين – قصور التحديد
Under-investment	sous-investissement	قصور الاستثمار
Under-invoicing	sous-facturation	ابخاس الحسبنة – بخس الفاتورة
Under-nutrition	sous-alimentation	قصور التغذية – هزل
Under-populated country	pays sous-peuplé	دولة قليلة السكان
Under-population	sous-peuplement	قصور السكان – قلة السكان
	sous-population	
Under-production	sous-production	قصور الانتاج
Undertaking	entreprise	مشروع – منشأة
Under-utilised capacity	capacité sous-utilisée	طاقة قاصرة الاستخدام
Under-valued currency	monnaie sous-évaluée	عملة مبخوسة
Underwater resources	ressources sous-marines	موارد قاع البحار – موارد مغتمرة
Underwrite, to	garantir – souscrire	ضمن – أمن – اكتتب
Underwriter (*issues*)	garant (*émissions*)	ضمان تصريف – ضامن اصدار (اصدارات)
Underwriter	garant – assureur	ضامن – ملتزم – مؤمن – مكتتب
	souscripteur	
Underwriting agreement	accord de garantie	اتفاق ضمان – عقد اكتتاب
	contrat de prise ferme	
Underwriting commitment	engagement de garantie	تعهد ضمان – التزام اكتتاب
Underwriting house	établissement de garantie	مؤسسة ضمان – مؤسسة اكتتاب
Underwriting syndicate	syndicat de garantie	حلقة ضمان – دارة اكتتاب
Undeveloped land	terre vierge	أرض بكر
Undisbursed balance	solde non déboursé	رصيد غير مدفوع – رصيد متبق
Undistributed profits	bénéfices non distribués	أرباح غير موزعة

Undrawn balance	solde disponible	رصيد غير مسحوب – رصيد متاح – رصيد متبقي
Undrawn portion of a loan	partie non utilisée d'un prêt	الرصيد غير المسحوب من القرض
Unearned income	revenu immérité – rente	دخل غير مكتسب – ريع
Unemployed	chômeur	عاطل – متعطل
Unemployment	chômage	بطالة
Unemployment benefits	allocations-chômage	اعانات بطالة – مخصصات بطالة
Unemployment insurance	assurance-chômage	تأمين ضد البطالة
Unemployment rate	taux de chômage	نسبة البطالة – معدل البطالة
Unemployment relief	assistance-chômage	اعانة بطالة
Uneven development	développement inégal	نمو غير متكافئ
Unfair commercial practices	pratiques commerciales déloyales	أساليب تجارية غير مشروعة
Unfair competition	concurrence déloyale	منافسة غير مشروعة
Unfair price	prix exagéré prix inéquitable	سعر غير عادل – ثمن جائر
Unfair trade practices	pratiques commerciales déloyales	اجراءات تجارية غير مشروعة
Unforeseen contingencies	éventualités imprévues imprévus	احتمالات غير مرتقبة – فجاءات
Unfreeze funds, to	débloquer des fonds	اطلق أموالاً – افرج عن أموال
Unification of tariffs	unification des tarifs douaniers	توحيد التعرفات الجمركية
Uniform tariff	tarif unique	تعرفة موحدة – رسم موحد
Unilateral transfers	transferts unilatéraux	تحويلات فاردة – تحويلات غير متبادلة تحويلات بلا عوض
Unilateral repudiation of a debt	répudiation unilatérale d'une dette	نبذ فارد للدين – الغاء فارد للدين
Unincorporated entreprises	entreprises individuelles	مشروعات فردية – مؤسسات فردية
Unissued shares	actions non-émises	أسهم غير مصدرة
Unit cost	coût unitaire	تكلفة الوحدة – متوسط التكلفة
Unit of account	unité de compte	وحدة حساب – وحدة تقييم
Unit price	prix unitaire	ثمن الوحدة – متوسط الثمن
Unit trust	fonds d'investissement ouvert société d'investissement à capital variable (sicav)	صندوق استثمار مفتوح
Unit value	valeur unitaire	قيمة الوحدة
Unit wage cost	coût unitaire des salaires coût salarial unitaire	التكلفة الاجرية للوحدة متوسط الكلفة الاجرية
Unlading costs Unloading costs	frais de déchargement	تكاليف التفريغ
Unlisted securities	valeurs non admises à la cote officielle	أوراق مالية غير مقيدة
Unmatured coupons	coupons non échus	قسائم غير مستحقة
Unnegotiable securities	titres non négociables	أوراق مالية غير قابلة للتداول
Unofficial market	marché hors-cote	سوق غير رسمي
Unpacking of imported technologies	démontage des technologies importées déglobalisation des technologies importées déségrégation des technologies importées	افضاض التكنولوجيات المستوردة – تفضيض الفن الانتاجي المستورد

Unpaid capital	capital non libéré	رسمال غير مدفوع
Unpaid labour	travail non rémunéré	عمل بلا عوض
Unproductive labour	travail improductif	عمل غير منتج
Unproductive land	terre stérile terre improductive	أرض جدباء – أرض جدبة
Unprofitable	non rentable	غير مربح – غير مجز
Unqualified agreement to reimburse	garantie irrévocable de remboursement	تعهد مطلق بتغطية الدفع
Unrealised capital gains	plus-value non réalisée	نماء غير محصل أرباح رسمالية غير محصلة
Unredeemable debentures	obligations non remboursables	سندات غير قابلة للسداد
Unrequited transfers	transferts sans contrepartie transferts unilatéraux	تحويلات بحتة – تحويلات بلا عوض
Unsecured loan	prêt sans garantie prêt non gagé	قرض بلا ضمان
Unsecured loan stocks	obligations ordinaires non garanties	سندات عادية بلا ضمان
Unskilled labour	main d'oeuvre non qualifiée	عمل غير مؤهل
Unspent balance	solde non dépensé solde non utilisé	رصيد غير منفق – رصيد غير مستخدم
Unstable equilibrium	équilibre instable	توازن غير مستقر
Unstable market	marché instable	سوق غير مستقر
Untapped resources	ressources inexploitées ressources vierges	موارد غير مستغلة – موارد عاطلة موارد بكر
Untied aid	aide non liée	معونة مرسلة – معونة غير مقيدة
Untying of aid	déliement de l'aide	اطلاق المعونات – تحرير المساعدات
Unused capacity	capacité non utilisée	طاقة عاطلة – طاقة غير مستغلة طاقة غير مستخدمة
Unused credit	crédit non utilisé	ائتمان غير مستخدم
Unweighted index	indice non pondéré	مؤشر غير مرجح
Unweighted mean	moyenne non pondérée	وسط غير مرجح
Updating of the plan	actualisation du plan	تحديث الخطة
Upper class	haute société	الطبقات العليا – علية القوم
Upper quartile	dernier quartile	الربيع الأعلى
Upstream operations	opérations à l'amont	عمليات خلفية
Upsurge	hausse marquée	ارتفاع ملموس
Upswing	hausse	صعود – ارتفاع
Upturn	reprise	انفراج – صعود
Upward trend	tendance à la hausse	اتجاه ارتفاعي – اتجاه صعودي
Urban agglomeration	agglomération urbaine	تجمع حضري
Urban centre	centre urbain	مركز حضري

Urban community	communauté urbaine	جماعة حضرية
Urban development	aménagement urbain	انماء حضري – تنمية حضرية
	aménagement des agglomérations urbaines	
Urban economy	économie urbaine	اقتصاد حضري
Urban explosion	explosion urbaine	انفجار حضري
Urban growth	croissance urbaine	نمو حضري
Urban planning	planisme urbain	تخطيط حضري – تخطيط المدن
Urban population	population urbaine	سكان الحضر – سكان المدن
Urban poverty	paupérisme urbain	الفقر الحضري
Urban sprawl	extension urbaine	زحف حضري
Urban transport	transport urbain	نقل حضري
Urbanisation	urbanisation	تحضّر
Use value	valeur d'usage	قيمة الاستعمال
Useful life of equipment	durée utile du matériel	فترة استخدام المعدات
Users	usagers	منتفعون
Users benefits	avantages aux usagers	منافع المنتفعين – مزايا المنتفعين
User cost	coût d'usage	كلفة الاستعمال
Usufruct	usufruit	حق الانتفاع
Usurer	usurier	مرابي – مراب
Usurious interest	intérêts usuraires	فوائد ربوية – فائدة ربوية
Usurious loan	prêt usuraire	قرض ربوي
Usurious price	prix usuraire	ثمن ربوي
Usury	usure	ربا
Utility	utilité	منفعة
Utility function	fonction d'utilité	دالة المنفعة
Utility maximisation	maximisation de l'utilité	تعظيم المنفعة – اذراء المنفعة
	maximation de l'utilité	اقصاء المنفعة
Utopia	utopie	خيال – عالم خيالي – فردوس
Utopian socialism	socialisme utopique	الاشتراكية الخيالية – الاشتراكية الفردوسية

Vacancies	emplois disponibles	وظائف خالية
Valuation	évaluation	تقييم – تقدير القيمة
	estimation	
Valuation of assets	évaluation des actifs	تقييم الاصول
Valuation of risks	appréciation des risques	تقدير المخاطر
Value	valeur	قيمة

Value to	évaluer	قيّم – قدّر
Value added	valeur ajoutée	قيمة مضافة
Value-added tax (vat)	taxe à la valeur ajoutée (tva)	ضريبة القيمة المضافة
Value at cost	valeur d'achat	قيمة الشراء – قيمة التكلفة
Value date	valeur – date de valeur	تاريخ الاستحقاق
Value in exchange	valeur d'échange	قيمة المبادلة – قيمة التبادل
Value of exchange		
Value in use	valeur d'usage	قيمة الاستعمال
Value index	indice de valeur	مؤشر قيمي
Value judgment	jugement de valeur	حكم قيمي
Value-maintenance provision	clause de maintien de la valeur	نص حفظ القيمة
Value of goods	valeur des biens	قيمة السلع
Value of money	valeur de la monnaie	قيمة النقود
Variable	variable	متغير
Variable capital	capital variable	رسمال متغير
Variable costs	coûts variables	تكاليف متغيرة
Variable rate bonds	obligations à taux variables	سندات متغيرة المعدل – سندات ذات سعر
		فائدة متغير
Variance	variance	التغير – التباين
Variate	variable	متغير
Variations	variations	تغيرات
Variants of the project	variantes du projet	بدائل المشروع
Vector	vecteur	متجه
Vegetable crops	cultures maraîchères	حاصلات خضارية – محاصيل الخضراوات
Vegetation	flore	نبات
Veil of money	voile monétaire	ستار نقدي – قناع نقدي
Velocity of circulation (*money*)	vitesse de circulation (*monnaie*)	سرعة التداول (نقود)
Venture capital	capital de participation	رسمال مساهم
Vertical integration	intégration verticale	تكامل رأسي
Vested interest	droit acquis	مصلحة مكتسبة – حق مكتسب – حقوق ثابتة
Viability of a project	validité d'un projet	سلامة المشروع
	rentabilité d'un projet	
Vicious circle	cercle vicieux	حلقة مفرغة
Vicious circle of poverty	cercle vicieux de la pauvreté	حلقة الفقر المفرغة
Village commune	commune villageoise	جماعة قروية – مجمعة قروية
Village community	communauté villageoise	مجتمع قروي
Villagisation	villagisation	تجميع قروي
Vintage model	modèle de cru	نماذج جيلية
	modèle de longévité différentielle	
Virgin land	terre vierge	أرض بكر
Visible trade	commerce visible	تجارة منظورة
Visible transactions	opérations visibles	عمليات منظورة

Vital statistics	statistiques démographiques	احصاءات سكانية
Viticulture	viticulture	زراعة الكروم
Vocational guidance	orientation professionelle	توجيه مهني
Vocational training	formation professionelle	تدريب مهني
Volatile market	marché inconstant	سوق متقلب
Volume-index	indice-volume	مؤشر الحجم
Volume of aid	volume de l'aide	حجم المعونات – حجم المساعدات
Volume of business	volume des affaires	حجم الأعمال – حجم النشاط التجاري
Volume of trade	volume du commerce	حجم التجارة
Volume of transportation	volume des transports	حجم النقل
Voluntary colonialism	colonialisme volontaire	استعمار رضائي
Voluntary contributions	cotisations volontaires	مساهمات اختيارية
***Vostro* account**	compte *vostro*	حسابكم
Voting shares	actions à droit de vote	أسهم مصوتة – أسهم متمتعة بحق التصويت
Voting stock	actions portant droit de vote	
Voucher	reçu – document	ايصال – مستند – سند
	bon	
Vulgar economics	économie vulgaire	الاقتصاد الدارج – اقتصاد العامة
Vulgar economists	économistes vulgaires	الدوارج من رجال الاقتصاد
		الاقتصاديون الدوارج

Wage	salaire	اجر
Wage and price control	contrôle des salaires et des prix	رقابة الاجور والأسعار
Wage-price control		
Wage bill	masse salariale	مجموع الاجور
Wage costs	coût de la main-d'oeuvre	كلفة الاجور
Wage demands	revendications salariales	طلبات زيادة الاجور – شكاوي الاجور
Wage determination	formation des salaires	تكوين الاجور
Wage differentials	différences de salaires	فوارق الاجور
Wage discrimination	discrimination salariale	تمييز في الاجور – تمييز أجري
Wage-earner	salarié	اجير
Wage freeze	blocage des salaires	تجميد الاجور
	"gel" des salaires	
Wage-fund theory	théorie du fonds des salaires	نظرية مخصص الاجور
Wage-goods	biens salariaux	سلع عمالية – سلع استهلاك عمالي
	biens de consommation ouvrière	
Wage in kind	salaire en nature	اجر عيني
Wage incentive	prime de salaire	علاوة تشجيعية

Wage index	indice des salaires	مؤشر الاجور
Wage indexation	indexation des salaires	تأشير الاجور
Wage-inflation	inflation-salaires	تضخم اجري
Wage-labour	travail salarié	عمل اجير – عمل مأجور
Wage level	niveau des salaires	مستوى الأجور
Wage policy	politique des salaires	سياسة الاجور
Wage-price freeze	blocage des salaires et des prix	تجميد الاجور والأسعار
Wage-price spiral	spirale salaires-prix	لولب الاجور والاسعار
	spirale prix-salaires	تسابق الاجور والاسعار
Wage-push inflation	inflation-salaires	تضخم اجري
Wage rate	taux de salaire	معدل الاجر
Wage settlement	accord de salaires	تسوية اجرية – اتفاق اجري
Wage structure	barème des salaires	هيكل الاجور – سلم الاجور
Wage system	système salarial	النظام الاجري – نظام الاجور
Wage tax	impôt salarial	ضريبة الاجور
Wage-worker	salarié	اجير
Waiting-line theory	théorie de la file d'attente	نظرية صف الانتظار
Waiver	dispense – renonciation	اعفاء
	dérogation	
Walk-out	grève	اضراب
Wants	besoins	حاجات
War debt	dette de guerre	دين ناشيء عن الحرب – دين حربي
War economy	économie de guere	اقتصاد حرب
War loan	emprunt de guerre	قرض حرب
War reparations	réparations de guerre	تعويضات حرب
War risks	risques de guerre	مخاطر الحرب
Warehouse	entrepôt	مستودع
	magasin	
Warehouse receipt	certificat d'entrepôt	ايصال ايداع – شهادة ايداع
Warrant		
Warrant	garantie	ضمان – خيار شراء أسهم
	option d'achat de titres	
	warrant	
"Warranted" rate of growth	taux de croissance équilibrée	معدل النمو المتوازن
Warranty clause	clause de garantie	شرط ضمان – شرط كفالة
Wastage	gaspillage	ضياع – اضاعة
Waste	gaspillage	ضياع – اضاعة – فضلات – فاقد
	déchets	
Waste land	terre inculte	أرض موات – أرض بور
Waste of natural resources	gaspillage des ressources naturelles	اضاعة الموارد الطبيعية
	sur-exploitation des ressources	نبذرة الموارد الطبيعية-تبذر الموارد الطبيعية
	naturelles	
Wasting assets	biens consomptibles	اصول هالكة

Watch and clock making	industrie de l'horlogerie	صناعة الساعات
Water charges	tarification de l'eau charges de consommation d'eau	رسوم المياه
Water collection	captage des eaux	تجميع المياه – قلد المياه
Water planning	planification des eaux	تخطيط الموارد المائية
Water resources	ressources hydrauliques	موارد مائية
Water shortage	stockage d'eau	خزن المياه
Water supply	adduction d'eau	توفير المياه
Water supply network	réseau de distribution des eaux	شبكة توزيع المياه
Watering of stocks	dilution du capital	تذويب الرسمال
Watering techniques	méthodes d'arrosage	أساليب الري
Waterways network	réseau fluvial	شبكة الطرق النهرية
Ways and means	avances budgétaires	اعتمادات مالية
Way of life	mode de vie	نمط الحياة-اسلوب الحياة
Weak market	marché faible	سوق ناعس – سوق ضعيف
Weakening of prices	fléchissement des prix	تراجع الأثمان – انخفاض الأسعار
Wealth	richesse	ثروة
Wealth-income ratio	rapport richesses-revenus	نسبة الثروة إلى الدخل
Wealth distribution	répartition des richesses	توزيع الثروة
Wealth tax	impôt sur les fortunes	ضريبة على الثروات – ضريبة الثروة
Wear and tear	usure	بلى – قدم – بلاء
Weight	poids coefficient de pondération	وزن – عامل ترجيح – راجح – مرجح
Weighted average Weighted mean	moyenne pondérée	وسط مرجح
Weighted index	indice pondéré	مؤشر مرجح – أرقام قياسية مرجحة
Weighted regression	régression pondérée	ارتداد مرجح
Weighing	pondération	ترجيح – وزن
Weighting coefficient	coefficient de pondération	معامل ترجيح – معامل وزن
Weighting procedure	procédure de pondération	اسلوب الترجيح-أسلوب الوزن
Weighting system	système de pondération	نظام الترجيح – نظام الأوزان
Welfare	bien-être	رفاهية – رفاهة
Welfare criteria	critères de bien-être	معايير الرفاهية
Welfare economics	économie de bien-être	اقتصاديات الرفاهية
Welfare payments	prestations d'assistance sociale prestations de la sécurité sociale	اعانات اجتماعية
Welfare programme	programme social	برنامج خدمات اجتماعية
Welfare services	services sociaux	خدمات اجتماعية
Welfare State	Etat-providence	دولة الارفاه – دولة الرفاهية
Well-being	bien-être	رفاهة – رفاهية
Well-conceived and well-prepared project	projet bien conçu et bien préparé	مشروع حسن الصياغة والاعداد
Western way of life	mode de vie occidental	نمط الحياة الغربية
Westernisation	occidentalisation	تغرب – تفرنج

Wharf dues	droits de quai	رسوم رصيف
Wharfage	quayage	
White coal	houille blanche	الفحم الأبيض – الكهرباء
White-collar workers	col-blancs	عمال غير يدويين – موظفو المكاتب
	travailleurs non-manuels	أصحاب الياقات البيضاء
	employés de bureau	
"White elephant" project	projet de prestige	مشروع ارائي – مشروع اراءة
Wholesale price	prix de gros	سعر الجملة – ثمن الجملة
Wholesale price index	indice des prix de gros	مؤشر أسعار الجملة
Wholesale trade	commerce de gros	تجارة الجملة
Wholesaler	grossiste	تاجر جملة
Widening of capital	extension du capital	توسيع الرسمال – بسط الرسمال
Wildcat capitalism	capitalisme sauvage	رسمالية متطرفة
Wildcat strike	grève sauvage	اضراب فجائي
Willingness to pay	consentement à payer	استعداد للدفع
	disposition à payer	
	acceptation de payer	
Windfall profits	profits imprévisibles	أرباح طارئة
	profits fortuits	
Winding up	liquidation	تصفية
Window dressing	fardage – maquillage	تزيين – ازيان
Wipe off a debt, to	épurer une dette	تسوية دين – تصفية دين
"With-and-without" test	test "avec et sans"	اختبار الفرضين (تقييم المشاريع)
(project appraisal)	*(évaluation de projets)*	معيار الفرضين
Withdraw a sum, to	retirer une somme	سحب مبلغاً
Withdrawable	retirable	قابل للسحب
	disponible	
Withdrawal	retrait – tirage	انسحاب – سحب
Withdrawals	retraits – tirages	سحوبات
Withdrawal application	demande de retrait	طلب سحب
Withdrawal schedule	calendrier des tirages	برنامج سحب – جدول سحب
	calendrier des retraits	
Withholding system	système de retenue à la source	نظام الحجز عند المنبع
Withholding tax	impôt retenu à la source	ضريبة عند المنبع
Wood and cork products industry	industrie du bois et du liège	صناعة منتجات الخشب والفلين
Wood-pulp industry	industrie de la cellulose	صناعة لباب الخشب
Works-contract	marché de travaux	عقد اشغال
Work-force	main d'oeuvre	قوة عاملة
Work group	groupe de travail	مجموعة عمل – ثبة عمل
Working party		
Work incentives	stimulants au travail	حوافز عمل
Work-leisure trade-off	échange travail-loisir	مبادلة العمل والفراغ
Work stoppage	arrêt de travail	وقف العمل – ايقاف العمل

Worker	ouvrier – travailleur	عامل
Worker participation	participation ouvrière	المشاركة العمالية
Working assets	capital roulant	أصول متداولة
Working balance	fonds de roulement	رصيد التشغيل – رصيد الاستغلال
Working capital	fonds de roulement	رسمال متداول – رسمال تشغيل
Working class	classe ouvrière	الطبقة العاملة
Working conditions	conditions de travail	ظروف العمل
Working day	jour ouvrable	يوم عمل
Working hours	heures de travail	ساعات العمل
Working group	groupe de travail	فريق عمل
Working population	population active	العاملون – السكان العاملون
Workshop	atelier	ورشة – حلقة دراسة عملية
	session d'études pratiques	
	séminaire	
World consumption	consommation mondiale	الاستهلاك العالمي
World economic community	communauté économique mondiale	الجماعة الاقتصادية الدولية
World economic crisis	crise économique mondiale	أزمة اقتصادية عالمية
World economic stability	stabilité de l'économie mondiale	استقرار الاقتصاد العالمي
World economic system	système économique mondial	النظام الاقتصادي العالمي
World economy	économie mondiale	الاقتصاد العالمي
World energy supplies	ressources énergétiques mondiales	موارد الطاقة العالمية
		الموارد العالمية للطاقة
World liquidity	liquidité mondiale	سيولة دولية
World markets	marchés mondiaux	أسواق عالمية
World modelling	modélisation mondiale	نمذجة عالمية – نمذجة دولية
	modélisation globale	
World monetary system	système monétaire international	نظام النقد الدولي
World of finance	monde de la finance	عالم المال
World payments	paiements mondiaux	مدفوعات عالمية
World prices	prix mondiaux	أسعار عالمية – أثمان دولية
World production	production mondiale	انتاج عالمي
World reserves	réserves mondiales	أرصدة دولية – أرصدة عالمية
World trade	commerce mondial	تجارة عالمية – تجارة دولية
World trading system	système du commerce mondial	نظام التجارة العالمية
Worthless check	chèque sans provision	شيك بلا رصيد – شيك بدون رصيد
Write down doubtful debts, to	réduire la valeur des créances douteuses	حطّ الديون المشبوهة
Write off a debt, to	défalquer une dette	اسقط ديناً
	annuler une dette	
Write off capital, to	amortir le capital	استهلك الرسمال
Write up the value of assets, to	réévaluer l'actif	اعاد تقييم الأصول

212

| Xeno-currencies | xéno-devises
xéno-monnaies | عملات أجنبية |

Yankee bonds	obligations yankees	سندات دولية امريكية – سندات «يانكي»
Yearling bonds	obligations à un an	سندات حولية
Yield	rendement	عائد – ردة
Yield, to	rapporter	ادّر
Yield curve	courbe de rendement	منحنى العائد
Yield gap	écart de rendement	فرق العائد – فجوة العائد
Yield rate	taux de rendement	معدل العائد
Yield test	critère du rendement	اختبار العائد – معيار العائد
Yield to maturity	reustement à l'écliéance	العائد عند الاستحقاق
Yielding interest	productif d'intérêt	مدّر لفوائد

Zakat tax	*zakat*	الزكاة
Zero-base budgeting	élaboration *ab ovo* du budget budgétisation *ab ovo*	اعداد الموازنة من الصفر – اعداد الموازنة من الأساس
Zero-economic growth	croissance économique nulle	لا نمو اقتصادي
Zero-population growth	croissance démographique nulle	لا نمو سكاني – ثبات السكان
Zero-sum game	jeu à somme nulle	مقارعة صفرية – مقارعة صفرية النتيجة
Zollverein	*zollverein*	اتحاد جمركي
Zone pricing	tarification par zones	تسعير اقليمي